W9-DFJ-754

# SINNERS, LOVERS,
## and
# HEROES

SUNY Series in Communication and the Struggle for Identity
in Postmodernity

Mick Presnell, Editor

*Sinners, Lovers, and Heroes*
Ancient Cemetery, Hartford, Connecticut

# SINNERS, LOVERS,
# and
# HEROES

An essay
on memorializing in three American cultures

RICHARD MORRIS

STATE UNIVERSITY OF NEW YORK PRESS

Cover Photograph of Clyde du Vernet Hunt's "The American Spirit" (1938) is reprinted by permission of The Bennington Museum, Bennington, Vermont.

Published by
State University of New York Press

© 1997 State University of New York

All rights reserved

Printed in the United States of America

No part of this book may be used or reproduced in any manner whatsoever without written permission. No part of this book may be stored in a retrieval system or transmitted in any form or by any means including electronic, electrostatic, magnetic tape, mechanical, photocopying, recording, or otherwise without the prior permission in writing of the publisher.

For information, address the State University of New York Press,
State University Plaza, Albany, NY 12246

Marketing by Nancy Farrell
Production by Bernadine Dawes

**Library of Congress Cataloging-in-Publication Data**

Morris, Richard Joseph, 1953–
    Sinners, lovers, and heroes : an essay on memorializing in three American Cultures / Richard Morris.
        p.     cm. — (SUNY series in communication and the struggle for identity in postmodernity)
    Includes bibliographical references (p. 183) and index.
    ISBN 0-7914-3493-1 (HC : alk. paper). — ISBN 0-7914-3494-X (pbk. : alk. paper)
    1. Lincoln, Abraham, 1809-1865—Monuments. 2. Lincoln, Abraham,—1809-1865—Public opinion. 3. Memorials—United States. 4. Memory—Social aspects—United States. 5. Group identity—United States.
I. Title. II. Series.
E457.6.M7    1997
973.7'092—dc21                                                         97-13019
                                                                              CIP

1  2  3  4  5  6  7  8  9  10

*For all my relations, with loving memories of*

*Dorothy Louise Morris*
*Robert Stanley Morris*
*and*
*Gary Robert Morris*

# CONTENTS

Preface ix

Acknowledgments xiv

List of figures xvii

1. Introduction • 1

2. Sinners • 45

3. Lovers • 77

4. Heroes • 115

5. Conclusion • 153

Notes 175

References 183

Index 227

# PREFACE

I happened upon the subject of this book by accident. The finer details of that accident are irrelevant now, but the larger contours reveal significance and purpose.

One warm autumn day in 1984, while driving from Rutgers University to Temple University, where I had agreed to deliver a talk on nineteenth-century responses to Lincoln's assassination, I stopped by the roadside to collect my thoughts. Across the road was the entrance to a country cemetery, which somehow seemed an appropriate location to contemplate the subject of my talk. I crossed the road, entered the cemetery, and meandered about aimlessly.

Sometime later I discovered I had wandered absentmindedly into an unfrequented, ill-kept corner of the cemetery littered with early to mid-nineteenth-century tombstones. This low-lying, unattended section, which, I noted, had been "reserved" for people of color, had been well segregated from the meticulously attended sections higher up that would not lend themselves to flooding. By the logic of land use, this was the least desirable piece of land and had been set aside for the community's least desirable dead. I had wandered into a climatological and sociological drain.

As I turned to leave I noticed for the first time a tombstone that moments before I had walked past but failed to notice. By most (perhaps all) aesthetic standards this stone would be unremarkable. Among the vast array of carefully carved and sculpted memorials that filled the upper portions of the cemetery, those in the section where I stood were poor aesthetic imitations. And this particular stone manifested little aesthetic sensitivity and less artistic skill—merely an irregularly shaped, smallish boulder of approximately eighteen inches in height and width and ten inches thick, with a roughly hewn but discernibly surfaced face on which the memorializer has crudely but deeply and boldly inscribed "MAN." And yet this stone struck me as enormously expressive and overwhelmingly powerful.

My immediate interpretation was that this crude stone marked the burial place of a male slave who had not been "given" an anglicized name or whose real name the memorializer for some reason could not inscribe. My own interpretation, I then realized, was a source of what I had initially considered the stone's evocative power. My understanding of America's torrid history—especially the treatment and marginalization of people of color, then and now—my recognition of the stark contrast between the manifest lack of concern amply illustrated by the disparities between this and other sections of the cemetery, and the poignant concern of the memorializer had all clothed this stone in layers of meaning and significance that would be equally obvious to some viewers and not at all obvious (even plausible) to others. A second source of evocative power came much more directly from the stone. Although crudely carved, each of the stone's three letters was a full six inches deep. The memorializer had sought to ensure that this "MAN" would be remembered.

*Sinners, Lovers, and Heroes* is not about the "MAN" stone. Others have admirably begun the task of investigating the memorial efforts of the marginalized and the forgotten (see, for example, Combs 1972; Cunningham 1989; Gosnell and Gott 1989; Kruger-Kaholoula 1989; Little 1989; Tashjian & Tashjian 1989). Nevertheless, I begin with a recounting of my accidental encounter because that brief autumnal moment has lead me on a curious journey through diaries, newspapers, public records, discursive memorials, elegies, poems, religious tracts, scholarly works produced by individuals in a variety of different disciplines, and more than five hundred cemeteries in forty states where I have encountered, pondered, photographed, measured, examined, analyzed, and been perplexed and frustrated by memorials dating from 1632 to the present.[1] In one sense, that journey and my effort here are footnotes dedicated to the "MAN" stone, to the memorializer who carved it with huge care and concern, and to the individual who inspired the memorializer; for my accidental encounter has engendered questions enough for a lifetime, some of which I attempt to answer in these pages.

In a second sense, however, this book is an addendum to past and present scholarship. As I explain in greater detail in the introduction and elsewhere, although numerous scholars have acknowledged the cultural and rhetorical (or communicative) significance of American memorials, their analyses have focused almost exclusively on issues other than the cultural and rhetorical bases of American memorializing. This is not inherently wrong or wrongheaded, but it has left a considerable gap in our understanding of memorials as instances of memorializing—an understanding that must encompass and account for the cultural and rhetorical power of instances like the MAN stone, which aesthetic and historical approaches have either ignored or dismissed. Even those who have been atypically sensitive to the importance of these bases—for example, Dickran and Ann Tashjian, whose superb *Memorials for Children of Change* (1974) has informed much of my thinking—

have tended to assume that memorials are fundamentally aesthetic objects (see, for example, Ludwig 1966), that location or period (or some other external source) immediately and explicitly announces a memorial's "culture" (see, for example, Duval and Rigby 1978), and that shifting visual patterns across time reveal the evolutionary nature of that culture and its "collective memory" (see, for example, Deetz 1989).

My effort here provides a reversal that challenges these assumptions and advances the thesis that memorials are fundamentally rhetorical and cultural forms of expression, that a careful examination of American memorializing discloses the contours of at least three distinct American cultures, and that shifting visual and discursive memorial patterns across time reveal the ascendancy and subordination of these three cultures and their cultural memories. Rather than a sequence of aesthetic and/or historical movements that presumably explains the "evolution" of a single, monolithic "American culture," then, what we find is a mode of human expression that embodies the *ethoi* and worldviews of divergent American cultures—each of which has possessed and continues to seek to possess America's hegemonic voice and to become (or remain) the custodian of America's collective memory.

The three American cultural groups (that is, Religionists, Romanticists, and Heroists) that constitute the focus of the present work unquestionably are not the only American cultures one might identify through an examination of American memorializing. For various reasons, many remain beyond my grasp. Some, for example, have had and have little or no voice. Their dead lay buried under markers conceived by members of other cultures, in mass graves, in unmarked graves, in no graves at all. Their *ethoi* and worldviews often are either unarticulated or so vaguely insinuated that their voices are silent or muted. As modes of rhetorical and cultural expression, memorials continue to speak largely because living members of a specific culture continue to speak; and those memorials that survive do so in large part because the living have deemed them worthy of preservation. Inherently, memorials are not representative of all individuals or cultures.

On the other hand, those memorials that do survive, that the living have deemed worthy of preservation, often tell us as much about the present as they do about the past. My aim here is not to describe or develop a typology of all memorials, of all American memorials, or even of a majority of American memorials, but to use American memorial efforts as a means of identifying and describing three American cultures. This, in turn, allows us to offer some interesting insights about the rhetorical and cultural bases of American memorializing, about the nature and scope of cultural conflict and resolution, about memorials as sites for ideological struggle, about cultural memory, and about the uses of "collective" memory.

# ACKNOWLEDGMENTS

Even a cursory glance at the pages of this book would reveal my indebtedness to a great many people. On a more personal level, however, I would like to express my sincere gratitude to several people who have generously shared with me their time, their advice, their acuity, and their encouragement. First and foremost, my son, Ian Morris, sacrificed his time, followed me through scores of cemeteries, helped me collect and catalogue photographs and information, mercifully tolerated my obsessive behaviors year after year, and provided me with an unending supply of support and encouragement. Edwin Black skillfully guided me through my graduate education, instilled in me a stout appreciation for scholarship, and helped me lay the foundation for this book. Kenneth Burke provided me with hours of amusement and a full dose of encouragement when this book was nothing more than a faint dream, a dream that his kindness helped make a reality. Philip Wander provided me with an appreciation of the ideological implications of lived experience and, much more important, was my friend unconditionally during the most desperate moments. Jay and Elizabeth Mechling kindly listened to my endless ramblings and helped me to think more seriously about questions of context. Kathleen Jamieson singlehandedly reshaped my concept of audience, graciously provided me with the time and the environment that I needed to give this work shape, and in the end showed me the meaning of courage. Herb Simons lent me his insight and wisdom and told me an important thing or two about structure. Marsha Seifert listened without complaint to my ill-formed ideas, helped give those ideas shape, and helped give that shape meaning. Mary Stuckey graciously read and made valuable suggestions for repairing languished chapters. Robin Moremen helped make the proofreading process less painful. And Clifford Geertz (or should I say his works?) has been an endless source of insight and inspiration. I also extend my heartfelt thanks to the many cemetery superintendents, cemetery personnel, funeral home directors, and library staff who candidly talked with me, gave me direction, and provided me with access to their experiences, records, and environments. Finally, I owe a great debt of gratitude to Mick Presnell, Lois Patton, Bernadine Dawes, and four anonymous manuscript reviewers whose keen sight and kindness and patience have made this work possible.

These few words cannot do justice to the people who have assisted me; for whatever I say is necessarily an act of forgetting even as it is an act of remembering. Nevertheless, I am certain that whatever good this work contains is largely a consequence of their efforts. I alone am responsible for what remains.

# LIST OF FIGURES

Following page 114

2.1.   Religionist gravescape. Old Colony Burying Ground; Norfolk, Connecticut
2.2.   Headstone of Richard More, 1692. The Burying Place; Salem, Massachusetts
2.3.   Headstone of Jane Second, 1686. The Burying Place; Salem, Massachusetts
2.4.   Headstone of Roger Hooker, 1698. Ancient Cemetery; Hartford, Connecticut
2.5.   Headstone of Josiah Hayward, 1736. South Burying Place; Concord, Massachusetts
2.6.   Headstone of John Haynes, 1895. Eakins Cemetery; Ponder, Texas
2.7.   Headstone of Elizabeth Mockridge, 1940. Woodlands Cemetery; Philadelphia, Pennsylvania
2.8.   Headstone of Ella Brock Sinkler, 1960. Woodlands Cemetery; Philadelphia, Pennsylvania

xvii

2.9.    Headstone of Lowell M. Clucas III, 1986. Woodlands Cemetery; Philadelphia, Pennsylvania

2.10.   Memorial of Nathanael Mather, 1688. The Burying Point; Salem, Massachusetts

2.11.   Headstone of Doraty Cromwell, 1673. The Burying Point; Salem, Massachusetts

2.12.   Headstone of Joseph Barrett, 1763. South Burying Place; Concord, Massachusetts

2.13.   Sideplate of Robert Rad sarcophagus, 1753. Church Burying Ground; Williamsburg, Virginia

2.14.   Detail of Samuel Adams' headstone, 1728. King's Chapel Burying Ground; Boston, Massachusetts

2.15.   Detail of George Ropes' headstone, 1755. The Burying Point; Salem, Massachusetts

2.16.   Memorial of Humphrey Barrett, 1783. South Burying Place; Concord, Massachusetts

2.17.   Memorial of Jonathan Melven, 1737. Old Hill Burying Ground; Concord, Massachusetts

2.18.   Detail of James Barrett memorial, 1779. Old Hill Burying Ground; Concord, Massachusetts

2.19.   Purves memorial, 1931. Woodlands Cemetery; Philadelphia, Pennsylvania

2.20.   Bewster memorial, 1888. Woodlands Cemetery; Philadelphia, Pennsylvania

2.21.   Webb memorial, 1980. Woodlands Cemetery; Philadelphia, Pennsylvania

2.22.   Bowser memorial, 1882. Restland Memorial Park; Dallas, Texas

2.23.   Memorial of Alice Jones, 1792. South Burying Place; Concord, Massachusetts


3.1.    Headstone of Ephraim Jones, 1756. South Burying Place; Concord, Massachusetts

3.2.    Headstone of Catherrine Conant, 1780. South Burying Place; Concord, Massachusetts

3.3.    Headstone of Joseph Watson, 1806. Ancient Cemetery; Hartford, Connecticut

3.4.    Headstone of Andrew Conant, 1813. South Burying Place; Concord, Massachusetts

3.5.    Headstone of Abigail Dudley, 1812. Old Hill Burying Ground; Concord, Massachusetts

3.6.    Headstone of Judith Archer, 1801. The Burying Point; Salem, Massachusetts

3.7.    Headstone of Paul Reed, 1799. The Burying Point; Salem, Massachusetts

3.8.    Headstone of Luke Roberts, 1780. King's Chapel; Boston, Massachusetts

3.9     Granery Burial Ground subsequent to reorganization and beautification efforts. Boston, Massachusetts

3.10.   Romanticist gravescape. Mount Auburn Cemetery; Cambridge, Massachusetts

3.11.   Bigelow Chapel. Mount Auburn Cemetery; Cambridge, Massachusetts

3.12.   The Tower. Mount Auburn Cemetery; Cambridge, Massachusetts

3.13.   Entrance. Elm Grove Cemetery. Mystic, Connecticut

3.14.   Entrance gate of the Confederate Section of the Old City Cemetery in Lynchburg, Virginia

3.15.   James Lawrence memorial, 1855. Mount Auburn Cemetery; Cambridge, Massachusetts

3.16.   William Perkins Walker memorial, 1892. Mount Auburn Cemetery; Cambridge, Massachusetts

3.17.   Memorial for the Preservation of the Union. Mount Auburn Cemetery; Cambridge, Massachusetts

3.18    Martin memorial, 1876. Woodlands Cemetery; Philadelphia, Pennsylvania

3.19.   A.D. Harris memorial, 1917. Eakins Cemetery; Ponder, Texas

3.20.   Schluter memorial, 1916. Eakins Cemetery; Ponder, Texas

3.21.   Warren Cone memorial, 1856. Old Colony Burying Ground; Norfolk, Connecticut

3.22.   William Frederick Harden memorial, 1845. Mount Auburn Cemetery; Cambridge, Massachusetts

3.23.   Chickering memorial, ND. Mount Auburn Cemetery; Cambridge, Massachusetts

3.24.   Emmert Hamilton memorial, 1909. Church Burying Ground; Williamsburg, Virginia

3.25.   Nathan and Isabel Sargent memorial, 1907. Arlington National
        Cemetery; Arlington, Virginia
3.26.   Thomas and Nancy McKee memorial, 1924. Arlington National
        Cemetery; Arlington, Virginia
3.27.   Cottrell memorial, 1865. Elm Grove Cemetery; Mystic, Connecticut
3.28.   Annie E. Mallory memorial, 1864. Elm Grove Cemetery; Mystic,
        Connecticut
3.29.   Eliza Smull memorial, 1864. Elm Grove Cemetery; Mystic,
        Connecticut
3.30.   Mary R. Swain memorial, 1877. Old Colony Burying Ground;
        Norfolk, Connecticut
3.31.   Front view of Graceland. Memphis, Tennessee
3.32.   Memorial wall outside Graceland. Memphis, Tennessee
3.33.   Memorial to Dr. Martin Luther Kind, Jr. and plaque outside the
        Lorraine Hotel. Memphis, Tennessee

4.1.    Albin Thomas and Mary Moore memorial, c. 1879. Woodlands
        Cemetery; Philadelphia, Pennsylvania
4.2.    Nathaniel and Lucy Tucker memorial, c. 1865. Church Burying
        Ground; Williamsburg, Virginia
4.3.    William Worth Belknap memorial, 1890. Arlington National
        Cemetery; Arlington, Virginia
4.4.    Memorial for Confederate soldiers of La Fayette County.
        Oxford, Mississippi
4.5.    Andrew Dunlap memorial, 1914. Arlington National Cemetery;
        Arlington, Virginia
4.6.    Heroist memorials in a Romanticist gravescape. Mount Auburn
        Cemetery; Cambridge, Massachusetts
4.7.    Washington Monument, 1848–1884. Washington, D. C.
4.8.    The Jefferson Memorial, 1943. Washington, D. C.
4.9.    Memorial statue of Thomas Jefferson, 1943. Washington, D. C.
4.10.   Ulysses S. Grant memorial. Washington, D. C.
4.11.   Civil War memorial. Washington, D. C.
4.12.   Marine Corps memorial, 1954. Arlington, Virginia
4.13.   Ironwork fencing with gate. Mount Auburn Cemetery; Cambridge,
        Massachusetts

4.14.   Ironwork enclosure. Rosehill Cemetery; Concord, California

4.15.   Heroist gravescape. Princeton Memorial Park; Princeton, New Jersey

4.16.   Heroist gravescape. Oaklawn Memorial Park; Washington, New Jersey

4.17.   Arlington National Cemetery. Arlington, Virginia

4.18.   Price memorial, 1989. Eakins Cemetery; Ponder, Texas

4.19.   Milton C. Broad memorial, 1939. Restland Memorial Park; Dallas Texas

4.20.   Joseph H. Kelly memorial, 1985. Princeton Memorial Park; Princeton, New Jersey

4.21.   William H. Buchanan memorial. Oaklawn Memorial Park; Washington, New Jersey

4.22.   Nolia E. Floyd memorial, 1886. Restland Memorial Park; Dallas, Texas

4.23.   Funerary art in the Heroist gravescape. Princeton Memorial Park; Princeton, New Jersey

# 1

## INTRODUCTION

*Fortune favoured him . . . in the opportune moment of his death.*

—Tacitus, *Agricola*

The ascendancy of one cultural group over other cultural groups that are competing for dominance typically is a gradual, nearly imperceptible process.[1] This is not difficult to fathom. In times and/or places where members of a cultural group are conscious of their marginalization and subordination, when they are alert and attuned to their membership in their culture, and when they have the means and the conditions and the power to organize and to work against the forces that have created the conditions of their marginalization and subordination, the possibilities for cultural transformation are great. Remove, block, thwart, or stifle any of these—as occurs almost by definition in any multicultural nation, especially in those that manifest the ingredient of the postmodern condition we recognize as fragmentation—and the possibilities immediately diminish toward nothingness.

Events that rupture the social structure of a nation so dramatically that they thoroughly call into question the totality of

1

cultural arrangements that were in place before the event are rare. When such events occur, however, they create conditions that are consummate for cultural transformation, for providing an opportunity for well poised cultures to assume the position of the hegemonic bloc (Gramsci 1971). Within the frame provided by these extraordinary events we are privileged to witness within the span of a brief time what ordinarily we must trace across broad spans of time. I know of no other event that so exactly marks the dramatic rupture of the social structure of a nation and that so clearly lays cultural transformation open to observation than the death of Abraham Lincoln.

The possibilities of cultural transformation had been building long before Lincoln's assassination, of course. Immigration, the exaggerated importation of European deportments, the stabilization of the political environment, economic restructuring, and a myriad of other indicators point undeniably to gradual and sometimes ephemeral shifts in the status of American[2] cultures.[3] But at the moment of Lincoln's death—and the nearly simultaneous end of a terrible, bloody war—those possibilities emerged, through a peculiar synchronicity, as actualities. Embedded within those actualities we find the voices of citizens who responded to Lincoln's death, who announced for others to hear that the great, fallen leader was, without question, a member of *their* cultural group, and that, therefore, they were entitled to carry on his work, to assume the mantle of his position and power, and to guide the nation toward a future that *their* Lincoln had helped create and toward which the nation was destined to travel.

Just below I have pieced together what *appears* to be a coherent narrative, a cogent story of a single culture singularly struggling to respond to a national tragedy. Yet, "the term 'narrative,' like 'beauty,' or 'order,'" as Arnold Krupat (1992) recently has remarked, "represents a determination as to what counts as signal or figure; narrative, beauty, and order are sociolinguistic constructs, which is to say that only those exchanges of information we take as fulfilling the conditions we posit for narrativity can be taken to constitute a narrative" (76). Just so, a reading informed by the perspective that I am advancing here allows us to hear and bear witness to the voices of disparate cultures seeking to ascend in this rare opportunity for cultural transformation. To hear those disparate voices, to listen to them clamoring to lay claim to Lincoln and his legacy sets the stage here for understanding three consistently potent and powerful American cultures whose *ethoi* and worldviews constitute the central focus of this book. That some readers will hear a ring of familiarity in some of the voices— or will be repulsed or altogether unable to hear other voices—is a portentous indication that these three cultures are still very much with us. Responses to Lincoln's assassination thus serve here and throughout this work not so much as addenda for enhancing our understanding of Lincoln or of Lincoln's place in history, but as instructive media through which we can begin to understand the rhetorical and cultural bases of memorializing, the struggle to control and maintain public memory, and the interplay of cultures and cultural boundaries.

Following this brief narrative, I sketch and then expand the circumstances immediately surrounding Lincoln's assassination. I then place Lincoln's death and the responses and central myths that his legacies generated in a broader context. Third, I set forth the analytic framework that I later bring to bear on those responses and legacies. Finally, I conclude with a preview of the remaining chapters of this work.

## LINCOLN'S DEATH

At ten-thirty on the evening of April 14, 1865, while Maj. Henry Reed Rathbone, Clara Harris, Mary Todd Lincoln, and Abraham Lincoln watched the third act of *Our American Cousin* from the State Box in John Ford's theater, twenty-six-year-old John Wilkes Booth entered the box, aimed his derringer, and discharged a shot that struck the left side of the President's head. The ball then traveled "obliquely forward, towards the right eye, crossing the brain obliquely, a few inches behind the right eye, where the ball lodged" (Barnes 1865, 71). Having "heard the discharge of a pistol behind him," Henry Rathbone "then turned to the President."

> His position was not changed. His head was slightly bent forward and his eyes were closed. Deponent [Rathbone] saw that he was unconscious, and supposing him mortally wounded, rushed to the door for the purpose of calling medical aid. . . . Deponent removed the bar and the door opened. Several persons who represented themselves to be surgeons were allowed to enter. . . . Deponent then returned to the box and found the surgeons examining the President's person. They had not yet discovered the wound. As soon as it was discovered it was determined to remove him from the theatre. He was carried out, and this deponent then proceeded to assist Mrs. Lincoln, who was intensely excited, to leave the theatre. On reaching the head of the stairs deponent requested Major Potter to aid him in assisting Mrs. Lincoln across the street to the house to which the President was being conveyed. (Rathbone 1865, 62–63)

Across the street in "the house of a Mr. [William] Petersen" [sic], Lincoln's moribund frame lay stretched across a double bed "with his head at the outside" (Shea 1865, 69). Within minutes "the pillows were saturated with blood, and there was considerable blood upon the floor immediately under him. There was a patch-work coverlet thrown over the President,"

> which was only so far removed, from time to time, as to enable the physicians in attendance to feel the arteries of the neck or heart, and he appeared to have been divested

of all clothing. His eyes were closed and injected with blood, both the lids and the portions surrounding the eyes being as black as if they had been bruised by violence. He was breathing regularly, but with effort, and did not seem to be struggling or suffering. (Field 1865, 69–70)

Throughout the night a continuous stream of visitors inspected Lincoln's unconscious form—sixteen different physicians, cabinet members, various government officials, "senators, congressmen, army officers, personal friends," William T. Clark, the young Massachusetts soldier in whose room Lincoln lay, "the four other Peterson House boarders and their landlord, Mr. Lincoln's son Robert and his mother's circle of comforters, actors from the interrupted *Our American Cousin*, and just plain people who had slipped in somehow to watch Abraham Lincoln die" (Kunhardt & Kunhardt 1965, 91).

In the midst of this continuous confusion the numerous physicians who had crowded into the small room vigilantly, diligently, incessantly monitored and recorded Lincoln's condition. By "five minutes past eleven," they noted, his pulse was forty-five "and growing weaker." At "thirty-two minutes past eleven" his pulse was forty-eight "and full." By "quarter past twelve" his pulse was forty-eight, his respiration had dropped to twenty-one, and the deeply bruised appearance around "both eyes" clearly indicated "ecchymosis." At "forty minutes past twelve" his pulse had increased to sixty-nine, his "right eye [was] swollen, and ecchymosis" was deepening and spreading. At "fifty-five minutes past twelve" his pulse had increased to eighty, and the physicians noted "struggling motions of arms." By "half-past one" his pulse had increased to eighty, but he was "appearing easier." At "twenty-five minutes past three" his respiration was forty-two "and regular." By "four o'clock" his respiration was "hard" and "regular." At "fifty minutes past five his respiration was twenty-eight," "regular," and he was "sleeping." But by "six o'clock" his pulse was "failing." At "half-past six" his respiration was "still failing," and his breathing was "labored"; by "seven o'clock" the physicians observed "symptoms of immediate dissolution"; and, finally, at "twenty-two minutes past seven—Death" (Abbott 1865a, 39; see also 1865b, 70 and 1865c, 71).

The expression on Lincoln's face "immediately after death," Maunsell Field (1865) noted, "was purely negative, but in fifteen minutes there came over the mouth, the nostrils, and the chin, a smile that seemed almost an effort of life. I had never seen upon the President's face," he continued, "an expression more genial and pleasing" (70). Mary Lincoln, the men present uneasily observed, was rather less than genial.

On at least three separate occasions during the ordeal, she attempted to be at her husband's side.[4] But "she was allowed to remain there only a few minutes, when she was removed in a sobbing condition, in which, indeed, she had been during all the time she was present" (Field 1865, 70). On the last occasion, at 3:00 A.M., Edwin M. Stanton, Lincoln's secretary of war, called for someone to "take that woman out of here" and declared that no one was to "let her in again" (as quoted in Kunhardt & Kunhardt 1965, 79). The First Lady's display of emotions was so offensive to Stanton and the physicians that they would not even allow her to be present "in the chamber of death" when Phineas Gurley delivered his deathbed prayer or to accompany her husband's corpse to the White House. After completing his prayer Dr. Gurley went into the front parlor, "where Mrs. Lincoln was, with Mrs. and Miss Kinney, and her son Robert, Gen. Todd of Dacotah (a cousin of hers), and Gen. Farnsworth, of Illinois. Here the reverend offered up another prayer," which "was continually interrupted by Mrs. Lincoln's sobs" (Field 1865, 69–70). Immediately following the prayer, officials escorted Mary Lincoln to her carriage, then took her to the White House, where a "doctor said she must go to bed immediately" (Randall 1953, 384).

As Mary Lincoln struggled to be near her husband, those

who thought themselves more suited to the tasks at hand removed
Abraham's corpse "to the White House, attended by a dense
crowd, and escorted by a squadron of cavalry and several distinguished officers." At the White House "Surgeon-General Barnes,
Dr. Stone, the late president's family physician, Drs. Crane, Curtis,
Woodward, Taft, and other eminent medical men" conducted a
postmortem examination (Shea 1865, 71). Following the examination,

> the embalmers proceeded to prepare [Lincoln's corpse] for
> the grave. Mr. Harry P. Cattell, in the employ of Doctors
> Brown and Alexander, who, three years before, had pre-
> pared so beautifully the body of little Willie Lincoln, now
> made as perpetual as art could effect the peculiar features
> of the late beloved President. The embalming was per-
> formed in the President's own room, in the west wing, in
> the presence of President Johnson. The body was drained
> of its blood, and the parts necessary to remove to prevent
> decay were carefully withdrawn, and a chemical prepara-
> tion injected, which soon hardened to the consistence of
> stone, giving the body the firmness and solid immobility
> of a statue. . . .
>
> The body was then placed in a beautiful mahogany cof-
> fin lined with lead, and with a white satin covering over
> the metal. It was finished in the most elaborate style, with
> four silver handles on each side, stars glistening between
> the handles, and a vein of silver winding around the whole
> case in a serpentine form. To the edges of the lid hung a
> rich silver tassel, making a chaste and elaborate fringe to
> the whole case. (Shea 1865, 111-12)[5]

In the short time between being sworn in as President and
witnessing the embalming, Andrew Johnson had met with his cabinet and had "determined that the funeral ceremonies in

Washington should be celebrated on Wednesday, the 19th of April, and all the churches throughout the country were invited to join at the same time 'in solemnizing the occasion' by appropriate observances" (Nicolay & Hay 1890, 317; see also Johnson 1865). Immediately, artists and workers began to prepare the East Room in the White House for the funeral, which greatly disturbed Mary Lincoln; for "every plank that dropped gave her a spasm and every nail that was driven seemed to be like a pistol shot" (Edgar T. Wells, as quoted in Randall 1953, 385).[6]

By Sunday, April 16, Washington was "shrouded in Black. Not only the public buildings, the stores and shops, and the better class of residences were draped in funeral decorations," but also "the poorest class of houses, where the laboring men of both colors found means in their penury to afford some scanty show of mourning" (Shea 1865, 112). Everywhere, observers repeatedly remarked, people draped their cities and towns "in mourning, and from every pulpit in the land came the voice of lamentation over the national loss, and of eulogy to the virtues of the good President who had been so cruelly murdered" (Holland 1866, 523).

On Monday, April 17, officials turned their attention to the details of interring Lincoln's remains. At noon "members of the 39th Congress then in Washington met in the Senate reception room, at the Capitol" to consider their options (Bancroft 1866, 55). "Some urged that he should be buried in the vault built for Washington under the national capitol dome; Mrs. Lincoln [reportedly] favored New York or Chicago, but Governor Richard L. Oglesby [sic] and the senators from Illinois were insistent on the burial being at Springfield" (Holmes 1930, 317).[7] At four o'clock that afternoon the committee publicly announced their decision to assume full responsibility for making the necessary funeral arrangements, to transport Lincoln's "remains to their place of burial in the state from which he was taken for the national service," and to send a copy of their decision "to the afflicted widow of the late President, as an expression of sympathy in her great bereavement" (Bancroft 1866, 57). Even before the committee had announced its decision, members of the Springfield City Council had met, "appropriated $20,000 to defray the expense of the funeral," and hired artists to embellish "the State House without and the Halls of the House of Representatives within" (Holmes 1930, 317). Without consulting Mary Lincoln, the Springfield committee paid $5,300 for "six acres of the Mather grounds in [Springfield] for a burial place for Lincoln" and had very nearly completed his burial vault "before Mrs. Lincoln telegraphed her refusal to have him buried there" (Randall 1953, 387). But the Springfield committee was in accord with its Washington representatives, who were in accord with the Congressional Committee.

Almost concurrent with the Congressional Committee's public announcement, the Illinois delegation in Washington issued its own set of resolutions in which they thanked "the Federal authorities for their cordial cooperation and concurrence with the citizens of Illinois in securing to that State the remains" of Lincoln; they also announced that his remains would "be interred at the capitol of the State so long his residence" (Haynie et al. 1865, 136-137). Within a matter of hours "every town and city on the route begged that the train might halt within its limits and give its people opportunity of testifying their grief and their reverence," although the Congressional Committee eventually determined "that the funeral cortege should follow substantially the same route over which Lincoln had come in 1861" (Nicolay & Hay 1890, 319).

By ten o'clock the following morning, April 18, federal workers had prepared the White House to be "thrown open, to give the people an opportunity to take their farewell of the familiar face, whose kind smile death had for-ever quenched. At least twenty-five thousand persons availed themselves of this liberty; and thousands more, seeing the crowd, turned back unsatisfied" (Holland 1866, 524). Churches the next day recorded attendances that exceeded the record attendances of "Black Easter" three days prior—perhaps as many as "25,000,000 people" (Holmes 1930, 318). In the nation's capital the official ceremonies began at noon in the East Room of the White House, where the casket containing Lincoln's remains rested on a meticulously designed catafalque:

> The floor of the catafalque was about four feet in height, and approached by one step on all sides, making it easy to view the face of the honored dead. Above was a canopy, in an arched form, lined on the underside with white fluted satin, covered otherwise with black velvet and crepe. This was supported by four posts, heavily encased with the emblems of mourning. The canopy, the posts, and the main body of the catafalque were festooned with crepe and fastened at each fold with rosettes of black satin.
>
> On the top of the coffin lay three wreaths of moss and evergreen, with white flowers and lilies intermingled. At the head of the coffin, standing upon the floor of the catafalque, and leaning against the metallic case, stood a beautiful cross, made of japonicas, lilies, and other white flowers, as bright and blooming as though they were still on their parent stem, and had not been plucked to adorn the house of the dead, its pure and immaculate white furnishing a strong contrast with the deep black on all sides. . . . Here, then, were the emblems of the dead, the marks of rank, the tokens of grief, deep and sorrowful, the signs of love and affection, and the living emblems of purity and happiness hereafter, as well as hope and immortality in the future. (Shea 1865, 112–13)

Around the equally ornamented room sat "governmental and judicial dignitaries, and such high officials from the states as had gathered to the capitol to pay their last tribute of respect to the illustrious dead" (Holland 1930, 524). While Albert Hale, Matthew Simpson, Phineas Gurley, and E. H. Gray presented scriptures, prayers, and funeral addresses, "Robert Lincoln sat . . . with his face in his handkerchief, weeping quietly, and Little Tad, with his face red and heated, cried as if his heart would break. Mrs. Lincoln, weak, worn, and nervous, did not enter the East Room nor follow the remains" (Shea 1865, p. 114).

At the conclusion of the ceremonies pall bearers solemnly carried the casket to an elaborate two-tiered hearse, "built expressly by G. R. Hall," that permitted "a full view to all spectators" (Shea 1865, 128).[8] Then began the lengthy procession on its deliberate march toward the Capitol: "All of the pomp and circumstance which the Government could command was employed to give a fitting escort from the White House to the Capitol where the body of the President was to lie in State." And, "to associate the pomp of the day with the greatest work of Lincoln's life, a detachment of colored troops marched at the head of the line" (Nicolay & Hay 1890, 317 and 318). At the Capitol, amid more richly ornamented emblems of mourning, "Dr. Gurley completed the religious exercise of the occasion. Here the remains rested, exposed to public view, but guarded by soldiery, until the next day" (Holland 1866, 526).

At the end of the day many citizens began to insist that this pageant "was never paralleled upon this continent. Nothing like it—nothing approaching it—had occurred in this country, if, indeed, in the world" (Holland 1866, 526). Nor did the pageant end here. Through the following day thousands of citizens filed past Lincoln's open casket to pay their final respects before federal authorities took his remains "along a track of more than fifteen hundred miles" to Illinois "to be buried among the scenes of his early life" (Holland 1866, 526–27). On the morning of "April 21, with Lincoln's coffin" and "the coffin of Willie Lincoln, the son, who had died at Washington in February, 1862," the funeral train began its deliberate journey toward Springfield (Holmes 1930, 319).

In Baltimore and Harrisburg on April 21, in Philadelphia from April 22 to 23, in Cleveland on April 28, in Columbus on

April 29, in Indianapolis on April 30, in Chicago from May 1 to 2, mourners solemnly repeated the funeral pageant: elaborate funeral processions, specially designed hearses, funeral services, splendorous catafalques, addresses, sermons, prayers, speeches, viewings of the remains, and emblems of mourning everywhere (Morris 1865, 155–218; Shea 1865, 168-222; Williamson 1865, 233–42). And where the train did not stop, "in out-of-the-way places, little villages, or single farm-houses, people came out to the side of the track and watched," showering the train with flowers and handing funeral wreaths to the train's passengers as they slowly passed: "Every five rods along the whole line were seen these mourning groups, some on foot and some in carriages, wearing badges of sorrow, and many evidently having come a long distance to pay this tribute of respect, the only one in their power, to the memory of the murdered President" (Shea 1865, p. 168).

Nearly three weeks after his death "the mortal remains of Abraham Lincoln, the sixteenth President of the United States, arrived in Springfield, the capital of Illinois, on Wednesday morning, the 3rd of May, 1865" (Morris 1865, p. 219), where the funeral scene began anew, as though it were being performed for the first time. Again authorities transferred the casket from the train to an ambitiously designed hearse; again a funeral procession bore the remains to an honored place where it would lie in state upon a grand catafalque adorned with the symbols of mourning; again "the citizens of the place, with thousands who came pouring in by every mode of conveyance, sought to gaze on the face of the corpse" (Shea 1865, 227). And again the morning light brought with it complementary ceremonies. From the Capitol in Springfield a funeral procession bore Lincoln's corpse "over the gently undulating suburbs, across the beautiful meadows, to the cemetery. Oak Ridge Cemetery, if it has not the grandeur of Greenwood or Mount Auburn, is yet a beautiful resting place for the dead, covering an area of thirty-eight acres. Nature made the spot beautiful, and the artificial landscaping has been made with much taste and skill, in conformity with the natural outlines. The original growth of small oaks still stands, and there are a score of towering elms along the banks of the brook which flows across the southern side" (Morris 1865, 223-24).

At Oak Ridge Cemetery Lincoln's casket, "hidden in the beauty of flowers," rested "atop a bier inside a thoroughly adorned limestone vault prepared for the temporary reception of his remains" (Morris 1865, 224).[9] Then came a prayer by Albert Hale, a dirge composed for the occasion by L. M. Dawes and George F. Root, a reading of scriptures by N. W. Miner, a choral presentation of "To Thee, O Lord," a reading of Lincoln's "Second Inaugural Address" by A. C. Hubbard, a metic performance of Otto's "As When Thy Cross Was Bleeding," a funeral oration by Matthew Simpson, a choral presentation of "Over the Valley the Angels Smile," some well-chosen remarks and a closing prayer by Phineas Gurley, a metic performance of a funeral hymn and doxology, and Phineas Gurley's benediction (Morris 1865, 219-37; Shea 1865, 225-41; and Williamson 1865, pp. 242-54). On June 1, 1865, by special proclamation, millions of citizens met publicly to pay tribute once again to Abraham Lincoln.[10]

## AN IMMEDIATE CONTEXT

From a vantage point situated long after the fact, some may find it difficult to imagine that Lincoln's contemporaries would not have responded to his death with as much pomp and circumstance and devotion as they could command. Because Lincoln has become such an integral part of the nation's image, and because citizens have witnessed similar tributes during the intervening years, the pageantry and emotionality occasioned by his death, although distant, somehow seem appropriate, inevitable, and, therefore, perhaps rather unremarkable. But this vantage point overlooks an immediate context that makes both nineteenth century responses to his death and his current status as one of the nation's most beloved and legendary presidents entirely remark-able.

In the best of times before his death Lincoln was only a mod-erately popular president. At other times, at William Hanchett (1983) has pointed out, "Lincoln was the object of far more hatred than love" (7). Consider, for instance, the election results of 1860 and 1864. In the election of 1860 Lincoln received only 39 percent of the popular vote—the second lowest percentage of anyone ever elected to the presidency.[11] Lincoln not only failed to carry a sin-gle slave state in this election, he also received only 26,388 of the 2,523,428 votes cast in the slave states (Cole 1986, 303–307; and Potter 1976, 442–43). Nor did he fare well in the urban North. As David Potter (1976) has noted, "whereas the North as a whole gave him 55 percent of its votes, in seven of the eleven cities with pop-ulations of 50,000 or more, he failed to get a majority" (443). Further, although Lincoln received 180 of the 303 electoral votes, which gave him twenty-seven more than he needed to win the election, his margin of victory very likely was more a result of good strategists and of William Seward's support than of Lincoln's pop-ularity (429–47). This is particularly telling in light of the fact that the electoral college inflates the margin of victory.

In the election of 1864 Lincoln received 55 percent of the popular vote and 212 of the 233 electoral votes, which seems to imply that his popularity increased significantly during his first term in office. However, several points strongly suggest the oppo-site. Given the generally accepted belief that changing leaders in the middle of an all-consuming war invites catastrophe, for exam-ple, 55 percent of the popular vote and 212 of the electoral votes hardly seem resounding expressions of confidence or popularity. Consider, also, that the population of the United States increased by more than four million between 1860 and 1864, that there were many more potential voters in 1864 than there had been in 1860, that the states that had seceded did not participate in the election of 1864, and that Lincoln actually received nearly 700,00 *fewer* votes in 1864 than he had received in 1860 (Cole 1986, 303–307; and Potter 1976, pp. 442–43).

Even more telling indicators of Lincoln's status in the eyes of many of his contemporaries before his death are the attacks people so frequently and openly made against his character, the constant threats to his life, and the glaring references, even in eulogies, to his flaws. In eulogizing Lincoln, for example, Ralph Waldo Emerson (1878) recalled that "All of us remember . . . the surprise and disappointment of the country at his first nomination by the Convention at Chicago. . . . It seemed too rash, on a purely local reputation, to build so grave a trust in such anxious times; and men naturally talked of the chances in politics as incalculable" (308–309). However incalculable his chances may have been, Lincoln won the election, which prompted the Richmond (VA) *Enquirer* to insist that the election of a Black Republican was tantamount to "a declaration of war" (as quoted in Hanchett 1983, 7). Whether Southerners widely shared that sentiment is not difficult to discern, for, as David Potter (1976) pointed out, "secession had begun, after all, not as a response to anything done or left undone by Congress, but rather as a response to the election of Lincoln" (552).

Secession was not the only concrete product of Lincoln's election. When Lincoln arrived in Philadelphia on February 21, 1860, on his way to be inaugurated, he was warned that someone planned to make an attempt on his life in Baltimore. Having ignored the warning initially, Lincoln later received a message directly from William Seward and Gen. Winfield Scott urging him to take the threat seriously. On their advice Lincoln altered his plans and took a different train through Baltimore to Washington. After Lincoln's death many would remember this as Lincoln's "hair-breadth escape from the hand of the assassin as he passed through the notorious city of Baltimore" (Miner 1865, 282). At the time, however, many citizens regarded Lincoln's "escape" as "an anticlimactic and even ignominious ending to a journey that had been in some respects an extended celebration." As David Potter (1976) observes, "opposition newspapers seized gleefully on the episode and made the president-elect a target of ridicule and cartoons. His prestige, never extraordinarily high, sank probably to its lowest point since his election" (562).

Nor did his prestige rise very much soon afterward, for Lincoln was persistently the object of derision throughout his first term in office. Some ridiculed Lincoln for his awkward and peculiar mannerisms—what George Hepworth (1865) referred to as "a certain want of refinement" (113). Rather more explicitly, James Davidson called Lincoln "the vulgar monkey who now rules Washington" (as quoted in Hanchett 1983, 11-12). J.D. Fulton (1865), a Boston minister, pointed to Lincoln's "official awkwardness" (362). Another, who claimed to have visited Lincoln in the White House, insisted that he found Lincoln "seated in shirt sleeves, his feet on the mantelpiece, his hat on his head, amusing himself by making huge semicircles with tobacco juice that he squeezed out of his quid" (as quoted in Hanchett 1983, 11-12). J. M. Manning (1865) drew attention to Lincoln's "philosophy of jacoseness," which many thought unbefitting an American president (65). George Templeton Strong, a New York diarist, thought Lincoln was "a barbarian, Scythian, yahoo, or gorilla" (as quoted in Hanchett 1983, 11-12). And A. N. Littlejohn (1865) remarked that "as a writer he was singularly deficient in the ordinary graces of style," "destitute of methodological training, utterly without what is technically known as culture" (151-152).

Others ridiculed Lincoln's competence, intelligence, and policies. In New York a member of the state House of Representatives remarked that "many of the measures that [Lincoln] adopted for the suppression of the bloody contest, had, in some instances, as was to be expected, passed through the ordeal of severe criticism" (Redington 1865, 27). Speaking on the same occasion, another New Yorker blandly remarked that Lincoln "was not, in the common acceptance of the term, a great man" (Murphy 1865, 82).

Warren Cudworth (1865) later recalled that many of those in Lincoln's own administration had vigorously opposed his policies on "the confiscation of property, the unconditional abolition of slavery, the extension of the right of suffrage, and the publication of an act of amnesty offering pardon to everybody willing to renew alliance" (207). The Reverend A. N. Littlejohn (1865) insisted that Lincoln "had not the severe dignity of Washington, nor the acumen and breadth of Hamilton, nor the versatility of John Quincy Adams. He had not the electric eloquence of Clay, nor the matchless finish of Everett, nor the massive strength of Webster" (151). A New York editor insisted that Lincoln was "an uneducated boor. He is brutal in all his habits and in all his ways. He is filthy. He is obscene. He is vicious" (as quoted in Hanchett 1983, 12). Another Northerner criticized Lincoln because "he hesitated to put his foot down. There can be little doubt," he proclaimed, but that "thousands of lives were sacrificed because of his slowness" (J. D. Fulton 1865, 374). And the *New York World* flatly declared that "The conspicuous weakness of Mr. Lincoln's mind on the side of imagination, taste, and refined sensibility, has rather helped him in the estimation of the multitude" (as quoted in Shea 1865, 80).

As the election of 1864 approached, Lincoln was denounced in Chicago "as a tyrant and usurper, and compared to Nero and Caligula, and every other vile wretch whose black deeds darken the page of history" (as quoted in Colfax 1865, 216). Maria Daily wondered if "our countrymen can be so blind, so stupid, as to again place such a clod . . . in the presidential chair"; and Marcus "Brick" Pomeroy, the infamous editor of the LaCross (WI) *Democrat,* prayed to "Almighty God [to] forbid that we are to have two terms of the rottenest, most stinking, ruinworking small pox ever conceived by friends or mortals." Pomeroy was also hopeful that "some bold hand" would piece Lincoln's "heart with a dagger point for the public good" (as quoted in Hanchett 1983, 17 and 18).

Pomeroy's hope was by no means isolated. The *New York Copperhead* told Lincoln to "behave yourself, boss, or we shall be obliged to make an island of your head and stick it on the end of a pole. Then, for the first time, Lincoln's cocoanut [sic] will be posted" (as quoted in Turner 1982, 69). In the South, or so many Northerners believed, "the assassination of the President" was such a common topic of conversation that few were terribly surprised when "one of the Southern papers actually offered a reward for the assassination of the President, Vice-President, and Secretary of State" (Shea 1865, 56). That infamous advertisement, as Schuler Colfax (1865) noted in his eulogy for Lincoln, was "published in the Selma (AL) *Dispatch* of Last December [1864], and copied approvingly into other rebel organs":

> ONE MILLION DOLLARS WANTED, TO HAVE PEACE BY THE FIRST OF MARCH.—If the citizens of the Southern confederacy will furnish me with the cash, or good securities for the sum of one million dollars, I will cause the lives of Abraham Lincoln, W. H. Seward, and Andrew Johnson to be taken by the first of March next. This will give us peace, and satisfy the world that cruel tyrants cannot live in a "land of liberty." If this is not accomplished, nothing will be claimed beyond the sum of fifty thousand dollars in advance, which is supposed to be necessary to reach and slaughter the three villains.
>
> I will give, myself, one thousand dollars toward this patriotic purpose. (206)

Both North and South, Thomas Reed Turner (1982) notes, "newspapers were filled with suggestions for violence against the president" (69). And, as William Hanchett (1983) has observed, "threatening letters arrived [at the White House] continuously and in large numbers" (23). It is difficult to know whether these constant threats would have been acted out or whether persistent rumors of organized efforts to kidnap or assassinate Lincoln had any firm basis in reality (Hanchett 1983, 7–124; and Turner 1982, 125–50). One assassination effort obviously did come to fruition, and even then criticisms of Lincoln did not cease.

When an individual dies, as Freud (1953) knew so well, the living typically "suspend criticism of [them], overlook [their] possible misdoings, issue the command: *De mortus nil nisi bene*, and regard it as justifiable to set forth in the funeral oration and upon the tombstone only that which is most favourable to [their] memory" (16). Most citizens appear to have abided by that dictum; or, at least, most manifested some degree of restraint subsequent to Lincoln's death. Others did not. With complete disregard for the belief that one should not speak ill of the dead, the *Texas Republican* insisted that "from now on until God's judgment day the minds of men will not cease to thrill at the killing of Abraham Lincoln, by the hand of Booth, the actor." The Chattanooga (TN) *Daily Rebel* gladly proclaimed that "Abe has gone to answer before the bar of God for the innocent blood which he has permitted to be shed, and his efforts to enslave a free people" (as quoted in Turner 1982, 95 and 96).

Although often less jubilant, some Northerners were no less direct. A Boston minister remarked in his eulogy for Lincoln that, had Lincoln lived, "being in our midst, and not always the representative of our ideas, no doubt he would often have failed of appreciation, had he not provoked opposition, and some of his measures or recommendations would have been sharply criticised, if not severely censured" (Cudworth 1865, 208). Some of the more extreme members of Congress "did not among themselves conceal their gratification that [Lincoln] was no longer in their way" (Nicolay & Hay 1890, 315–16). Everyday citizens, both "men and *women*," Charles Robinson (1865) noted in his eulogy to Lincoln, "clap their hands in applause of this murder," and some "will declare that this murder in cold blood of a man in the presence of his wife is *chivalrous!*" (97, 103-104). Many even among those who were sympathetic to

Lincoln's policies were inclined to believe that "perhaps he would have been too gentle with evil-doers in the time to come," for Lincoln clearly was "not sufficiently stern" (Bartol 1865, 55). In all, during his time in office and to a lesser extent even after his death, Lincoln was, as Henry Foote (1865) remarked in his eulogy for Lincoln, "the object of such contumely and violent hate as no other in our history has ever had to bear" (185).

None of this is to suggest that Lincoln was hugely unpopular, that a majority of citizens disliked him or disapproved of his policies or politics, or that the often frustrated rhetoric of his contemporaries is somehow inaccurate. On the other hand, because Lincoln was the object of much hatred and anger and frustration, because rumors of plots and conspiracies were incessant, because threats to his life were constant, because violence and subterfuge were everpresent, and because some people openly and publicly hoped for his death while others had been fearfully anticipating his assassination "for four years and more" (Bartol 1865, 53), Lincoln's contemporaries were not entirely surprised when they learned of his death. But they were shocked. Northerners were shocked in part because the news they had been receiving during the week preceding Lincoln's assassination suggested that the end of the war was in sight. As Alfred T. Jones (1927) recalled in his eulogy to Lincoln,

> How brightly opened the days of that eventful month in 1865. Four years of bloody warfare, with its attendant vicissitudes and horrors, had passed, when came the joyful tidings of the evacuation of Petersburg; then quickly followed the flight of our enemies from Richmond; next the unconditional surrender of the Rebel army and its greatest General.
>
> What a universal jubilee prevailed throughout the loyal States. Joy sat enthroned on every countenance, each glance shone with expectation bright, friend greeted friend

with heartfelt warmth; political opponents, with united
hands, joined in the universal exultation; women wept for
joy, and children shouted in exuberant delight. (156)

Particularly significant in helping to create an atmosphere of
celebration was Lee's surrender to Grant at the Appomattox Court
House on April 9, 1865. "We remember," Richard H. Steele (1865)
lamented, "how the daily papers greeted us that morning with the
broad capitals—Union—Victory—Peace—The surrender of General
Lee and his whole army" (5). Throughout the North people were
either already celebrating or preparing to celebrate, and, some people believed, there was a general sense that "the rancor of party feeling was fast dying out in the nation; men were fast honorably sub-
mitting to the voice of the people expressed through the ballot box;
and they were gradually yielding to the conviction that Abraham
Lincoln was an honest and a good man." The possibility that victory
and peace were at hand also seemed to suggest to many
Northerners that, whatever his flaws, Lincoln had been "pursuing a
wise and judicious policy, which would result in the restoration of
peace upon the great and immutable principles of truth, liberty, and
righteousness" (Rockwell 1865, 274). In short, however much they
might have anticipated or wished for Lincoln's assassination, many
Northerners were shocked that his death came when it did—in the
midst of celebration and when Lincoln's popularity was perhaps as
high as it had ever been (Turner 1982, 18–24).

Against this backdrop one of the things that most impressed
and perplexed citizens was the unprecedented character of Lincoln's
death. Perhaps because human beings are "fated to puzzle out what
it actually means to feel 'right,'" as Ernest Becker (1975, 104) so aptly
put it, Lincoln's contemporaries diligently sought some historical
precedent, some point of reference that would place the assassination of an American president in proper perspective. Some suggested a point of comparison between the deaths of Lincoln and
William of Orange.[12] Some saw a similarity between the deaths of

Lincoln and Moses or Christ.[13] Others sought to draw a parallel between the deaths of Washington and Lincoln.[14] As Merrill Peterson (1994) recently pointed out, "Lincoln's name was constantly coupled with Washington's. In fact that began before the President's death, but the apotheosis firmly enforced the pairing in the public mind" (27). Yet, even those who focused on what they thought might be historically or emotionally similar incidents eventually concluded that Lincoln's death and its consequences were simply unprecedented.

In considering that "President Harrison died in 1841, a month after his inauguration, and President Taylor held the office but little over a year, dying in 1850," O. E. Daggett (1865) also acknowledged that both of these deaths arrived "with the slow steps and premonitions of disease. The nation had made itself in part ready for the issue; bent its ear to listen for the tidings" (5).[15] "For the third time since our existence as an independent government," J. E. Rockwell (1865) recalled, "we have been called upon to mourn over the death of our Chief Magistrate. Yet, never before has the nation passed through such an experience as this" (273). Henry J. Fox (1865) noted that "Harrison and Taylor both died during their term of office. But in these instances death was ushered, if not invited, in, by disease and overwork" (342). Addressing his congregation in Bedford, Pennsylvania, Robert F. Sample (1865) simply declared that "we must accept the sad truth, and write a chapter in our national history unlike any that has gone before" (8). Witnessing before his congregation in New York, A. P. Rogers (1865) even more overtly stated the conclusion to which many people increasingly were drawn: "It has no precedent in all our history, and we reel and stagger under the unexpected and mighty catastrophe" (241).

## THE LINCOLN MYTH AND BEYOND

The assassination of Abraham Lincoln presents us with an extraordinary case. Despite his status then and now, here is an individual whose contemporaries continued to criticize and deride him even after his death. Yet, a great many of those same contemporaries memorialized his death and life as if he had been an intimate member of their family, sparing neither expense nor effort. A partial explanation of this disparity, no doubt, is that the death of a significant individual, even under the least objectionable conditions, necessarily places the living squarely at the center of a nexus of disorganized emotions.[16] As Ernest Campbell (1969) concludes, "we should expect the volume of grief occasioned by a death to be, indeed, proportional to the number of persons whose role systems are dislocated or threatened, and to the sum of the severity of the dislocation" (221).

In such an exceptional case, of course, it would be entirely too simplistic to imagine that Lincoln's contemporaries responded to his death as they did solely out of fear for the status and stability of their social roles—or, for that matter, out of sheer admiration for Lincoln, or out of political considerations necessarily drawn into focus by the fact of and circumstances surrounding his death, or out of guilt that he had been placed in such an impossible position, or out of shame that so many had openly and persistently hoped and prayed for his death, or out of remorse that he had been constantly the object of threats and ridicule and derision, or out of shock for the unprecedented manner of his death, or out of the possibility that his death would provide an opportunity for cultural transformation. Much more likely, all these forces were at work within Lincoln's contemporaries, who were bound together in their extraordinary efforts to commemorate his death not by any singular emotion or motive, but by a set of intense discomforts that derived from a number of sources and that impelled the living to go to extremes to attach their emotions to something concrete.

"While we don't know exactly how the mind works in relation to emotion, how deeply words go when dealing with reality or repressions," Ernest Becker (1975) once wrote, we do know that

the death of an intimate occasions rhetoric, the meaningful articulation of symbols, through which "one tries to deny oblivion and
to extend oneself beyond death in symbolic ways" (104). In the
liminal moments surrounding the death of a significant individual, especially, those symbols finely articulate the ethos and worldview that make life and death meaningful and that define how one
*ought* to feel and how one can best deal with the way one actually
feels. One consequence of such efforts in the present case is a clear
legacy of the *ethoi* and world views of Lincoln's contemporaries.

On the other hand, even given intense discomforts at a variety of levels, it is implausible that the rhetorical and cultural
efforts of Lincoln's contemporaries immediately and permanently
created the images of Lincoln that now occupy places of honor and
reverence in the nation's "collective memory." Immediate
responses to Lincoln's assassination and corresponding opinions
of his character varied much too dramatically to have crystallized
immediately and permanently into an untarnished hero-image
(Campbell 1973, Gerzon 1992, Segal 1990). Equally important,
even if those responses and opinions had been singular, creating a
seemingly permanent element of the symbolic code that constitutes collective memory requires time as well as intensity
(Berkovitch 1993, Bodnar 1992, Kammen 1991, Nerone 1989,
Shudson 1989). How, then, did Lincoln come to occupy such a special place in collective memory?

A large part of the answer, as Merrill Peterson's (1994) recent
*Lincoln in American Memory* roundly demonstrates, is that a myriad of citizens, working from different assumptions and different
motives, have sought to appropriate—and often have successfully
appropriated—Lincoln's image over time. And it is through just
such efforts that Lincoln has continually "belonged to the nation's
cultural heritage as well as to its civil history" (375).[17] This in no
small measure helps to explain why the same three conflicting
images that dominated contemporaneous rhetoric about Lincoln
later became the three dominant elements of the Lincoln myth—

namely, "the rail-splitter," the man who journeyed "from a log cabin to the White House," and "the American Christ/Moses."[18] Indeed, what Peterson (1994) observes about scholars can be taken as a truism about Lincoln's image more generally: "Scholars maintained, of course, that their Lincoln was the historical Lincoln—the *real* Lincoln—and they could not help it if he resembled the idealized Lincoln" (374). Looking specifically at how and why various cultural groups have sought to advance *their* Lincoln explains how and why those same three elements, which were part of the symbolic code in Lincoln's time, survive as distinct parts of the present symbolic code.

Before turning to that task, however, we would do well to bear in mind that America—even if we restrict our use of this term to the United States—is not and never has been monocultural, and that the continuous struggle to gain access to and control of America's collective memory is hardly a benign process (Berkovitch 1993, Bodnar 1992, Kammen 1991, Miller 1992). Clearly, the assumption that collective memory within any multicultural society is singular too readily presumes that the various cultures within a multicultural society endorse and/or embrace the same collective memory and that the interactions of cultures do not result in cultural interchange, exchange, influence, and/or transformation. As Michael Shudson (1989) has suggested, thinking that collective memory is infinitely available for reinterpretation is naive. At the very least, "full freedom to reconstruct the past according to one's own present interpretation is limited by three factors: the structure of available pasts, the structure of individual choices, and the conflicts about the past among a multitude of mutually aware individuals or groups" (105). Further, as Bodnar (1992) maintains, collective memory serves as "a cognitive device to mediate competing interpretations and [to] privilege some explanations over others" (14).

Here it will be useful to distinguish between "public memory" and "cultural memory" (see also Berkovitch 1993, Bodnar

1992, Kammen 1991, Miller 1992). Whereas cultural memory reflects the particularized world view and ethos of the members of a *particular* culture, public memory is perhaps best conceived as an *amalgam* of the current hegemonic bloc's cultural memory and bits and pieces of cultural memory that members of other cultures are able to preserve and protect. The struggle to obtain and retain public memory being constant and constantly a signifier of the possibility of cultural transformation, significant shifts in the character of public memory thus point sharply to the actualities of such transformations. To witness, for example, the dominance of Lincoln's image as a rail-splitter give way to an image that celebrates Lincoln's meritorious movement from a poor boy with limited prospects to a man with virtually unlimited prospects signals a moment of cultural conflict, a moment of cultural transformation, and, because the rail-splitter element persists, an amalgam of two conflicting efforts to install (and preserve) elements of cultural memory within public memory.

In these pages I seek to demonstrate that the extraordinary efforts of nineteenth-century citizens not only helped to ensure "the future fame of 'the martyr President,'" as Charles Stewart (1964, 307; see also Stewart 1963 and 1965) has established, but that they also contributed specifically to the formation and perpetuation of the three dominant elements of the Lincoln myth. These three dominant elements, I also argue, emerged and have survived the test of time not because of any inherent superiority, but because they embody key tenets of three distinct memorial traditions, each of which reveals the rhetorical outlines of three equally distinct cultures that historically have vied for control of public memory, three cultures that are roughly parallel to those identified in *Habits of the Heart,* the remarkable work by Robert Bellah, Richard Madsen, William Sullivan, Ann Swidler, and Steven Tipton (1985): "From its early days, some Americans have seen the purpose and goal of the nation as the effort to realize the ancient biblical hope of a just and compassionate society. Others have struggled to share the spirit of their lives and the laws of the nation in accord with the ideals of republican citizenship and participation. Yet others have promoted dreams of manifest destiny and national glory" (27–28). What we see in the transformation of Lincoln's image, then, is not a single people creating and later transforming an element of the symbolic code of collective memory, but the rise and fall of different cultures, each of which positions Lincoln within a different world view and ethos.[19]

From another angle, the very fact that Lincoln's death called forth memorials that embody a host of voices from many cultures makes this moment in time especially well suited to an exploration of the rhetorical and cultural bases of American memorializing. At the macroscopic level, as Farrell (1980) notes, "Death is a cultural event and societies as well as individuals reveal themselves in their treatment of death" (3). Further, "one general connection between death and the organization of human culture[s] [that] has been repeatedly observed and analyzed since the turn of the present century," as David Stannard (1975a) points out, "is the tie between attitudes toward death and the sense of community purpose and a meaning a people may or may not enjoy" (x). Then, too, as Mandelbaum (1959) observes, "Rituals for death can have many uses for life. And the study of their rites can illuminate much about a culture and a society" (215). In the context of those voices, then, we witness the articulation of each culture's worldview and ethos, of the desire to make Lincoln the embodiment of that worldview and ethos, of the need to perpetuate one's culture by attaching that worldview and ethos to something concrete yet so much less susceptible to oblivion than fragile life, and of the struggle to install one's own culture as the proprietor and gatekeeper of the nation's public memory.[20]

The connection here between worldview and shifting images of Lincoln across time and place derives from the nature of culture, and the connection between culture and collective memory derives from the nature of memorializing. Borrowing from Clifford

Geertz (1973), I use the term "culture" to refer to "an historically transmitted pattern of meanings embodied in symbols, a system of inherited conceptions expressed in symbolic forms" whereby individuals "communicate, perpetuate, and develop their knowledge about and attitudes toward life." Within such a system, memorials are in a fundamental sense sacred symbols, which "function to synthesize a people's ethos—the tone, character, and quality of their life, its moral and aesthetic style and mood—and their world view—the picture they have of the way things in their sheer actuality are, their most comprehensive ideas of order" (89). Embedded within an identifiable tradition, sacred symbols created through the process of memorializing thus recapitulate culture and constitute a vivid record of cultural memory.

## MEMORIALIZING AMONG AMERICANS

Those who have studied American memorials persistently have acknowledged the cultural and rhetorical (or communicative) significance of their subject.[21] Despite having generated a solid and lively body of research somewhat loosely organized around a common set of assumptions and observations, however, researchers in this area have not examined the communicative dimensions of American memorializing in a way that would encourage us to make sense of memorials as fundamentally rhetorical sacred symbols; nor have they systematically applied the concept of culture in a way that would allow us to make sense of memorials as fundamentally cultural. As a consequence, we now have a impressive body of research that says a great deal about the work of individual memorial artists, individual icons and iconographic motifs, and shifting visual patterns across time and place, but we still understand far too little about American memorializing.

The first part of this twofold problem is that researchers overwhelmingly have assumed that a memorial is best understood if we conceive of it as being something other than a memorial, a sacred symbol. For a variety of reasons, that is to say, some researchers have assumed that memorials are best understood as aesthetic objects, while others have assumed that memorials are best understood as historical data.

Those who have approached memorials as aesthetic objects explicitly or implicitly have focused on how and/or how well memorials and their creators have realized their aesthetic potential. Early on in the development of this body of research, for example, Allan Ludwig (1966) concluded in his impressive pioneering work that, after the decline of Puritan influence, memorializers fell prey to diseases of fashion:

> Before the introduction of neoclassical motifs into New England the Yankee enthusiastically pictured the flight of the soul to heaven upon his gravestone. Later it was no longer fashionable to portray the naive joys of Christianity, when shiny new neoclassical sentiments had just been imported from England. A mark of a culturally provincial people is the degree to which they abandon their own values and become slaves of one imported fashion after another. . . .
>
> The bumptious aspirations of a newly emerging America are nowhere more appallingly revealed than in the transformation of style from the natural rural idiom of abstraction to a hollow provincialized one. (337 and 338)

What might in other terms be understood as significant rhetorical and cultural differences or as fundamental cultural transformations or as sites of cultural conflict here reduce to a dilution of aesthetic sensibilities. Enthusiastic, naive, value-oriented, natural, aesthetic abstractions give way, according to this view, to "shiny new neoclassical sentiments," to the slavery of "one imported fashion after another," to "bumptious aspirations," to "the transformation of [an appropriate] style" into "a hollow and provincialized one." Just so, memorials cease to be sacred symbolic expressions of a culture and become mere manifestations of aesthetic sensibilities.

Seeking to expand Ludwig's interpretive framework, Dickran and Ann Tashjian (1974) convincingly argued that an understanding of memorials can occur only if one first understands the culture(s) from which they emerge, for such an understanding "requires a recognition of the artifact first as a manifestation of culture in its own right, then as part of an intangible network of ideas, attitudes, and values that brought it into being" (xiv). From this perspective memorials "not only commemorated the deceased individual but also confirmed the broad cultural goals and ideals" of the cultural members for whom they were significant (10). The point is well taken, but as Tashjian and Tashjian explicitly acknowledge, the primary goal of their research was not to understand the cultural significance of memorials, but to resolve a number of "long-standing misconceptions" so that scholars could begin to consider memorials more seriously as works of art (5).

The widespread influence of Ludwig's early work and the expanded interpretive framework that Tashjian and Tashjian later introduced largely explain why so many scholars so consistently have celebrated "interesting" memorials; why they have ignored and even been repulsed by "mass produced" memorials; why they have focused so intensely on attempting to determine whether memorials are instances of "art," "folk art," or "debased" or "degraded art which exhibits more confusion than symbolism" (Foster 1977, 10); and why so much of the work in this area concerns "talented" memorial artists.[22]

However interesting and illuminating such issues and foci may be in their own right, the assumption that memorials are best understood as aesthetic objects has led to the imposition of fundamentally inappropriate evaluative and interpretive criteria in the following sense. A memorial's *cultural* significance derives from its status as a sacred symbol to those for whom it is literally significant, not from its status as an aesthetic object or from the aesthetic talents of its creator or from aesthetic standards that fail to take into account its sacred status. A "poorly wrought" sacred symbol is just as sacred as a "well wrought" sacred symbol, even if members of the culture for whom that symbol is sacred acknowledge that the latter may be "more beautiful" than the former. Within the mutable boundaries of a particular culture, for example, a crucifix would not cease to be sacred simply because it is a mass-produced piece of painted plastic. This is why works of art may be defamed whereas defamation becomes desecration in the presence of the sacred.

To render a negative evaluation of an aesthetic object, to defame it, is to reveal only that the object does not satisfy specifiable aesthetic standards; but to render a negative evaluation of a sacred symbol, to desecrate it, is to commit an offense and to reveal, more often than not, that one is not a member of the culture for whom that symbol is sacred. When critics of the Vietnam Veterans Memorial in Washington, D.C., caustically described it as "a urinal" and worse, they did so under the guise of aesthetic criteria. But the passion of their evaluations and the equally passionate responses that those evaluations elicited from those for whom the Memorial is a sacred symbol reveal that the conflict was cultural, not aesthetic (Morris 1990, esp. 211–14). Similarly, when scholars render positive or negative evaluations of sacred symbols as aesthetic objects, they are in effect announcing their membership in a culture that either does or does not regard that particular symbol as sacred. In either case, to render an aesthetic judgment of a sacred symbol is to impose fundamentally inappropriate interpretive and evaluative criteria: A sacred symbol cannot mean what it means or be valued culturally unless we first allow it to be what it is. Attempting to comprehend a given memorial tradition or memorializing more generally with the unwarranted assumption that memorials are aesthetic objects in hand simply compounds the problem.

The assumption that memorials are bits of historical data, by contrast, has led other researchers to focus attention on the repetition of symbols and symbol types. James Deetz and Edwin Dethlefsen (1967), for example, argued in their pioneering efforts that the emergence of the death's head, the cherub motif, and the willow and urn motif correspond to historical periods dominated by Puritanism, the Great Awakening, and Unitarianism and Methodism, respectively.[23] Following additional research and reflection, Deetz (1989) abandoned the view that specific symbols attach to specific religious movements in the United States, though he still maintained that the appearance and disappearance of particular icons or iconographic motifs "are functions of a major change in the world view that occurred during the late eighteenth century" (xiii). Thus, knowing when a particular icon or iconographic motif appeared, reached its peak of popularity, and disappeared, he argues, correspondingly should tell us about a shifting or "evolving" of *America's* worldview.

This helps explain why so much of the research conducted with this assumption in mind favors documenting the existence of a particular symbol or icon to the exclusion of other symbols or icons, why the meaning of both repetitive and nonrepetitive symbols and icons is of little concern, why the investigation of specific memorial artists and their influence is a privileged focus of discussion, and why these scholars in particular are so concerned to maintain rigid control of space, time, and form.[24] Again, however interesting such issues may be methodologically, the assumption that memorials are best understood as historical data leads to unwarranted and misleading conclusions.

By concentrating intensely on repetitive symbols and icons, for instance, one readily can conclude that nonrepetitive symbols and icons are mere subtypes of what one takes to be prototypical. Yet, as David H. Watters (1979/80) points out, the identification of such prototypes rests on faulty assumptions because "the simplistic classification of certain images as death's heads or cherubs, combined with assumptions of which images are more or less hopeful to our eyes for the sake of 'proving' changes in religious and cultural attitudes, blurs [researcher's] perceptions of the stones themselves" (176). One consequence of relying on such faulty assumptions is that "too much time has been spent trying to match particular designs to such popular events as the Great Awakening, at the expense of recognizing much more basic, unchanging beliefs which gravestones express" (178). Rather than considering and investigating the possibility that multiple cultures may be using the same or similar symbols to say entirely different things about what, how, and why the living should remember, methodology subsumes and obscures "subtypes" as additional bits of data to substantiate the view that, as Deetz (1989) recently suggested, "the decline in popularity of the Death's head motif was a function of the decline in New England Puritan orthodoxy" (xiii). To argue that such memorials belong to related or even entirely different cultures or memorial traditions, as I argue here, calls into question the central hypothesis that undergirds this body of research.

A similar problem emerges when one focuses on the existence of specific symbols or icons to the exclusion of other symbols and icons, for this readily leads to the mistaken belief that the existence of that icon or symbol on a single memorial allows it to "count" as an instance of the prototype under investigation—regardless of what else that memorial may have to say about what, how, and why we should remember. Thus, for example, assuming that the presence of a winged death's head allows one to count any given memorial as an instance of the prototype encourages one to overlook transculturation, cultural exchanges, and other alterations that occur when cultures in close contact borrow from one another, in which case their seemingly univocal memorials may not be saying the same things at all. And if they are not saying the same things, if one recommends that we remember death while the other recommends that we remember the specific person for whom the memorial was erected, as I also argue here, then both clearly cannot "count" as instances to prove the hypothesis.

To put the matter in a different light, the problem with assuming that memorials belonging to a particular period or place are indicative of a predefined culture is that it begs the question and reduces culture to a mere temporal or spatial intersection. This might not be especially problematic if what one seeks is an account of shifting aesthetic sensibilities across time, space, or both. But if we are to assign any rhetorical or cultural significance to such shifts, assuming the conclusion will obscure rather than illuminate. As Ludwig and Hall (1978) came to understand, to equate culture with aesthetic standards derived solely from considerations of time and place leads to the untenable conclusion that cultures wink in and out of existence almost instantaneously. Ultimately, we are on much safer ground if we "assume that fundamental belief patterns such as eschatological ones do not change over night. Rather, they may be said to evolve over centuries, and their waning can stretch over many decades, if not centuries" (18; see also Hall 1977)

To avoid this conclusion, some scholars lately have begun to use terminology that describes such shifts as "developmental" or "evolutionary."[25] Rather than the sudden and unexplainable demise of various cultures, then, we supposedly find a single, monolithic "American culture" moving through various evolutionary stages of growth and development. As James Slater (1977) acknowledged, beginning with this assumption tends to lead scholars by an "almost subconscious instinct to view [memorials] from an evolutionary standpoint" (11). Subconsciously or otherwise, beginning with the assumption that there is such a thing as an American culture—if we understand "culture" to refer to something more meaningful than physical or physiological characteristics—is wrought with confusion.

Consider the matter this way. The twin assumptions that "culture" is either infinitely expandable or infinitely divisible are not opposites but belong to the same order of thinking—namely, that culture refers to a spatial and/or temporal intersection. In this sense "American culture," "Black culture," "Gay culture," "Native American culture," and other such notions effectively are demographic categories that have little or nothing to do with the ethos and worldview of the people to whom they ostensibly refer. One might just as easily—and undoubtedly more accurately—render "American culture" as "nation" without any loss of meaning. Terms such as "Black culture," although often politically useful and seemingly meaningful, thus turn out to be entirely problematic, to say the least, if one understands the term "culture" as referring to anything more than a spatial and/or temporal intersection; for if culture refers to a shared worldview and ethos (or to any other set of meaningful, nonphysiological, nonphysical, nondemographic categories), the term "Black culture," for example, posits the untenable position that all individuals with a particular skin tone or range of skin tones have the same worldview and ethos—that skin tone in such cases transparently identifies an individual's or demographically created group's values, principles, beliefs, modes of communication, and so forth. Viewed from this perspective, "American culture," "Black culture," "Women's culture," "peasant culture," and the like are far more than innocent abuses of an otherwise meaningful term. Beyond question, something more than demographic categories or the use of specific symbols unites individuals across space and time. As D'arcy McNickle (1973) astutely notes,

> to say that a culture persists or that a modal personality remains psychologically intact while adapting to change does not describe what it is that persists. It is necessary to define content or quality, at least in generalized terms, in order to determine what sets one culture apart from others, and possibly to distinguish stages within a sequential development. This is not easy because any culture is itself a generalization, an averaging out of many discrete modes, even

contradictions. When the problem is dealt with quantita-
tively by cataloging the known traits of a culture, the result
is an abstraction describing nothing human. (10)

If the term "culture" refers to something more than a demographic category and to something less than all of the individuals
about whom one might conceivably speak, then we might more pro-
ductively and empathically begin not with categories of people, but
with an identifiable ethos and worldview, with "an historically transmitted pattern of meanings embodied in symbols, a system of inherited conceptions expressed in symbolic forms" whereby individuals
"communicate, perpetuate, and develop their knowledge about and
attitudes toward life" (to return to Geertz's definition). Such an
approach to culture becomes increasingly necessary in a world that
increasingly is fractured and fragmented, where individuals increasingly see themselves as belonging either to categories that are not
especially meaningful to them or to nothing at all.

The alternative perspective of memorializing that I advance
here thus emerges from the assumption that members of identifiable
cultures share a worldview and ethos and that presupposed demographic categories do not and cannot establish the existence of any
given culture by fiat. I also begin with the precepts that cultures are
dynamic, that their memorial efforts must be understood as sacred
symbols, that those sacred symbols express a culture's presence
through a cultural and rhetorical imperative rather than through a
finite set of icons or symbols, and that cultural and rhetorical shifts
in dominant memorial expression signal the hegemonic rise and fall
of different cultures. The first step in positioning this explanation is
to come to a clearer understanding of memorializing.

## MEMORIALIZING AS PROCESS

That memorializing is a process wherein memory is engaged we
might gather from the Latin term *memoria* (memory) and its root

*memor* (mindful). But memorializing is never merely remembering. To be mindful of something (of anything) by way of memorializing is necessarily to engage in a creative, third-order, symbolic process that simultaneously is a concrete, abstract, incomplete, and evaluative effort to evoke or establish memory of the "memorable" (that is, the object of memorialization) in some specific way. At the risk of belaboring what may seem obvious, consider the matter further.

Memorializing does not simply come to be, nor is it passively coaxed into being. Neither is it the memorable (first-order) or even memory of the memorable (second-order); it is the result of a process that requires the creation of symbols in order to represent memory of the memorable. As a representation, memorializing is also necessarily concrete (albeit not necessarily palpable) because it is something one can experience and to which one can refer, and because it frequently yields something we can call a memorial. A statue, a monument, a bridge, a tombstone, a highway, a building, a mourning ring, a locket, a lock of hair, a room kept as it was, a tree, a park bench, a speech, even a silent prayer— all are concrete manifestations, memorials, brought about through a creative process of symbolization.

At the same time, because memorializing is a third-order process, both it and its manifestation(s) are necessarily abstractions: Both are drawn away from the memorable through memory. And, as symbolic, both are also necessarily incomplete. Through abstracting and symbolizing, one is left with a distillation of one's memory of the memorable. Since any such distillation cannot be identical to the memorable or to one's memory of the memorable, manifestation and process alike must be incomplete, partialized representations.

From this it follows that both manifestation and process are necessarily evaluative. The process is necessarily evaluative because distilling or abstracting invariably involves identifying features of the memorable that "deserve" to be in memory, which concomitantly identifies by negation those features that do not. (That is, since it is not possible to bring the memorable forward through memory in toto, even symbolically, one necessarily partializes the memorable evaluatively.) The manifestation is necessarily evaluative, first, because it derives from a necessarily evaluative process and, second, because any such symbolic formalization serves to evoke or establish features of the memorable that "deserve" to be in memory.

Of particular note here is the implication that purpose discloses itself specifically through the manifestation through which the memorable is symbolically but partially represented in order to evoke or establish memory of the memorable. Put differently, manifestation derives from purpose, and purpose (evoking or establishing memory of the memorable) is in turn signified through manifestation (that which deserves to be in memory). Yet, a memorial's disclosure is by no means transparent. A locket, for instance, may serve as a memorial for some individual but fail to evoke or establish in others what it evokes or establishes in the memorializer. Discerning what a memorial memorializes, why and how it serves as a memorial, or what memory a given memorial evokes or establishes may be possible in such instances only by consulting the memorializer.

None of this matters. Personal or private memorials are not public, not meant to be shared, to evoke or establish memory of the memorable in others. However idiosyncratically they may signify, the apparent or actual disparity between manifestation and purpose is consequently and literally insignificant. On the other hand, when memorials are meant to be shared, when they serve as memorials in the public domain and thereby rely on their rhetoricity, disparity between manifestation and purpose assumes much greater significance.

Unlike private memorials, public memorials "speak" publicly by attempting to shape and possess the present and the future by first shaping and possessing the past. As artifacts, memorials, "through a variety of complex and often interrelated manifestations," Richard Meyer (1989b) observes, "establish patterns of communication (and even dynamic interaction) with those who use or view them" (1); in so doing, they allow us to "achieve a better understanding of ourselves—what we are, what we have been, and, perhaps, what we are in the process of becoming" (5). And, as Dilip Gaonkar (1988) has noted in another context, "to possess the past is to possess the people. For those who possess the past command the sense of the community that enables them to authoritatively recognize the meaning of the present and the possibilities of the future. Thus, history as a systematic understanding of the past unavoidably becomes a site of ideological struggle to understand the past and to direct the future" (1). Thus, also, public memorials become sites of ideological struggle whenever they seek to shape and direct the past, present, and future in the presence of competing articulations.

In the public domain the concrete, abstract, functional, incomplete, and evaluative character of memorializing thus direct us to attend carefully to what a given memorial or memorial tradition says, to how and why it says what it says, to what it fails to say and why it fails to say it, and to the metric it evokes in arriving at its specific evaluation of the memorable. Further, acknowledging that memorializing is a creative, third-order, symbolic process directs us to attend carefully to the creative manner in which a given memorial or memorial tradition seeks to represent the memorable, which in turn directs us to comprehend the culture through which the creativity and symbolicity of that memorial or memorial tradition find their "voice."

No doubt Heidegger (1962) was correct in saying that tradition "takes what has come down to us and delivers it over to self-evidence; it blocks our access to those primordial 'sources' from which the categories and concepts handed down to us have been in part quite genuinely drawn" (42). Yet, by coming to understand the tradition and culture to which something belongs and from which it emanates we can retrace and revitalize in the present those very same sources, and we can begin to comprehend how the past manifests itself in the present by encouraging and enabling those in the present to see themselves as part of a greater whole. Memorials and memorial traditions do not exist simply because scholars describe them. Nor do they require the acknowledgment or consciousness of the individuals or collectivities who perpetuate them. Memorials and the traditions and cultures to which they belong persist because they continue to answer needs—because they are emotionally, psychologically, culturally, and/or rhetorically satisfying to those for whom they are literally significant—even if in answering those needs they obscure their own "primordial sources."

This is doubly true insofar as individual and collective responses to death reveal world views, cultural premises—manners of organizing, parsing, combining, interpreting, and responding to the world.[26] May and Becker were both correct. The "sacral power of death," as May (1969, 1973) calls it, is so enormous that we marshal all our energies to cope with the chaos. And in attempting to thwart the chaos, as Becker (1975) observed, we bring to bear all the resources at our command—our knowledge, our beliefs, our principles, our experiences, our attitudes: The culture that has nurtured and perplexed and shaped our lives (120). Human confrontation with the death of someone or something who/that matters bodies forth concentrations of the culture(s) we are. Literal constructions of reality, memorials "speak" through cultural and rhetorical forms, and their "speaking" is a signification of the culture(s) to which they belong.

## SUMMARY AND PREVIEW

Individually, each memorial is a gift, a sacred symbol, given both to the deceased and to the living. As a sacred symbol—and as the product of a symbolic and necessarily evaluative process—each memorial partially represents the ethos and worldview of the gift-giver. Each manifests concretely what/who is memorable and how and why the memorable ought to be remembered. In so doing, each memorial privileges, preserves, and advances the gift-giver's ethos and worldview over all others.

Considered collectively, memorials coalesce into describable traditions that reflect richer, more complex, more complete images of the *ethoi* and worldviews they seek to perpetuate. Deliberately located in sanctified public space, memorials and the traditions to which they belong endeavor to speak to present and future generations not only of how and why that past ought to be remembered, but also of how and why the present and future ought to be shaped and lived.

Considered macroscopically, memorial traditions conflict, struggle against one another, offer contrary, even contradictory images of what the past was like and of what the present and future should be like. Implicitly, viewers are drawn into a struggle for cultural survival: To accept a memorial as pleasing or beautiful or appropriate signals more than an aesthetic or moral response to an object; it signals the viewer's membership in the tradition and culture to which the memorial belongs, and it marks the continuation of that culture's ethos and worldview. Passing from one person to the next, through contiguous generations, this "historically transmitted pattern of meanings embodied in symbols" helps to ensure the culture's survival as well as the possibility of its continuing influence on public memory.

Diachronically tracing the contours of American memorial traditions, from 1632 to the present, thus provides us with a nearly cinemagraphic representation of the ebb and flow, the movement and moment of cultural transformation and dominance, which allows us to explore why the content of public memory at any given moment in a multicultural society depends largely on the needs and inclinations, the values and norms, the ethos and worldview of the culture that is dominant at that moment.

Within this interpretive frame, nineteenth-century responses to Lincoln's assassination—considered as a synchronic balance—provide us with hundreds of images akin to still photographs of a specific moment and place.

Charged at the very least by an intense set of discomforts that Lincoln's death helped to create, a cultural group that I call "Religionists" (whose memorial tradition and cultural contours I trace in chapter 2) circumscribed Lincoln's life and death within their view of reality, creating an image of Lincoln as the American Christ/Moses. Similarly charged and following a different cultural logic, a cultural group that I term "Romanticists" (whose memorial tradition and cultural configuration I detail in chapter 3) clothed Lincoln in their worldview and ethos to create an image of Lincoln as the rail-splitter. A third cultural group that I designate "Heroists" (whose memorial tradition and cultural adumbration I sketch in chapter 4) measured and fit Lincoln within the logic of their culture, memorializing him as the man who had worked his way from a log cabin to the White House.

Contesting not simply to lay claim to Lincoln as their own, but to lay claim to the nation's public memory through their value-laden portrayals of Lincoln, members of all three of these cultural groups sought to confront the chaos created in part by Lincoln's death by attempting to create an order made in their own image. Understanding the continuity across time between the ascendance and decline of these memorial traditions and disparate images of Lincoln, I argue in chapter 5, reveals a great deal more than the distant sentimentality of nineteenth-century citizens; it reveals an historically embedded cultural struggle that has significant implications for how we interpret cultural conflict in past, present, and future America.

Before moving to those discussions, however, two final caveats are in order. First, the terms I have chosen to represent the three American cultures under discussion, it seems obvious, are somewhat problematic because referring to any culture as

"Religionist" might suggest that this culture and this culture alone values religion and/or that all people who consider themselves religious are by definition Religionists. Referring to a cultural group as "Romanticist" similarly might suggest that this culture and this culture alone privileges romantic values and that all those who privilege such values must be Romanticists. Referring to a cultural group as "Heroist" might suggest that this culture and this culture alone values and celebrates its heroes and that all those who value and celebrate heroes must be Heroists.

These are legitimate concerns. I have pondered numerous alternatives that conceivably would alleviate the problem in some measure. Yet, I can imagine no other terms that so remarkably capture the *ethoi* and worldviews under discussion as appropriately as the terms I have chosen. More to the point, cultures, especially in a multicultural society, are not entities, discrete or otherwise. They do not possess incomparable characteristics and are not mutually exclusive categories. Their members move in and out, sometimes existing in more than one culture simultaneously, sometimes existing betwixt and between. As Claire Farrer (1991) puts it, "a culture cannot remain static and never-changing and still be vital in a changing world. Culture is continually emerging, continually changing, and continually being reaffirmed" (127). Perhaps it will suffice to say that Religionists can be thoroughly romantic and do celebrate their heroes; Romanticists can be thoroughly religious (and even embrace the same religious tenants as members of other cultures) and lionize heroes made in their own image; and Heroists can be fully religious and romantic in their own way. But each of these cultures communicates, perpetuates, and develops these tendencies differently, through a very distinct worldview and ethos; and that is the central concern that has guided my use of the terms.

Then, too, these terms (and their cognates) are already well used in a variety of different ways, which may invite confusion. Because one might say with some legitimacy that "religious,"

"romantic," and "heroic" impulses exist to some extent simultaneously in many if not all of us, that is to say, it might seem reasonable enough to conclude that these impulses are strands or threads
rather than "cultures." For all that, I consider myself a student of
culture and ethnology and hardly an "authority" on what culture
is/must be. Just the same, if we look more deeply into the matter,
it seems to me obvious that some people venerate, communicate,
develop, and perpetuate a worldview and ethos (to return yet
again to Geertz's definition) that emerge from such "impulses."
Further, because people individually and collectively also elevate
and practice and seek to persuade others to elevate and practice
such worldviews and *ethoi*, it seems to me equally obvious that we
may speak sensibly of those who embrace such worldviews and
*ethoi* as belonging to identifiable cultures—even to the extent that
members of the same family may embrace and belong to different
cultures, and even to the extent that, in a world renown for fragmentation and alienation, individuals do not see themselves as
belonging to anything more specific than "American culture." At
the risk of inviting confusion, which I think often is a sign of vig-
orous intellectual health, I have retained these analytical categories
as a matter of convenience.

# 2

# SINNERS

*Miserable riddle, when the same worm must be my mother, and my sister, and my self. Miserable incest, when I must be married to mine own mother and sister, beget and bear that worm, which is all that miserable penury, when my mouth shall be filled with dust, and the worm shall feed, and feed sweetly upon me.*

—John Donne, "Death's Duel"

Among the cultural groups that might benefit from the possibilities of cultural transformation brought about by Lincoln's death, none were as anxious for an opportunity to regain their hegemonic position as the group I am calling Religionists. Having held hegemonic sway over social life (and therefore having been largely in control of public memory), members of this cultural group by the turn of the century had begun to lose ground to other cultural groups; by the time of Lincoln's assassination, their position was further problematized by portentous changes (a point well illustrated by the analysis of cemeterial forms, below). The rise of materialism, naturalism, and positivism; changes in the social status of African Americans, women, children, clerics, and professionals; medical, technological, and scientific advances; shifts in ethical and aesthetic standards; economic, educational, and political changes—all point in significant ways to the transformation of America from the old to the new, from what it had been in the hands of the initial immigrants to what it was becoming in the hands of subsequent waves of immigrants.[1] Yet, even in the face of often radical changes, those who had for so long maintained hegemonic authority continued to wield considerable political and social power into and beyond the nineteenth century—due in no small measure to the fact that their central clarion call—religion—had been and continued to be both a marker around which citizens rallied during times of localized and widespread crises and a set of condensation symbols through which those same citizens defined themselves during less anxious times. Indeed, for the cultural members of this group, to be a citizen was and is to embrace a very specific worldview.

Perhaps the first thing to notice about this particular worldview is the centrality of the belief that the genesis, structuring, ordering, and termination of all things belongs to and derives from the moral structure of the universe. The intensity of this belief varies widely among cultural members. Regardless of how intensely any given individual might hold this belief, what is beyond question within this frame is that things do not happen by chance or by nature or by dint of human will; they happen because of a larger master plan, and that plan is the construct of a personal deity whose hand is visible in every action and event. Cultural members thus understand actions and events as divine significations that members of the community are to decipher, with some members of the community being more or less properly attuned to and trained for the task. Things are not what they appear to be.

## LINCOLN AS A RELIGIONIST

Working within this rhetorical and cultural tradition, nineteenth-century cultural members across the country insisted that they saw in Lincoln the "appropriate" ethos and in his assassination every reason to prepare for death religiously. To encourage auditors to embrace their perspective in dealing with the turmoil associated with Lincoln's death, for example, cultural members were intensely concerned to illustrate the manifold ways deity had shaped, guided, and manifested "Himself" through the circumstances surrounding Lincoln's life and death. This intense concern especially provided cultural members with a vehicle for making Lincoln's humble beginnings culturally and rhetorically meaningful. Matthew Simpson (1865a), for instance, told his auditors that, "by the hand of God," Lincoln "was especially singled out to guide our government in these trouble-some times, and it seems to me that the hand of God may be traced in many events connected with his history" (233). Among those things that Simpson regarded as being of particular importance was Lincoln's early "physical education, which he received, and which prepared him for herculean labors. . . . His education was simple. . . . He read few books but mastered all" (233). Henry B. Smith (1865) similarly saw the hand of deity in Lincoln's humble origins, for deity knows, he reminded his audience, that "hard work requires strong muscles" (373). Warren H. Cudworth (1865) made the point even more explicitly when he told his auditors that

> we must never forget that God gave us President Lincoln in the first place. That He led his father to move across the Ohio River when he was yet but a child, leaving that condition of semi-bondage in which all poor white were then compelled to live in the slave States, and settling down where he could breathe the air of freedom. Let us remember the struggles, labors, and aspirations of his boyhood, youth and early manhood; how he toiled as a boatman, up and down the great rivers of that region . . . how signally he has been directed and sustained through his official career thus far, and how really he has not been taken from us until his work was done; his enemies scattered, the rebellion put down, the Union restored, the country saved. (202)

It is not that Lincoln did not accomplish these things; rather, it is that deity enabled Lincoln to accomplish these things to fulfill a part of the larger plan. For if deity had given Lincoln humble origins and had provided him with struggles that would prepare him for later hardships, cultural members insisted, the hand of deity was equally apparent in Lincoln's brief political career. Speaking as one who had opposed Lincoln's candidacy, Robert F. Sample (1865) reminded his audience that "when the candidates for that high office passed in review before us, as Jesse's sons before the prophet, we thought another was God's choice, but He who never errs, selected the noblest, the wisest, the best" (21). Having recognized unquestionable signs of divine influence in Lincoln's life, Sample was willing to acknowledge that "good men have differed in their opinions of certain official acts, but as we look calmly over the administration which is for ever closed, taking it all in all, we may see in it the guiding hand of God" (22). Matthew Simpson (1865b), who was more positively disposed toward Lincoln, asserted that deity "didst give him unto us so pure, so honest, so sincere, and so transparent in character." God gave Lincoln "wisdom to select for his advisers, and for his officers, military and naval, those men through whom our country has been carried through an unprecedented conflict" (13). Even more positively disposed, Phineas D. Gurley (1865a) exclaimed that "God raised him up for a great and glorious mission, furnished him for His work, and aided him in its accomplishment. Nor was it merely by strength of mind, and honesty of heart, and purity and pertinacity of purpose, that He furnished him." Divine wisdom gave Lincoln "a calm and abiding confidence in the overruling providence of God, and in the ultimate triumph of truth and righteousness, through the power and blessing of God" (22).

Beyond their efforts to point to clear signs that deity had shaped and guided Lincoln from the cradle to the presidency, cultural members saw equally clear signs that, as Robert Lowry (1865) put it, Lincoln "was God's gift for the crisis," "the appointed instrument of God" (304 and 305). Lincoln was deity's gift not simply to lead a physical battle, Stephen Higgison Tyng (1865a) explained, but to lead a spiritual battle:

The moral greatness of the President,—his meekness,—
his faith,—his gentleness,—his patience,—his self-posses-
sion,—his love of the people,—his confidence in the people,—his higher confidence in God,—his generous temper
never provoked,—his love fearing no evil, provoking no
evil,—are such an elevation of human character, such an
appropriate supply for our very want, that I cannot but
adore the powers of that God, whose inspiration giveth
man wisdom, as the one author of this gift, bringing an
unknown, a reproached, a despised man, to reveal a greatness of ability, and a dignity of appropriation, which surrounding men had not suspected. (78-79)

Portraying and promoting Lincoln as an individual whose
entire life divine inspiration had shaped and guided served partly to
identify him as "the minister of the nation," as "the servant of God"
(Robinson 1865, 87)—in short, as a significant cultural member. This
much they agreed was beyond doubt; as a subcultural text, however,
they did not always agree on the particular institutional affiliation
to which deity had appointed Lincoln. Richard Steele (1865) told his
audience that Lincoln was "a sincere Christian," which is obvious
"from the frequent declarations of his lips, and the acts of his life"
(13). Schuyler Colfax (1865) reported to his audience a conversation
that Lincoln had with "a clergyman who asked him if he loved his
Savior in which Lincoln said: 'When I was first inaugurated I did
not love Him; when God took my son I was greatly impressed, but
still I did not love Him; but when I stood upon the battlefield of
Gettysburg, I gave my heart to Christ, and I can now say I do love
the Savior'" (212).

With equal certainty, Sabato Morais (1927b) announced that
he "was amazed and chagrined at the late efforts of some eminent
orators to prove our martyr's high sense of religious duty, by his
reported avowal of certain religious dogmas." Lincoln's inclinations,
Morais insisted, were clear; for "if the essence of religion is what the

great Hillel taught us, then I unhesitatingly say that the breast of our lamented President was ever kindled with that divine spark" (9). Isaac M. Wise (1927), like Schuyler Colfax, detailed his personal knowledge of Lincoln's inclinations: "The lamented Abraham Lincoln believed himself to be bone from our bone and flesh from our flesh. He supposed himself to be a descendant of Hebrew parentage. He said so in my presence" (98).

Despite disagreement over Lincoln's exact cultural location, cultural members were convinced that he was a "godly man" (Morais 1927a, 3), "a good man, a truly pious man" (Neale 1865, 165), a man who possessed "a profound religious faith; not simply a general recognition of the law of order in the universe, but a profound faith in a Personal God" (M'Clintock 1865, 136). Not all were equally enthusiastic in their endorsements, of course, but endorsement nevertheless clearly and unequivocally identified Lincoln as a cultural member. To press the point further, those who were positively disposed toward Lincoln consistently compared him with one or more of the most significant cultural figures—Moses and Christ being the most popular choices. J. D. Fulton (1865) lamented that, "like Moses, he has died, not because of disease, nor of advanced age; his eye was not dim, nor was his natural force abated. He died because his work was done" (361). E. P. Rogers (1865) told his auditors that "when our Moses led the people through the wilderness to the borders of Canaan and saw as from Mount Pisgah the glorious land of Promise, and laid him down to die," deity had "another Joshua to take his work upon him and to clear this beautiful land of the last remnant of the rebellious tribes" (475). Bernard Illowy (1927) similarly declared that Lincoln "was permitted to see but not to enjoy" the fruits of his labors, "and like unto the great Teacher of mankind, the Redeemer of Israel," deity had told Lincoln "Get thee up on this mountain; from there shalt thou see the land which I have given unto thy people, and when thou has seen it, then thou shalt be gathered unto thy fathers who are gone before thee" (162).

Lincoln's martyrdom reminded others of Christ. Lincoln's

heart, a member of the New York House of Representatives told his colleagues, was "as all-embracing as the country, and his arms as outstretched for love and good will, as if they had been nailed, like the arms of the dying Lamb of God, to the traverse sections of the Cross" (Wilbur 1865, 54). William Ives Budington (1865) similarly mourned publicly that "we have lost a friend who was a father to the humblest in the land, and the Ruler who was the Savior of the country" (111). But Lincoln was no ordinary savior: "No man's life is to be compared with Christ's, and no man's death with His; but he comes nearest to the Divine Man who receives a trust for humanity, carries it to a successful issue, and at last dies for it, making his life to culminate and triumph in death. This is the high calling of men treading after and next the person of Christ! This is the crown of martyrs. This is the calling and the crown of Abraham Lincoln" (126). Defending Lincoln against detractors, John M'Clintock (1865) retorted, "We had no fear about Abraham Lincoln, except the fear that he would be too forgiving. Oh! what an epitaph—that the only fear men had was that he would be too tender, that he had too much love; in a word, the he was too Christ-like! And how Christ-like he was in dying" (139).

Beyond identifying Lincoln as an exemplary cultural member, portraying and promoting him as a messiah served at least three other cultural purposes. First, it enabled cultural members to draw attention to the cultural meaning of Lincoln's death. As William Ives Budington (1865) saw the matter, divine wisdom had not only guided and shaped Lincoln's life, but had also permitted or caused his death because "God needed . . . the blood of Abraham Lincoln" (125). Bringing about Lincoln's death thus was a message to the nation. Some insisted that this divinely encoded message was a reminder that deity is utterly sovereign, that "in the midst of our rejoicings we needed this stroke, this dealing, this discipline, and therefore He has sent it. Let us remember our affliction has not come forth of the dust, and our trouble has not sprung out of the ground" (Gurley 1865a, 19). Others, like O. E. Daggett (1865), understood this message as a reminder that "events are providential not merely sometimes as independent of human agency, but always as never independent of the divine control; as always under God's permission, and within the scope of his plan, and hence provided for in his all comprehending administration" (12). Henry J. Fox (1865) concluded that the message was designed to tell the world that "He doubtless saw that it was best that Abraham Lincoln be taken from us; that he should be taken from us at the time and in the very manner in which he was taken" (352).

Calling attention to the messages deity had embedded in Lincoln's death allowed cultural members to address not only criticisms of Lincoln, but also fears that the circumstances attending his death might be interpreted as a divine indication of deity's displeasure toward Lincoln. Because Lincoln died in a theatre (indicative of choosing a physical life over a spiritual life), because he died suddenly, and because sudden death from this perspective is readily interpreted as a sign of divine displeasure, in other words, cultural members needed to reassure one another that the timing and manner of Lincoln's death were not ignominious. Because "God raised him up for a grand purpose, for a great and noble work" (Lothrop 1865, 252), because deity "has permitted a vile assassin's hand to destroy [Lincoln] in one fell blow" (Robbins 1865, 216), because he was "so religious a being" (Isaacs 1927, 74), and because he was a cultural messiah, speakers insisted again and again, Lincoln could not be held responsible for the manner and timing of his death. Such ignominious circumstances, cultural members repeatedly explained, pointed not to Lincoln but to the community. In this sense Lincoln's death is an omen predicated on the past (through projection backward from the present), but it is also an omen in the present projecting forward into the community's future.

That deity's message was intended for the community brings us to a third purpose underlying the insistence that Lincoln was a cultural member. Without question, W. R. Nicholson (1865) proclaimed, "It is God's call to us for yet a deeper self-humiliation"

(125). Phineas Gurley (1864a) similarly insisted that deity's message "demands of us that we lie very, very low, before Him who has smitten us for our sins" (20). For A. P. Rogers (1865) deity's message to the community was even more explicit:

> Had our lamented President died by the process of ordinary disease, we should have seen a sufficient explanation of the catastrophe in the immediate instrument, and would have been content, perhaps, to leave the matter there. But this sudden, unexpected, awful death by the cowardly hand of a vile assassin, drives the bewildered and afrightened mind back to this great eternal truth, and forces an appalled and stricken people to reflect that God is sovereign on his throne, and that even the machinations and crimes of wicked men are but the agents of his will. (246)

Deity brought about Lincoln's death (from this perspective) not only because His/his divine work was done or because Lincoln clearly merited immortality, but also because the sins of the community required a stern message, a devastating reminder that the living are frail, that life is a temporary journey toward death and judgment, that judgment depends on the individual's religious worth, that the individual's religious worth determines whether that individual will merit immortal bliss or eternal damnation, and that only by preparing religiously for death while living can one hope to earn the former while avoiding the latter. "Creatures of a day, as we are," cultural members relentlessly recited, "whose habitation is in the dust, and who are crushed before the moth, whose strength is weakness, and whose wisdom is folly, we often presumptuously rebel against the absolute sovereignty of an infinitely perfect God, and desire to find out some more palatable and less humbling reason for occurring events than his single, sovereign, indisputable will" (Gurley 1865a, 20). From "the absolute sovereignty of an infinitely perfect God" emerges the view that deity clearly had warned the nation "how suddenly the paths of worldly ambition and activity may terminate in the tomb," that deity was simply using Lincoln's death to remind the living that "the young, the busy, and the eager, and the giddy" should "be startled amid these funeral solemnities, to bethink themselves of that eternity, of which we are but too easily and generally forgetful" (Williams 1865, 29). This then leads to an inescapable cultural imperative: Remember "the need of immediate preparation for that eternity to which we are all hastening" (Rockwell 1865, 287).

Given the cultural logic at work here, there is every reason to suspect that cultural members would have arrived at this dictum regardless of the particular circumstances of Lincoln's life and death.[2] Nevertheless, they were predisposed to portray Lincoln as one of their own—for various reasons, but especially as a means of setting forth a positive example of their ethos and worldview so that others would begin to contemplate more humbly the necessity of preparing themselves for death.[3]

Consider the matter in closer detail.

### "Be Still And Know That I Am God"

Standing firmly at the pulpit in front of his congregation in Boston, Massachusetts on Easter Sunday, April 16, 1865, Edward Norris Kirk (1865) begins his sermon by describing two sets of circumstances that have evoked conflicting emotions in the audience.[4] People were joyful because of the North's recent military victories, especially the recent capitulation "of the rebellious forces . . . to General Grant." Then came widespread grief when the nation heard the news of Lincoln's unprecedented assassination. This sudden shift in emotions, Kirk says, resulted in confusion, frustration, helplessness, anxiety, and anger:

> Which way shall we look? What shall we do? What becomes
> a people so afflicted,—so great a nation under so great a

calamity? . . . We had fondly hoped the experience of four such years as we have passed would give us guaranty for the four years to come. But our hopes are blighted, our plans are frustrated. We are stunned by the suddenness of the blow; confounded by the awful wickedness of the deed. Murder is abroad; murder, that seeks the highest mark; that dashes down one of the noblest of our race; that blots out the brightest star in our heavens; that strikes at the wisest, kindest, gentlest of us all; that strikes at the life of the nation in the man to whom the nation has entrusted that life.

We are sad,—we are sick at heart. We feel as if our globe had lost its course, and were drifting down toward the Botany Bay of the Universe. The reign of Justice, of Law, of Order, seems to be past. We seem to be struggling like drowning men,—the black chill waters are blinding our eyes, stiffening our limbs, stifling our breath. (33-34)

Such emotions are to be expected, Kirk concedes, because circumstances have thrown the living abruptly from joy to sorrow. People are justifiably "stunned by the suddenness of the blow" because this was no ordinary death, for Lincoln was "basely assassinated; with no last words, no time to tell us where his hope was anchored, and wither he was going" (35). This alone would be cause for concern, Kirk acknowledges, because Lincoln virtually invited the manner of his death: "his clemency was harboring the villains that were plotting his destruction" (38). But Lincoln cannot be held responsible for time or manner.

Lincoln died as he did and when he did because it was deity's will. Lincoln was the nation's Moses, who "had led us so wisely, so firmly, so kindly, through such a wilderness, and brought us out as God's minister into so large a place and so great a deliverance"; through this death deity has announced that Lincoln's "work was finished, nobly finished. And I have removed him from the turmoil and confusion of earth to the peace and rest of heaven." To believe

Lincoln's sudden death an ignoble reflection on him would be to call divine wisdom into question, and this no mortal can do: "My thoughts are not your thoughts, neither are your ways my ways. For, as the heavens are higher than the earth, so are my ways higher than your ways, and my thoughts than your thoughts." Through this death deity proclaims "Mourn for yourselves but rejoice for him" (35-36).

As Kirk envisions the possibilities, such emotional intensity might lead people to do much more than mourn their fallen member: "We are liable to indulge in *murmurings*"; some would foolishly dare to "complain of the divine government" (36). Some would "make the wrongdoer suffer" (39). Some would call "for fire from heaven to fall upon the monsters," to destroy "a miscreant race, that prove themselves unfit to breathe the air of heaven" (40). But such people are confused, frustrated, helpless, anxious, and angry. Their judgment is not to be trusted.

Considered only to this point, the initial emphasis on the audience's supposed emotional response to circumstances appears to be no more than the speaker's effort to identify with his auditors. But the matter is not so simply stated, for this worldview is undergirded by and receives it sensibility from a clearly structured vertical metaphor in which the uppermost extreme represents absolute good, the lowermost extreme represents absolute evil, and all that lies between represents the natural world. Because of its position between these two extremes, the natural world is neither absolutely good nor absolutely bad (in the Latin: *non valdi boni et non valdi mali*). All things belonging to the natural world—with the notable exception of human beings—are morally neutral, which is why Kirk insists that nature is one of deity's creations but is not synonymous with deity: Deity causes "the great and strong wind," "the earthquake," "the fire," but "He is not in them." Nor are deity and nature contrary forces. Nature is part of deity's language, a means through which mortal beings receive deity's word: "Nature quivers in agony under such a blow," not because nature is morally responsible for deeds done, but because of deity's absolute power.

Unlike nature, humans are accorded special status in the natural world because they are fallen from grace, from necessary
immortality, even from moral neutrality. They are simultaneously
creatures of deity and creatures of nature: deity and dust. Theirs is a
life of constant struggle, of seeking to ward off the temptations of
absolute evil in order to regain grace, of striving to release the
immortal soul imprisoned within the natural dimension. Since
there invariably are those who achieve greater success than others in
this struggle, the natural world of humans, like the universe itself, is
morally structured. Those who are most *successful,* who are most
devoted to absolute good (hence: *devoti*), are nearest deity. Nearest
the *devoti* in this hierarchy are those who have not yet learned how
to overcome their natural instincts but who are simple in the eyes
of deity (hence: *simplices*) because they have demonstrated their
faith in deity by constantly striving toward the good (hence: *sancta
fides*). Below both of these are the avaricious (hence: *avari*), who
have given in to their love of and faith in life (hence: *secula fides*).
Furthest from absolute goodness and nearest absolute evil are the
*vani,* who, as the English cognate "vain" suggests, are "devoid of real
value, worth, or significance; of no [good] effect, force or power;
fruitless, futile, unavailing; empty, vacant, void" *(Oxford English
Dictionary).*

This structure suggests that the initial mood of Kirk's sermon
is an extension of the auditors' emotional condition, that the auditors, not Lincoln's death, established the tone and tenor of this discourse, that the auditors are its subject, its reason for being.
Auditors are desperately and immediately in need of instruction
and direction. The evidence, from this perspective, is obvious.
Consumed by their love of life, auditors might imagine that they
should "catch and execute a thousand vile assassins or their viler
employers," but those who are devoted know that such actions cannot "bring back our lost." Some might conceive that it would be sen-
sible to "fill the air with our clamors" and "put forth our strength
in some mighty deeds of vengeance," but such people are "struggling

like drowning men" and cannot comprehend "the duty and work of the hour,—of this holy Sabbath." Those who are not sufficiently devoted cannot determine what to do, where they are, or where they are going; nor do they seem to understand how tenuous and frail life is, despite the fact that they are witness to the assassination of "one of the noblest of our race," "the brightest star in our heavens," "the wisest, kindest, gentlest of us all." This does not bode well for the community.

Since sudden death reflects ignominiously on either the deceased or the community (or both), and since Lincoln cannot be called into question, the community obviously is the object of divine displeasure. Through natural circumstances "He informs us in his word that He chastens us for our own good, though we cannot always see how the end is secured" (for lack of devotion). This death comes as a divine message that "God's providence is rebuking the pride of men's hearts. That is what He is doing to-day among us" (37). Since immortality must be merited religiously, and since deity has granted Lincoln immortality, Lincoln *must* merit praise: "Around him the tenderest cords of our hearts were bound. We had placed in his hands the most sacred of earthly trusts. . . . We had seen in him so much of magnanimity, of sound judgment, of gentle kindness, of robust manliness, of tender sympathy, of lofty principle, we could not but love him, strongly, tenderly" (35).

Praise for the dead, then, is related not only to the status of the deceased and the degree to which the living are still attached to the deceased, but also—especially—to the moral character of the deceased and the moral circumstances of the deceased's death. Had Lincoln been an ordinary individual who had died under mundane circumstances, lavish praise would have been unnecessary and unlikely. Yet, even in this instance—where the circumstances surrounding death required cultural members to provide extraordinary explanations, and where they found it necessary to depict his moral character as unimpeachable (given their desire to lay claim to Lincoln as a significant cultural member)—the role of the deceased is critical but subordinate. His death is subordinate because death and judgment are synonymous, because the deceased has gone beyond the world of "turmoil and confusion" and, most important, because deity's providence is one of "moral judgment." The living still have time to do what they must in order to be worthy of favorable judgment, but they must not allow the urgency of this task to go unattended.

Rather than serving simply to identify the speaker with the auditors, then, characterizing the audience in this way serves two considerably more significant purposes. The first is to complete the speaker's description of the vertical structure of the universe. Lincoln clearly serves as one of the *devoti* (or, at the very least, one of the *simplices*), Kirk implicitly identifies himself as one of the *simplices* (since he admits to having had volatile feelings, and since his advice would be worth considerably less were he one of the *avari*), the "vile assassins and their viler employers" serve as *vani*, and the auditors serve as *avari* or, at least, *simplices* doomed to become *avari* if they do not soon change their ways. The authority to speak morally—and this applies especially to the *devoti* and the *simplices*—thus derives from the locus and status of deity, who has given the power of speech to the "righteous." Deity, serving as a supreme sovereign who holds jurisdiction over the entire universe, transmits this power to any given individual only to the degree that the individual demonstrably is devoted. Hence, the evangelical behavior of the individual is not only a sign of the individual's status as "chosen" (hence: as authority), but also an index of the individual's right (and obligation) to speak authoritatively.

The second purpose that negative characterization of the auditors serves is to shift their focus from the deceased (and the emotions they might be experiencing) to themselves, to make them humble, to humiliate them, to show them that they are "drifting down to the Botany Bay of the Universe." Whether a particular auditor might be an *avarum* or a *simplex* is one of the few inferences left to individual cultural members—a matter of small significance under the circumstances. In either case, auditors are where they are in this moral scheme because they have loved life too well, because *secula fides* has been more important to them than *sancta fides*. Again, the evidence from the perspective of the *devoti* and *simplices* is obvious.

Auditors have been so preoccupied with their daily activities, Kirk admonishes, that they have neglected their sacred duties to deity; they have forgotten deity's "person" and "attributes": "The Lord says—do so no more. . . . Be not blind, amid the works of my hands, to my glory. Be not deaf when I speak to you in my word. Treat me as having a heart, an intelligence, a will, of which your own is an imitation" (43). Deity takes offense at recent behaviors because "God attaches a supreme importance to the personal faith of each individual" (46). "He informs us in his word that He chastens us for our own good, though we cannot always see how the end is secured" (37). Just so, the rebellion, the apparent ignominity of Lincoln's sudden death, and the abrupt shift in emotions that has caused confusion in the auditors "are all revelations of God" (47).

By itself, Kirk acknowledges, the "love of life" is a natural instinct—hence, *non valdi boni et non valdi mali*. But the living have allowed this instinct too much freedom; the love of life has "become so mingled with our selfishness, and so perverted that we cannot properly exercise it at all in personal matters, and scarcely in public affairs" (39). The living have given in to moral limitations and are now in danger of succumbing to the deceptions and temptations of absolute evil. They have replaced or confused "Our Father" with "our father," trust in and love of deity with trust in and love of mere mortals; "the peace and rest of heaven" with "the turmoil and confusion of earth," deity's thoughts and ways with human thoughts and ways, the "eternal throne" with "human affairs," "faith" with "murmuring unbelief" and the "pride of our hearts," deity's hand with "an arm of flesh," deity with "generals" and "brave defenders" and a "magnanimous leader," "duty" with "vengeance," deity's judgment with human justice. In all, the living are guilty of pretentiousness, of hubris, of succumbing to "that master-passion, the pride of our hearts," of believing too much in their own creaturely significance (36–38).

Given their pretensions, the living clearly are in no position to judge the *vani*. Auditors may acknowledge, as does Kirk, that the *vani* "wear much of the image of their father, who was a liar, and a traitor, and a rebel, and a secessionist, and a murderer, from the beginning" (39). Auditors also may proclaim that the *vani* are "villains," who plotted Lincoln's "destruction"; "traitors," who will "carry personal revenge into their treatment of us"; thieves, who have stolen not only "forts, and ships, and arms," but also "the territory purchased by our common treasury"; designing criminals, who enlisted "the selfishness of foreign nations against us"; malefactors, who have abused "our brave soldiers, when made prisoners of war"; cunning varlets, who have "withered all the finer sentiments of the human soul and turned the very fountains of religious life into poisonous springs"; miscreants, who fully "prove themselves unfit to breath the air of heaven" (39–40).

Even with such evidence weighing so heavily against the *vani*, auditors are in no position to judge, for they "should cheerfully acquiesce in [Heaven's] decrees, and in its permissions; for it gives the devil the length of his chain, and makes him, in doing his own work, accomplish the purposes that infinite wisdom and love have formed" (36). Only deity is competent to pass final judgment on "nations, communities, individuals bringing them to [deity's] bar, to make every man answer for deeds done in the body" (40). Further, the living cannot judge the *vani* because their position in this moral structure is dangerously close to the position of the *vani*, which means that their condition necessarily must be of greater and more immediate concern than even their "perverted" instincts or feelings of grief. This is why deity has used "the language of an event which arouses the turbulent emotions of the heart, exciting grief or fear or anger" to say " I have come forth from my hiding place, to show you I am God" (47).

Although it is true within the parameters of this worldview that "individuals live forever," it is also true that immortality must be achieved through divinelike attitudes and activities and that those who live and die as *vani* or *avari* "shall be as stubble" on the day of judgment (45). With the burden of responsibility for present circumstances resting squarely on the shoulders of the community, with the responsibility for Lincoln's sudden death pointing directly at the living, with their direction and position in the moral universe having been fully and explicitly identified, and with their immortal souls clearly and immediately in danger, auditors have sufficient reason to shift their focus from the deceased to themselves (and others within the community; hence, again, the evangelical impulse) and to consider very carefully their values, beliefs, principles, and attitudes: "He does not make up the full issue for any individual until death occurs" (47).

The first and most important step auditors must take points us to a key attitude of this worldview: *"Suppress or modify all natural impulses by the controlling power of religious feeling"* (35). To do otherwise would prevent auditors from hearing the word of deity. Thus: "Suppress all murmurs. Suffer, weep, but do not murmur" (36). "Quiet the agitated sea of your heart. Feeling was not designed to hold the helm, but simply to fill the sails. When trouble comes, be still, so that you can hear every syllable God is whispering" (42). Failure to "hear every syllable God is whispering" freely leads humans to put their confidence and trust in themselves. Had humans been listening to "God's word," they would have known that they must not "put trust in an arm of flesh, because, however strong to-day, to-morrow it may be crumbling back to dust"; "this terrible event proclaims, Man is Frail, God is eternal" (38). Those who were listening have heard deity declare that "Vengeance belongeth to me, I will repay" (39). Those who were not listening did not hear, and because they did not hear, they have tended toward "pantheism, polytheism, atheism, theoretic or practical" (43). And those who did not hear have failed to suppress or modify their *"nat-*

*ural impulses by the controlling power of religious feeling"* and have angered deity, who has punished the community to remind the living that "states and families, like the individuals that compose them, 'live and move, and have their being' in Him" (43).

Only by suppressing "all natural impulses" will humans be able to understand that "nations perish, individuals live forever" (46). Only by listening to the word of deity can humans demonstrate their faith, for "faith believes His statements and assurances," and "faith alone can walk on waves, and sing amid the tempest, 'In God is my salvation'" (37). Only by suppressing emotions and listening to the word of deity can the living confront the death of an intimate appropriately by making the day of death "a religious day, a day of thought, of such deep reflection . . . where you can, undiverted, hear the voice of God. Be still" (47).

Not surprisingly, we find the same perspective articulated in the graveyard.


RELIGIONISM IN THE GRAVEYARD
From the beginning of colonization until after the turn of the nineteenth century, as I previously indicated, Religionists held hegemonic sway over social life. This point is perhaps nowhere better illustrated than in the graveyard (see figure 1), which they owned, maintained, shaped, and controlled through the turn of the nineteenth century and beyond.[5] One significant consequence of this fact is that for a great many years "gravescapes"—memorials and the landscape containing them—uniformly presented visitors with the same rhetorical and cultural imperative: Remember death, for the time of judgment is at hand. Romanticists and Heroists, as we will see in later chapters, strenuously objected to Religionist burial and memorial practices, which they regarded as fundamentally "inappropriate" because Religionist gravescapes and memorials do not articulate either Romanticist or Heroist worldviews or *ethoi*. As Jacob Bigeolow (1859), one of the key spokespersons for gravescape

reform at the turn of the nineteenth century, insisted, "this objectionable, but inveterate custom" of haphazardly burying "friends in frequented parts" of cities and towns offends every possible sensibility; what people want, what they need, he continued, is a place where individuals can discover "almost a new pleasure in building and decorating their own tombs" (v-vi). Given the nearly uniform cultural imperative of this gravescape and its memorials, those who owned and/or controlled early graveyards obviously resisted change. As Blanche Linden (1979/80) observes, before a memorial can "receive community acceptance for placement in the common burial ground, the iconography [as well as inscriptions and general form] had to have a certain degree of resonance with the values, beliefs, and tastes of the society" (149).

Once they had gained sufficient social and political power, Romanticists insisted on "beautifying" and, later, Heroists insisted on restructuring and reordering Religionist gravescapes to suit their own sensibilities. As Stanley French (1975) disapprovingly put it, "It is obvious from the dearth of comments about early New England graveyards, from the nature of the comments that do exist and from the grim symbolism of the period's monuments, that graveyards were treated simply as unattractive necessities to be avoided as much as possible by the living. This attitude continued from the beginnings of settlement into the early years of the nineteenth century. . . . The neglected graveyard was characteristic not only of New England but was common throughout the other colonies and states" (70-71). For Religionists, however, the location and ostensibly neglected condition of their gravescape and the discursive and iconographic representations on their memorials were and are entirely consistent and appropriate, both culturally and rhetorically.

In the most obvious sense, of course, the graveyard serves as a convenient place to dispose of the dead. But its more significant purpose—its cultural and rhetorical significance within this worldview—derives from its formal capacity to evoke or establish memory of death, which serves to remind the living of their own fragility and, hence, of their urgent need to prepare for death. Macroscopically, as Charles Grandison Finney (1835) very well understood, locating the dead among the living helps to ensure that the living will witness the gravescape's message regularly as a reminder "to manifest that this world is not their home" and "that heaven is a reality" (132). Further, as Marcuse (1959) observes, "With the devaluation of the body, the life of the body is no longer the real life, and the negation of this life is the beginning rather than the end" (68). What members of other cultural groups most disliked and later most rapidly changed about this gravescape—its seemingly neglected, decaying condition—actually constitutes a significant part of its message, which clearly separates the here and now from the forever after. That separation, of course, is a necessary extension of the belief that humans should not "trust too much in an arm of clay"; for the day of death "is fast approaching. It hastens on,—it comes surely and steadily,—nothing can arrest, nothing can retard it! And are we prepared?—prepared to meet our God?" (Robbins 1886, 86, vol. 1).

To locate the dead away from the living, to enclose burial grounds with fences as if to separate the living from the dead, to decorate and adorn the gravescape, or to order the graveyard according to dictates of efficiency and structural linearity, which others would later accomplish, runs contrary to this worldview. The constant struggle to embrace and to encourage others to embrace the view that life is nothing more than preparation for death, that one's preparation for death is a preparation for eternity, a journey toward death, demands constant attention if one seeks to merit eternal bliss and avoid eternal damnation. This worldview thus unceasingly insists upon a clear and distinct separation of "real life" (spiritual life, eternal life) from "illusory life" (physical life; the liminal, transitory existence one leads in the here and now). The formal unity of memorials in this gravescape thus both ensures its identity and energizes and sustains its rhetorical and cultural purpose.

Even from a distance the common size and shape of such memorials speak to visitors of their purpose (see figure 2.1).

Although this gravescape provides ample space for variation, an overwhelming majority of the memorials belonging to this tradition are relatively modest structures (between one and five feet in height and width and between two and five inches thick), and most are variations of two shapes: single and triple arches. Single arch memorials are small, smoothed slabs with three squared sides and a convex or squared crown (see figures 2.2 and 2.6). Triple arch memorials are also small, smoothed slabs with three squared sides but feature smaller arches on either side of a single large arch, which gives the impression of a single panel with a convex crown conjoined on either side by similar but much narrower panels, or pilasters, with convex crowns (see figure 2.3).

Together with location and general appearance, such minimal uniformity undoubtedly helps to ensure that cultural members will not mistake this gravescape for a community pasture or a vacant lot. But the more specific link between manifestation and purpose—between the gravescape and its rhetorical and cultural significance—derives from the iconography, mottos, and inscriptions of the memorials, which in one form or another incessantly and almost univocally remind viewers of death and time—hence, of the limited time visitors have to prepare for their own death. "The gravestone," as Tashjian and Tashjian (1974) note, "not only commemorated the deceased individual but also confirmed the broad cultural goals and ideals" of the communities in which they were erected (10). In this sense, as Agosta (1985) points out, a gravescape "may thus be seen as an emblem book with each separate stone a page in that book" (48).

As a significant part of that book, marker inscriptions characteristically provide only the deceased's name, age, date of death, and, less frequently, date of birth, cause of death, and family or community status, with by far the largest number providing nothing more than a brief inscription. To do otherwise—to draw attention to the heroic deeds and accomplishments of the deceased or to implore visitors to remember the deceased through their emotive experience, for example—would run contrary to the cultural imperative of this worldview. The memorials for Jane Second (figure 2.3), Roger Hooker (figure 2.4), Josiah Hayward (figure 2.5), John Haynes (figure 2.6), Elizabeth Mockridge (figure 2.7), Ella Brock Sinkler (figure 2.8), and Lowell M. Clusca III (figure 2.9), for instance, not only point to a prototypical discursive pattern, but also illustrate the longevity of that pattern among cultural members over a three hundred year period, thus clearly demonstrating the constancy of this memorial tradition and making the view that Religionists simply disappeared with the introduction of "neoclassical" motifs hard to credit. In each instance the memorial presents viewers with discourse that speaks not of beauty or nature or emotions or heroic actions, but of the very limited time that these individuals existed in the natural world.

That scholars have largely ignored inscriptions (save as use for data) and inscription-only memorials (see figures 2.2, 2.3, and 2.4) is not extraordinary. Brief inscriptions and inscription-only memorials provide precious little information. The headstone of Richard More (figure 2.2), for example, is a small single arch variation bearing only the following inscription: "HERE / LYETH BURIED / YE BODY OF CAP / RICHARD MORE / AGED 84 YEARS / DYED 1692 / MAYFLOWER / PILGRIM." Similarly, the memorial for Elizabeth Mockridge (figure 2.7) suppresses any emphasis on "illusory life": "Elizabeth Mockridge / December 9, 1899 / January 15, 1940." Confronted with so little information, scholars typically and understandably have turned their attention to memorials that display "more interesting" iconographic images, despite the fact that inscription-only memorials may well constitute as much as one third of all the memorials erected in early graveyards. More to the point, to those steeped in the traditions that gave rise to this gravescape, brief inscriptions and inscription-only memorials add to an explicit chorus: "Let their memories live but let their ashes be forgotten" (Gray 1847, 24). Within this worldview, graveyards are, again, only secondarily places for the dead. By focusing on the deceased's age and date of death and by conspicuously excluding all or most of what occurred between birth and death, brief inscriptions and inscription-only markers draw attention away from the dead and toward the finality of death. In turn, the finality of death serves to teach or remind the living that "this world is not our abiding place":

> Our continuance here is but very short. Man's days on the earth, are as a shadow. It was never designed by God that this world should be our home. Neither did God give us these temporal accommodations for that end. If God has given us ample estates, and children, or other pleasant friends, it is with no such design that we should be furnished here, as for a settled abode; but with a design that we should use them for the present, and then leave them in a very little time. When we are called to any secular business, or charged with the care of a family, if we improve our lives to any other purpose, than as a journey toward heaven, all our labour will be lost. If we spend our lives in the pursuit of a temporal happiness; as riches, or sensual pleasure; credit and esteem from men; delight in our children and the prospect of seeing them well brought up, and well settled, &c.—All these things will be of little significance to us. Death will blow up all our hopes, and put an end to these enjoyments. (Bentley 1962, vol. II, 127)

Within the parameters of such attitudes it is entirely understandable that the inscriptions on such memorials draw attention to death rather than to the dead. Graveyards, like the churches and meetinghouses to which they are so frequently adjoined (especially before Religionists lost their hegemonic status), are places of instruction, institutions, where the living can be schooled. As Tashjian and Tashjian (1974) correctly observe, death within this world view is "an occasion for teaching the congregation a religious lesson as well as for commemorating the dead" (36). Brief inscriptions are only a part of the lesson.

Another part of the lesson comes through mottos such as *"memento mori"* ("remember death") and *"fugit hora"* ("time flies" or, more literally, "hours flee"), which are inscribed on countless early memorials and leave little room for doubt as to what viewers are to remember (see figure 2.10). To restate and reinforce the lesson, memorials from this tradition relentlessly confront viewers with time- and death-related icons—skulls, crossed bones, coffins, shovels, picks, funeral shrouds, leaves, vines, flowers, fruits, vegetables, crashing waves, assorted winged creatures, hourglasses, allegorical scenes, the curtain of death, and the exceptionally common winged death's head. As numerous scholars have maintained, such iconography seems especially dedicated to the presentation of what some might call "horrific" imagery.[6] Within this particular perspective, however, the icons of death are far from horrific. Their purpose, like the purpose of brief inscriptions and the gravescape of which they are such an integral part, is not to instill a mind-numbing fear, but to provide the living with continual reminders of the distinction between physical life and spiritual life, between the ephemeral and the everlasting. Early practitioners turned time and again to the winged death's head (and other similar symbols) not only because it was a "symbol of physical death and spiritual resurrection," as Tashjian and Tashjian (1974, 62) suggest, but also because it clearly stated the point *and* because it implied a certain hopefulness that shunned hubris yet invited comfort. Equally important, "the most common [people], the least educated, could understand the carvings and profit from their didactic import" (52). The headstone of Nathanael Mather (figure 2.10) is illustrative.

The tympanum, or upper portion of the center panel, of this small triple arch stone features a large winged death's head with scalloped feathers. At the crown of the tympanum, immediately above the head, is a curved frieze, or band, in which the carver inscribed the motto *"MEMENTO MORI"* in block letters. Each

pilaster is crowned with an eight-pointed flower (or sun) design
that surmounts a series of sculpted leaves, flowers, and gourds. Near
the bottom of the memorial the pilaster design joins a frieze containing a series of swirling leaves that meet at an eight-pointed
flower (or sun) design in the center of the frieze. The designs in the
tympanum, pilasters, and bottom frieze thus form a border that
encases the following inscription: "MR / NATHANAEL MATHER /
DECD OCTOBER YE 17 / 1688. / An Aged person, / that had been
but / Nineteen Winters / in the World."

By far the largest feature of this memorial, the winged death's
head demands and commands the viewer's attention. The head,
although seemingly a gruesome representation of death, is actually
a hopeful sign. The skull—representing the skull of the deceased—is
a human skull, not the skull of a demon; this is not Death, but the
earthly remains of the deceased, the now useless husk of a mortal.
Here, as on so many other such early memorials, the skull is
winged—a very hopeful and comforting sign that, perhaps, the only
truly important part of this person, his soul, has migrated and been
admitted to heaven where he will live out eternity as one of the chosen few. And the skull's position reinforces this glint of hope: above
the discourse ("above" meaning "morally superior to" in this worldview, as I have already indicated), which is tied directly to the
earthly remains of the individual through the discourse, and above
and more central than the life signs in the pilasters, which are now
outside and below the migrant soul. But the icon stops short of
declaring the destination of this person's soul, for the wings are
attached to the skull; and souls, within this worldview, do not
require skulls. The motto not only summarizes the memorial's
worldview, it also stands above all other things as a declaration to
visitors: Time flies; if you wish to avoid eternal damnation and hope
to achieve eternal salvation, ignore the trappings of temporal life
and keep death constantly before you as a reminder of what you
must accomplish and of what you must be before you die.

The triple arch headstone of Doraty Cromwell (figure 2.11) features a more simplified arrangement. In the tympanum is a death's head with truncated, unscalloped wings. Crowning each undefined pilaster is an hourglass, split in half, suggesting that time has run out. Immediately below the death's head is the inscription, "HERE LYES Ye BODY / OF DORATY WIFE TO / PHILIP CROMWELL / AGED 67 YEARS/ DECd. SEPTd. Ye 27 / 1673."

The pseudo triple-arch headstone of Joseph Barrett (figure 2.12) features a wider array of death- and time-related icons. The tympanum features either a skull surmounting crossed bones and surrounded by other death-related designs or a winged death's head whose ornamental wings form the border that encases the tympanum and its designs. In either case, the words *"Memento mori"* appear on either side of the head in a straight, narrow frieze. On each side of the crossed bones below the head are death masks, which are entwined in vines. Below these is a sculpted header that rests on two vertical columns, which define the pilasters. Outside the pilasters is a continuation of the tympanum vines, and inside the pilasters the inscription notes: "Here lies buried the Body / of Cap. JOSEPH BARRETT / Son of Deacon Humphry and / Mrs. Mary Barrett, who died / the 4th day of April, Anno / Dom. one Thousand Seven / Hundred and Sixty three, / in the Eighty fifth Year of / his Age."

The skull icon is repeated and given greater prominence on the sideplate of the Robert Rad sarcophagus (figure 2.13). Featuring an elaborately carved partial skull at the bottom of the plate, the skull peers at viewers from underneath the curtain of death. Toward the top of the plate the curtain becomes a covering for two cherubs with finely carved faces and scalloped wings, which are partially hidden by the shroud. The cherubs hold the top of the shroud in place at each upper corner.

The allegorical scene depicted in the tympanum of the Samuel Adams triple arch headstone (figure 2.14) relies on a similar pattern to communicate its lesson to viewers (see Tashjian and Tashjian 1974, 176). At the center of the tympanum is a lighted candle mounted on a pedestal. Just to the left of the candle stands a winged Father Time, who holds an hourglass in his extended right hand; the index finger of his raised left hand points toward a second figure, as if to instruct or exhort. The second figure, who stands opposite Father Time, is Death, portrayed as a wingless skeleton. In Death's left hand is the scythe of time, and in his right hand is a lamp cover, poised just above the candle's flame. Finally, like the previous memorials, the pilasters feature temporal icons—a bunch of grapes surmounting a cob of corn, a flower, and leaves—and the inscription again attends only to life and death information about the deceased.

What is most noteworthy about such memorials is not their specific designs—which vary according to the skills of the carver; the dictates of the members of the particular community; the economic, political, social and/or cultural standing of the deceased or the deceased's family, and so forth—but the pattern of relationships between death and time. On most such memorials, that is, temporal representations consistently appear in subordinate positions—both in location and in referential significance—relative to death-related representations. On the Nathanael Mather memorial (figure 2.10), for instance, the deceased's age and date of death explicitly represent time, and "the World," as well as the icons that adorn the pilasters, implicitly represent time. Superior to these in location and significance is the winged death's head, the largest, most prominent icon on the memorial. Finally, lest any viewer miss the obvious iconographic implication that "Death will blow up all our hopes, and put an end to these [temporal] enjoyments," the motto, "MEMENTO MORI," surmounts and summarizes the memorial.

On other memorials, however, the dominant-subordinate relationship between time and death is less obvious. Time on the Samuel Adams memorial (figure 2.14), for instance, appears to have dual status. In the inscription and the pilasters time assumes a typically subordinate postion, but the allegorical scene appears to reverse that relationship: Death, as the Grim Reaper, receives his instructions and, it would seem, his character from Father Time, who exhorts or instructs Death to extinguish the individual's life. Death also carries the scythe of Time, which insinuates that even Death is ruled by Time. Whether time is subordinate to death or death is subordinate to time, the lesson is the same: Remember death *(memento mori)* for time flies *(fugit hora)*.

With time—and perhaps through transculturation—cultural members increasingly moved away from skulls, winged death's heads, and such toward memorials whose imperative remained the same but whose iconography began to express this culture's imperative differently. Such images, as Diane George and Malcolm Nelson (1983) observe, "developed both artistically and philosophically from the earlier skull [image]" (13). The memorial for George Ropes (figure 2.15), for example, presents viewers with typical death- and time-related images in the inscription and pilasters and through the inscription *"memento mori"* at the bottom of the tympanum. But cultural members here transformed the winged death's head into a curiously abstract face. On the James Barrett memorial (figure 2.18) the icons and the motto *("Memento Mori")* express the imperative, while the discourse expresses hope: "Here / rests / in hope / ye Body of / Col. James / Barrett."

Pressing the range of expression further, the memorials of Humphrey Barrett (figure 2.16) and Jonathan Melven (figure 2.17) present viewers with a winged human head with unusually large eyes and a carefully detailed face—suggesting, it would seem, that each has gone on to his reward: blissful immortality. However hopeful they may be in relation to memorials like the Mather headstone (figure 2.10), such memorials nevertheless draw attention to time and death through their inscriptions, pilaster iconography, and mottos *("Memento Mori")*.

Just as often, however, cultural members erected memorials that adopted the same strategy manifested by inscription-only markers while using forms that adapted themselves to cemeterial environments controlled by individuals from other cultural groups—a clear indication both that Religionists were rapidly losing hegemonic control and that transculturation was emerging in and through their memorial tradition (see figures 2.19-2.22).

The tympanum of the triple arch headstone of Alice Jones (figure 2.23), for example, features a winged, transformed human situated between an open umbrella design at the crown and, immediately below the winged figure, a horizontal frieze containing the motto "Memento mori." Each pilaster's crown presents viewers with a Grecian (or Egyptian) vase design, which rests on top of a pillar—seemingly clear indicators that this memorial represents Romanticist values (a topic I take up in the next chapter). A convex frieze stretches between the pilasters to form an arch (or bridge) on which the tympanum designs rest. Inside the borders created by the arch above and the pillars at the sides is the following inscription: "SACRED / To the memory of Mrs. Alice Jones / Relic of / Capt. Ephraim Jones / Who died / Feb. ye 28th 1792 / Aged 62 years."

The ambiguity here is obvious. On one hand, the motto in the frieze and the softened representations in the tympanum instruct viewers to remember death. On the other hand, the inscription informs viewers that this memorial is "SACRED to the memory of Mrs. Alice Jones." Viewers thus address the expansive possibility of remembering death (hence: of remembering their need to prepare religiously for death) and of remembering the deceased as an individual (hence: of remembering the sense of loss and the emotions concomitant with that sense of loss).

## BODY AND SOUL

In the graveyard and beyond, cultural members struggle against the chaos that death continuously represents by filtering experience through a worldview that frequently finds its most salient memorial expression in the form of a dichotomy between body and soul. At the very least, that dichotomy serves as a synecdoche for primary cultural principles, values, and beliefs (for example, good/evil, eternal/ephemeral, reward/punishment, order/chaos, sacred/secular, clean/dirty, hope/fear, reality/illusion, health/disease, self/other, etc.) and as a vehicle for expressing primary cultural realities that constitute this worldview.

One of the overruling primary realities from which this culture's memorials emerge and in which they are ultimately meaningful is the view that life is a vertical journey through an ephemeral existence that constantly challenges and reinforces human frailty in order that diety may judge individual fidelity and worth. Each action, each event, each desire, each hope—in a word, everything—exists for this purpose and this purpose alone.

At the level of the individual, such a view mandates, among other things, that cultural members adopt an appropriate ethos, something akin to the ethos that cultural members attributed to Lincoln—namely, simple rather than complex, physically educated only to the extent that such education contributes to or otherwise aides spiritual education, pure, honest, sincere, transparent, meek, guided by a profound sense of religious faith, humble, conscious of the temptations of the secular world, and, above all else, conscious of the immediate and urgent need to prepare religiously for death *qua* judgment. Because such characteristics are inherently and inevitably vague and/or ambiguous, there is considerable latitude for interpretation, about which cultural members may and do disagree. That is in the nature of cultural logic; for ethos possesses possibility.

Within the cultural community, however, latitude of this sort has only a brief arch, for the vertical structure that stretches between evil and good—between body and soul—positions the collectivity such that their possibilities for investigating alternatives are considerably abbreviated. In one direction this means that cultural members live in a world so carefully controlled and delimited by definition that interpretation is scarcely problematic. The exact meaning of Lincoln's death, for example, might have been (and was) interpreted in a number of ways, but the direction of interpretation (that it was a divine message directed to the community/nation) was not in doubt within this frame of reference. In another direction, cultural members are continuously impelled to restrict the interpretations and alternatives of those outside the cultural community both for their own sake and for the sake of their obligation to demonstrate their cultural membership rhetorically by bringing others into the community.

At the social level, then, memorializing as a consequence of the evangelical impulse directly serves the individual and the collectivity The individual potentially benefits most directly from opportunities to evangelize, while the collectivity potentially benefits most directly from opportunities to install elements of cultural memory in public memory, thereby perpetuating and/or potentially restoring hegemony. Because the past represents order and because the present represents chaos, restoration of hegemony within the context of Lincoln's death (and more generally) thus is far more than a personal quest or a thirst for power.

Within this frame of reference, the moment of cultural transformation of which Lincoln's death was a significant part provided an opportunity for cultural members individually and collectively to contribute to their chances to gain favorable judgment from deity by gaining control of public memory as a means of transforming chaos into order, thereby responding appropriately to deity's message to the community/nation and ushering in the death of death. As the next chapter suggests, however, cultural members were unable to capitalize on this remarkable opportunity largely because members of other equally and more powerful cultures were unpersuaded by the call to "return" to something they did not regard as lost.

# 3

## LOVERS

*Even the death of Friends will inspire us as much as their lives. They will leave consolation to the mourners, as the rich leave money to defray the expenses of their funerals, and their memories will be incrusted over with sublime and pleasing thoughts, as monuments of other men are overgrown with moss; for our Friends have no place in the graveyard.*

—Henry David Thoreau, *A Week on the Concord and Merrimack Rivers*

Where the worldview and ethos that we examined in chapter two draw attention to the need to prepare religiously for death, the worldview and ethos that constitute our present focus draw attention from the deceased to the need to appreciate the emotionality and unity and beauty of death as a moment immersed in natural processes. This is how and why death for Thoreau and others who occupy this ideological space can be as inspiring as life, why grief and all the intense emotions that accompany death can be regarded as commodities capable of defraying "the expense of their funerals," why memory of the individual *qua* individual plays so central a role in their memorial efforts, why art and nature can combine in the presence of death to create "sublime and pleasing thoughts," and why "our Friends have no place in the graveyard." In opposition to the exacting vertical structuring of the moral universe so concisely disclosed by the Religionist worldview, members of a second cultural group, which I term "Romanticists," regard the universe as horizontally unified through Nature, which, when reconstituted through human effort, constitutes the metric against which cultural members measure all things.

## LINCOLN AS A ROMANTICIST

Against this metric Lincoln was particularly memorable, cultural members maintained, because he was thoroughly natural. He was "a quiet, native, aboriginal man, as an acorn from the oak," Ralph Waldo Emerson (1878) told his auditors, and following his death the world has come to understand that "rarely was a man fitted to an event" (308, 312). He was, Theodore L. Cuyler (1865) declared, a man of humble origins, a man who spent his youth splitting "rails in the Illinois forest." This admittedly gave Lincoln a rough appearance and a rugged sense of humor, which led some to believe that he was "a 'jester,' a 'clown' and a 'baffoon,'" but those who knew his true nature, Cuyler continued, knew clearly that his "humor was as natural to him as breathing" (163, 165, 167).

Even more important, cultural members continually pointed out, Lincoln's humble origins as a rail-splitter gave him a genuine appreciation of "Nature," from which he developed his natural wisdom, strength of will, moral unity, and honesty. Lincoln's "honesty," Richard S. Storrs, Jr. (1865) observed, "was not a separate trait, set mechanically into his nature, and governing what was alien to it. It was a part, living and inseparable, of his conscientious and ingenious mind." "His nature drew, through secret ducts, the wisdom of the Nation into itself; and the roots of his matured opinions were as wide as the country." From this natural source, Lincoln developed "the tenacity of his will" that "was like that of his muscle, which could hold an axe at arm's length without a quiver when others drooped." He understood the *true* unity of Nature, which allowed him to recognize "the poorest as his peer, and the black man as his brother," and which "gave a true moral unity to his administration" (434, 430, 455, 435). To understand Lincoln, and to understand what made him such a great and greatly loved individual, A. L. Stone (1865) proposed, one need only remember that he was always true to his nature, that "all his simple, plain, homely talk, kept him near us. He spoke our vernacular, the language of the fireside and common life, and not the dialect of courts. He did not leave us,"

> and wrap himself in official stateliness, when he went up the hill of the capitol. His kindly face and voice, his cheerful, humorous fireside English, his form and attitudes, and all his personal habits, made him seem of kin to each of us. . . . The humblest could go to him, finding an open door and an open heart. It seems to me that we have never held any other President so tenderly in our affections. And one reason is we have never found any other so accessible to our thoughts and sympathies, and never one so much of our own mold and substance. (341)

Given Lincoln's nature, cultural members incessantly told their auditors, one need not wonder why all hearts are broken. "Old as history is, and manifold are its tragedies," Emerson (1878) proclaimed, "I doubt if any death has caused so much pain to mankind as this has caused, or will cause on its announcement" (307, vol. X). "When the flowers have many times bloomed and faded on the grave of our martyred President; when the banner of peace floats over every acre of the broad territory of our glorious Union; when the hearts that felt the pangs of awful bereavement are still, men will assent to the facts recorded by the historian, but they cannot feel with them a generation whose bosom received the fiery darts, *unless they come in contact with their feelings*" (Prefatory 1865, viii; my emphasis).

Although it may not have been natural in the usual sense, Lincoln's death was a natural conclusion to his life. It was, they insisted, a blessing, a beautiful fate. Certainly, Lincoln's sudden death was a "far happier fate than to have lived to be wished away; to have watched the decay of his own faculties; to have seen,—perhaps even he,—the proverbial ingratitude of statesmen; to have seen mean men preferred" (Emerson 1878, 313). But Lincoln's death was more than that, for it came at the best of times—"in the power of his manhood, in the rich strength of his intellect, in the noontide of his glory, in the climax of his fame, ere old age had come upon him," and, therefore, all "must regard his life and death as fortunate" (Folger 1865, 78). As "his sun goes down in full-orbed splendor, without a cloud to mar its beauty," and "around the little green mound that marks his resting-place those storms" that Lincoln had weathered now "subside, and all is peace" (Gleason 1865, 42, 43). "His career closed at a moment when its dramatic unity was complete, and when his departure from life on earth was the apotheosis, and the translation by which, defended against all the shocks and mishaps of the time, he passed on to immortality" (Andrew 1865, 126). This is why the living should "not mourn that his departure was so sudden, nor fill [their] imagination with horror at its method," for "when one is ready to depart suddenness of death is a blessing" (Beecher 1887, 705).

The living should weep and grieve and mourn as never before—not for Lincoln, whose death was "a blessing," but for themselves; for "a heavy pall overhangs the land, and all hearts are united in the holy brotherhood of sorrow" (Carrington, et al. 1865, 148). They should grieve because they have been "robbed . . . of the kindest and truest friend, . . . of one of the ablest advocates of humanity and brightest ornaments of the age—to whose memory, virtues, and great qualities eulogy can never do more than justice" (Haynie, et al. 1865, 136). They should weep to add their "voices to the wail of lamentation that swells from the nation, without distinction of class or party" (Carrington, et al. 1865, 149). They should mourn in an attempt "to give some feeble expression to the feelings and emotions with which every heart seems to be filled" and to pay tribute to their fallen martyr, for "the highest eulogy of ABRAHAM LIN-COLN is found in the universal gloom and sorrow that pervades the land, and the emblems of mourning," which should be constant reminders of "the deep and all-pervading grief of every member of the community" (Angel 1865, 36–37). "We cannot change thee, oh, weeping April! Oh, month of tears! Pour down all thy warm showers: from our eyes the rain falls faster yet! Evermore, from henceforth, at thy return, those and the sorrowing nation shall weep together" (Stone 1865, 338).

Within such a worldview, intense feelings naturally lead to greater unity because "ABRAHAM LINCOLN belonged to the country; he was the constitutional head of the whole republic." Therefore, "in this general demonstration of our loss there is no division, no sect, no party, among us" (Murphy 1865, 81). Emotions heal homeopathically, naturally. Universally stricken with the finest and most sublime emotions, the living should "cultivate that nobler ambition, which, if it is conscious of high and splendid qualities, seeks place and power to be of use to the common wealth, . . . so that public good is achieved and the best interests of universal man advanced" (Folger 1865, 80). "From his grave there comes to us a voice. It bids us to forget our selfish aims, old jealousies and party hates, and consecrate ourselves renewedly and entirely to our country and to mankind" (Gleason 1865, 44).

Equally important, cultural members reassured, intense, natural emotions will lead to greater beauty, and across the nation individuals will create "those eulogies" that "take the poetic form which only intensity of feeling produces" (Storrs 1865, 422). People will "rear to his name monuments, found charitable institutions, and write his name above their lintels." Still, even the creation of beautiful works of art in response to Lincoln's death and in memory of his life will not equal in beauty "the universal, spontaneous, and sublime sorrow that in a moment swept down lines and parties, and covered up animosities, and in an hour brought a divided people into unity of grief and indivisible fellowship of anguish" (Beecher 1887, 705). Anguish, sorrow, grief, pain, sadness—all of the finer, more sublime emotions occasioned by the death of an intimate—are themselves naturally beautiful works of art.[1]

Even so briefly considered, the logic of the Romanticist ethos and worldview are beginning to emerge. Unlike Religionists, Romanticists were disinclined to portray and promote Lincoln especially as a religious figure or to regard his sudden death as ignominious in any sense. They were shocked, of course. But their shock did not lead them to discover and interpret divine messages in nature. Rather, sublime emotions impelled them to search for the various ways Nature had manifested itself in Lincoln's life and death through beauty, unity, and emotionality. In part, this allowed cultural members to claim that Lincoln was one of their own by focusing on particular qualities that they supposed him to have possessed. But what was of even greater significance was that their portrayal of Lincoln as a Romanticist would allow them to encourage others to embrace their ethos and worldview, thereby reinforcing the legitimacy of their hegemony.[2] The image of a man working and living in harmony with nature—a woodsman, a rail-splitter— was well-suited to this perspective, which we can explore in greater depth by examining, first, a sermon that James Freeman Clarke delivered to his Boston congregation on April 16, 1865, and, second, the cemeterial and iconographic forms cultural members created as a means of communicating, perpetuating, and developing their worldview and ethos.

### "Who Hath Abolished Death"

Imagine a small New England chapel filled with people anxiously awaiting the comforting words of their minister. "The entire chancel" is "covered with a rich purple fabric looped to the wall at different points with wreaths of white flowers." On the wall, above and behind the chancel, is "a large cross surmounted by a crown, and at the side" are "the words 'He is Risen,' each worked in foliage and flowers." Located all around the chapel are "numerous bouquets and single specimens of choice flowers and plants." The American flag, "draped in mourning," is "drooping from the gallery" to heighten "the general effect" (Clark 1865, 91).[3]

Upon reaching the pulpit, the minister begins to speak. But he does not speak of auditors' need to prepare religiously for death, of their need to merit immortality, of the hierarchical structure of the moral universe, of the struggle between good and evil, of human frailty, of their need to restrain emotions and "*natural impulses by the controlling power of religious feeling.*" He speaks instead of the outpouring of emotions that followed the death of Jesus Christ—of the sense of loss and alienation, of the fear of having been abandoned by deity and Christ, of the horror of having been left to Satan. Christ's presence on earth, Clarke insists, was a unifying force, for Christ was "the one being who knew God wholly and human nature exactly; who could say 'I and my father are one,' 'I and my brother are one.'" Christ promised unity and the possibility of regenerating a "world dying of weariness." But the death of this bringer of unity and regeneration, who was "so true, so gentle, so brave, so firm, so generous, so loving," seemingly brought only "the blackest day in the history of man" (92).

From this portentous beginning our speaker leads his audience to understand that Christ's death was not what it seemed, that it was in reality beautiful, and that death itself is beautiful. Christ's death was beautiful because it "abolished death; because evil that day destroyed itself; sin, seeming to conquer, was conquered" (92). Death is beautiful because it naturally, inevitably leads to blissful immortality, for "we pass through death to life, through sorrow to joy, through sin to holiness, through evil and pain to ultimate and perfect good" (92-93). Nature provides clear and irrefutable evidence of natural, blissful, inevitable immortality:

> Nature, every spring, renews her miracle of life coming out of death. The little, tender buds push out through

the hard bark. The delicate stalks break their way up through the tough ground. The limbs of the trees, which yesterday clattered in the wind, mere skeletons, are now covered with a soft veil of foliage. Earth clothes itself with vendure, and these spring flowers come, the most tender of the year. They come, like spirits, out of their graves, to say that Nature is not dead but risen. Look at these flowers,—living preachers! "each cup a pulpit and each bell a book," and hear from every one of them the word of comfort: "Be not anxious, be not fearful, be not cast down; for if God so clothe us, and so brings our life out of decay, will He not care for you and yours evermore?" (93)

Nature's lesson here serves to assure cultural members that Christ's death and resurrection brought about "the subjugation of the last enemy,—Death." Death is unreal, "emptied . . . of reality and substance"; it is "only a form" (93).

Still, if people fail to understand the unity of nature and, hence, the inevitability of immortality, death must seem terrible. It must seem terrible because it apparently "ends this life, and all the enjoyment and interest of this life" (84). It must seem terrible because death seems to cast individuals into an unknowable void, where they can no longer enjoy and find comfort in and through Nature:

We are made to be happy in the sight of nature; in this great panorama of sky and land, hill and plain, sea and shore, forest and mountain, rivers, clouds, day and night, moon and stars, work and play, study and recreation, labor and sleep. We are made to enjoy the society of friends, the love of the near and dear, the quiet of home, the march of events, the change of the seasons, the vicissitudes of human and national life.

> Death seems to be the end of all this; and so we shrink
> from death. . . .
>
>   Another thing which makes death a terror is our
> own consciousness of sin. The sting of death is sin. (94)

The fear of death seems natural, then; but an understanding of Nature's unity serves to subdue and abate that fear. An understanding of Nature's unity allows individuals to realize "that when surrounded by nature we are in the arms of God." And, as death cannot take individuals "away from God, so we shall not go away from all this beautiful variety and harmony, this majestic order and transcendent beauty of creation. We shall doubtless have more of it, know it better, enjoy it more entirely" (94). Nor do cultural members need to be concerned by the sting of death, for "Christ removes this sense of sin, by bringing to us the pardon of sin. The conditions are simple and practicable: repentance and faith. If we turn from our sin and renounce it, and then trust in the pardoning grace of God, we are forgiven our sin" (94–95).

Having thus led auditors to a place where they can rest assured "that death, instead of being a step down, is a step up," a natural and inevitable "passing on and up, through death, to a larger life," Clarke at last turns to Lincoln's assassination (95). Because "of the assassination of our President and of Mr. Seward, and the other murders which accompanied those acts," Clarke observes, "it seemed impossible to dress this church with flowers, impossible to keep Easter Sunday with joy to-day" (96). As with the fear of death, the fear of not being able to enjoy Nature after and even in the midst of death, and the fear of not being moral enough to merit immortality, the fear of not being able to respond appropriately to the occasion is unfounded.

It is possible to respond appropriately to the occasion, Clarke insists, because true cultural members are emotionally attached to the deceased. They do not confront the death of some nameless, faceless person. This cultural members know because

Lincoln's death was not merely assassination: "It was parricide; for Abraham Lincoln was a father to the whole nation." Emotional turmoil is natural, inevitable because "the nation felt orphaned yesterday, when the black tidings came; for during these four years we had come to depend on the cautious wisdom, the faithful conscience, the shrewdness, the firmness, the patriotism of our good President" (96).

To be sure, Clarke acknowledges, Lincoln was not perfect. "We have all quarreled with him at times; we wished he would go faster; we wished he had more imagination, more enthusiasm" (96–97). People must also certainly concede that "the chief fault of Abraham Lincoln was that he was too forgiving of his enemies, too much disposed to yield to those from whom he differed, and to follow public opinion instead of controlling it" (97). Even so, his "chief fault" and his numerous positive qualities undoubtedly sprang from a common source, from his natural love of unity:

> He could not bear to punish those who deserved it; and the man who will suffer most from his death is his murderer, for had Lincoln lived, he would have forgiven him. Simple in his manners, unostentatious, and without pretense; saying his plain word in the most direct way, and then leaving off; he yet commanded respect by the omnipresence of an honest purpose, and the evident absence of all personal vanity and all private ends. . . . We shall miss him often in the years to come, for when shall we find among politicians one so guileless; among strong men one with so little willfulness; among wise men one with so much heart; among conservative men one so progressive; reformers one so prudent? (97)

Lincoln's life, according to this cultural perspective, provides people with a portrait of a man struggling for natural unity. "And so we find him mourned equally by the conservative and the progressive wing of the loyal people, because he was in reality a thoroughly conservative and a thoroughly progressive man." Certainly, the nation could not have expected anything but a thoroughly emotional response following the death of such an individual, who began "as a splitter of rails," who studied "his grammar by the firelight of a log cabin when a boy," who was "tried by hardship, hardened by labor, toughened by poverty, developed by opportunity, trained by well-fulfilled duties," and who, in death, was "crowned with the martyr's halo, to be made immortal through all history and all time as the chief actor in the greatest drama of modern days" (98). People are immersed in their emotions because Lincoln exemplified the best of natural life, and because that life has taught them to look beyond "surface-differences," "through the rough shell to the rich kernel" (99).

This is the connection between the deaths of Christ and Lincoln. Christ's death appeared to be "the blackest hour in the history of the human race," yet it ultimately "abolished death" and reaffirmed natural immortality. This "black event," too, may seem entirely evil and portentous of future evil; yet, "as Abraham Lincoln saved us, while living, from the open hostility and deadly blows of the slaveholders and secessionists, so, in dying, he may have saved us from their audacious craft, and their poisonous policy. We are reminded again what sort of people they are" (101). Christ's life brought unity to the world, and his death unified life and death. Lincoln's life brought unity to the Union, and his death will unify "the people of the North, always hopeful and good-natured," against the unnatural actions and policies "of the slaveholders and secessionists" (100). Lincoln's death "was like the blow of a hammer descending on the heart of the nation. But such a hammer and fire welds together the soul of a people into a strong, righteous purpose." Through natural processes, then, "this crime will unite the whole North to make thorough work with the rebellion, and put it down where it can never stir itself again" (100–101).

Christ and Lincoln are not entirely comparable; this much Clarke implicitly acknowledges. Christ was "the one being who knew God wholly and human nature exactly." Lincoln, on the other hand, was "too forgiving to his enemies, too much disposed to yield to those from whom he differed, and to follow public opinion instead of controlling it." Christ was perfect; Lincoln was imperfect. But these and other differences to which one might point are unimportant within this moment. They simply signify that each individual is an individual, distinct.

What is more important than differences for cultural members is similarity, comparability, the bases on which Nature unifies things that are seemingly disparate. Christ and Lincoln are comparable, in part, because both were emotional, both explored their individual natures, both were people of gentle sentiments: caring, loving, concerned, forgiving, wise, able to see unity where others saw only division. Both struggled through adversity, hardship, narrowness, ignorance, disunity. Both fulfilled their natures and died tragically—gloriously, honestly—to give their worlds new unity, new harmony, new life.

The comparison between Christ and Lincoln is not a necessary component of this worldview, of course. Nor, for that matter, is it necessary to compare the deceased to anyone. What is more important from this perspective is that the deceased be portrayed romantically, tragically, so that auditors can immerse themselves in the fate of the "chief actor."

Consider the underlying logic. While from one perspective actualities might be regarded as opposites, from the perspective we are here considering those actualities cease to oppose one another, since all things belong to the unified whole. Deity and individual, individual and nature, Nature and deity, deity and art, Nature and art, art and individual, individual and community, individual and individual, death and life, emotion and reason—all belong to a unified whole, to Nature. Nature unifies. "My Friend is not of some other race or family of man," Thoreau (1906) insisted, "but flesh of my flesh, bone of my bone. He is my real brother. I see his nature groping yonder so like mine" (302). For cultural members, then, things that appear to be disjunctive are conjoined by virtue of their similar natures. In turn, part of what drives this worldview is the effort to comprehend Nature's unity.

Death is as inspiring as life because they belong to the same whole, the same continuum; they have similar natures. The deceased leaves "consolation to the mourners, as the rich leave money to defray the expenses of their funeral" because the relationship between the death of an intimate and the intense emotions occasioned by that death is homeopathic; grief is "natural" and can be resolved best by means of natural processes. Memories of the deceased "will be incrusted over with sublime and pleasing thoughts" because life is the beginning of death, because death is the beginning of life, and because grief and mourning "naturally," homeopathically lead cultural members to remember the beautiful pathetically and the pathetic beautifully.

Yet, the effort to comprehend and be pleased by Nature's unity is not the only driving force here. Insofar as what is natural is by definition good, what is not natural logically must be bad. Good and bad, natural and unnatural, exist together within a frame where linear, bipolar opposition is impermissible because such opposition contradicts unity. This is the contradiction that plagues cultural members and helps to drive their view of the world. That view thus is an effort to comprehend and to be pleased by nature and to drive out what is unnatural, thereby ensuring that all things are naturally unified.

Both of these impulses figured prominently not only in cultural members' efforts to commemorate Lincoln's death, as we have seen, but also in their efforts to advance their "natural" memorial tradition. Before they could encourage others to see the world through their eyes, for instance, cultural members were necessarily concerned to eliminate whatever they considered "unnatural" by altering and beautifying the Religionist gravescape. This is why they insisted, as Thoreau put it, that "our Friends have no place in the graveyard," for the dominant gravescape developed, maintained, and controlled by Religionists is "horrific" to cultural members and, therefore, is not conducive to "sublime and pleasing thoughts." Nearly simultaneously, Romanticists advanced their own cemeterial form and their own emotionally and "naturally" evocative iconography as communicative means of developing and perpetuating their ethos and worldview. Cultural members seem to understand very well that, as E. Douglas Branch (1962) once observed, "The greatest enticement into romantic melancholy was probably the graveyard" (154).

## ROMANTICISM IN THE CEMETERY

As early as the first decades of the eighteenth century, as Tashjian and Tashjian (1974) have shown, citizens who did not embrace the then dominant worldview and ethos introduced "elaborate" funerals that appalled Religionists, who responded by creating "sumptuary laws which attempted to restrict the amount of money to be spent on gloves, rings, scarves, and rum at funerals (and other unrelated social acts as well) throughout the eighteenth century" (27). At roughly the same time, gravescapes began to show definitive signs of different cultural influences—of markers that announce the ascendance of a cultural tradition undergirded by a substantively different view of the world. As we have already seen, with the introduction of the cherub, the transformed human, portraits, the willow and urn motif, and other similar icons, we find a cultural blending between Religionists and Romanticists, with the former borrowing images from the latter while retaining death as the object of memory. For Romanticists, however, the introduction of different images provided a clearly different focus for memory. Understandably, because Religionists controlled gravescapes and the social scene generally, the ascendance of this new tradition was at first ambiguous and vague.[4]

Consider the curious contrast between the Ephraim Jones (figure 3.1) and Catherrine Conant (figure 3.2) memorials. Both are triple arch stones that feature the softened representations of death in the tympana that we associate with the Religionist memorial tradition. However, while the Ephraim Jones memorial provides viewers with typically Religionist life representations in the pilasters and typically Religionist discourse, the Catherrine Conant memorial discards the life representations and introduces a completely other object of memory: "IN Memory of / Mrs. Catherrine / Conant, wife of Mr. / Abel Conant, who died March ye 24th 1780: / In the 29th year of / her age."

By retaining softened representations of death but eliminating Religionist representations and explicit mottos, memorials like the Catherrine Conant headstone help to ease the tension between manifestation and purpose by allowing the viewer to choose either death or the deceased as the object of memory. Yet, both vague and ambiguous markers participate in the same variety of cultural shading. Both attempt to serve two traditions, two disparate purposes at once. Both disclose an effort to alter purpose without fully altering manifestation—hardly surprising, given the continuing hegemonic influence of Religionists in that moment.

Other markers disclose much less cultural shading. The single arch variation headstone of Joseph Watson (figure 3.3), for example, echoes Religionist form both in its shape and in its inscription-only presentation, but its inscription informs viewers that this marker is "Sacred / to the memory / of Joseph Watson / son of Capt. Joseph / & Mrs. Eliza Watson / he died at the age of 3 years & 5 months / on the 17th March 1806." Below a horizontal line separating the epitaph from the lower portion of the marker, viewers find a poem that draws attention not to death but to the poignancy of loss. "Sweet opening rose bud / like the dew drops morn / Too soon alas from thy / fond Mother torn." Without mottos or iconographic references to death to confuse or distract the viewer, inscription-only markers of this sort directly and unambiguously draw attention to the deceased as the object of memory. Moreover, poems like the one that concludes this marker serve to instruct viewers to remember the deceased pathetically, to experience life and death through intense emotions, to understand that they cannot authentically heal themselves *"unless they come in contact with their feelings."*

Although inscription-only markers of this sort are relatively common, other markers that emerged during the same period more decisively announce the ascendance of this memorial tradition both discursively and iconographically, thus signaling a rejoining of manifestation and purpose. That is, by combining inscriptions identifying the deceased as the object of memory with icons borrowed from Greek and Egyptian cultures ("exotic" cultures being a clear fascination among Romanticists) and/or representations of nature, cultural members explicitly identified the memorable and its significance by wedding emotion and the individual in art and nature, art and nature in emotion and the individual.

Among the most common indicators of this formal and functional coupling are the weeping willow and amphora (or hydra) designs. The headstone of Andrew Conant (figure 3.4) is illustrative. In the tympanum is what appears to be a Grecian hydra jar shaded by the branches and leaves of a weeping willow tree. The tympanum designs rest on a horizontal bridge that connects two pillars. Between and connected to the pillars is an ovular panel bearing the following inscription: "ERECTED / IN memory of / MR. ANDREW CONANT / who died / Jan. 31, 1813 / E.T. 39 years."

The headstones of Abigail Dudley (figure 3.5) and Judith Archer (figure 3.6) feature similar but somewhat simpler designs. The tympanum of Abigail Dudley's marker, for example, features a Grecian hydra jar design encased by an oval frame. The barely legible epitaph below the tympanum notes that "This stone is designed / by its durability, / to perpetuate the memory, / and by its colour, / to signify the moral character / of / MISS ABIGAIL DUDLEY / who died June 4, 1812 / aged 73." Here, clearly, it has become important for externalized memory to remain as long as possible (as opposed to the view that memory of the individual is quite beside the point). On Judith Archer's marker the featured icon is a simplified tree, and the inscription again calls attention to the deceased as the object of memory: "In Memory of / JUDITH ARCHER / Daughter of / Capt. Geo. & Mrs. Judith Archer / Obt. March 14, 1801. / Aged 5 Years."

Like the Judith Archer marker, the headstone of Paul Reed (figure 3.7) relies on a symbol of nature. Here, a stylized anthropomorphic sun occupies the tympanum, and the epitaph reminds viewers that this memorial was erected "In Memory of / PAUL REED / of Boothbay / died Jan. 24, 1799." Depending on the direction of movement one attributes to the sun, one might interpret this icon as representing the end or the beginning of the individual's life. On the triple arch headstone of Luke Roberts (figure 3.8), however, the iconographic implication is clear. Here, the tympanum features a large phoenix with a human head (presumably representing the deceased). A rectangular frieze adorned with swirling designs truncates the pilaster crowns and encases the inscription, which informs viewers that this memorial was carved "In Memory of / Mr. LUKE ROBERTS / who Died Sept. 25th / 1780." To reinforce the regenerative significance of the phoenix, each truncated crown contains a single stylized lily just beginning to blossom.

Although the emergence of markers such as these unquestionably announced the ascendance of the Romanticist memorial tradition, even the most innovative of these memorials did not and could not alter the Religionist gravescape. To be sure, as softer representations and divergent memorials increased in frequency and number, the lessons taught by the graveyard expanded. But four factors mitigated against authentic reform. First and foremost, Religionists still owned, maintained, and controlled community gravescapes. Second, although in proportionally decreased numbers, Religionists continued to produce markers (and through rules and regulations required others to produce markers) that echoed their ethos and worldview. Third, although Romanticist markers are generally larger than and divergent from Religionist markers, they are nonetheless markers. Finally, although Romanticist memorials announce the ascendance of a new memorial tradition, they do so within the confines of the Religionist gravescape, which was still located among the living, still "neglected," and still taught its original lessons to the living; its manifestations continued to reaffirm a Religionist ethos and view of the world.

Eventually, Romanticists would resolve this dilemma by developing a radically different cemeterial form that would express their worldview and ethos. Their initial efforts, however, focused on efforts to reform the graveyard, just as they had attempted to reform Religionist memorials (see figure 3.9). The development and subsequent redevelopment of Old Copp's Hill Burying Ground in Boston, Massachusetts is instructive.

On February 20, 1659, "the Selectmen of Boston" purchased a treeless "lot of land, 294 feet on the northerly side, 252 feet on the southerly side; in breadth on the easterly end 126 feet" from John Baker and Daniel Turell (*Suffolk Deeds*, lib. 53, fol. 153). On November 5, 1660, the town passed the following order, which officially recognized this lot as Boston's second graveyard: "Itt is ordered that the old burying place shall bee wholly deserted for some convenient season, and the new places appointed for burying only be made use of" (*Suffolk Deeds*, lib. 53, fol. 153). Fifty years later the graveyard had become so overcrowded with graves that enlargement "could no longer be postponed." The town appointed a committee, "consisting of Hon. Thomas Hutchinson, Timothy Thornton, and Edward Martyn," which purchased an adjoining parcel of land from Samuel and Hannah Sewall (*Historical Sketch*, 1901, 6). On December 17, 1707, the town thereby doubled the size of one of its most frequented graveyards for fifty pounds "and the release from payment of an annual quit-rent of 40 shillings for a certain ceder swamp in Brookline" (*Suffolk Deeds*, lib. 25, fol. 97).

Despite the fact that this small graveyard received "one-fourth the population of the town" from its inception through the middle of the eighteenth century, the town did not again increase its size until 1809 (*Historical Sketch*, 1901, 7). On December 18 of that year, "for $10,000, Benjamin Weld, and his wife Nabby, sold to the Town of Boston a parcel of land, bounded south-west on Hull Street 148 feet; north-west on the [present] burial ground, 148 feet 6 inches; north-east on land of Goodwin and others, 153 feet; south-east on land of Jonathan Merry, 123 feet; being land conveyed to Weld by Merry, October 21st, 1809, recorded" (*Suffolk Deeds*, lib. 231, fol. 199).

Although crowded conditions necessitated such occasional acquisitions, and although formally divergent markers began to emerge here as they did elsewhere throughout the eighteenth century and the first years of the nineteenth century, this place of the dead remained largely unaltered for nearly 160 years. Thereafter, however, we begin to glimpse the first in a series of attempts to alter Old Copp's Hill's appearance and purpose. Not surprisingly, the first modifications began to emerge at approximately the same time that Romanticist memorials began to emerge in Religionists graveyards.

The first significant change came in 1814, when "Charles Wells, later mayor of Boston, built 52 tombs" on land adjacent to the land the town had recently acquired from Weld. Five years later Wells purchased a small graveyard "usually called the Charter Street Burying-Ground," which also adjoined Old Copp's Hill Burying Ground (*Historical Sketch*, 7). After enclosing this graveyard with a fence, Wells erected another 34 tombs.[5] Then in 1827 "Edward Bell built 15 more [tombs] on the site of the old gun-house of the Columbian artillery." Like Wells' graveyards, this "new ground was laid out symmetrically in tiers and several bodies were interred in each grave" (*Historical Sketch* 1901, 7).

Having reconceptualized and refigured the grounds, cultural members then turned their attention to beautifying and naturalizing the graveyard. In May of 1833 "fifty dollars was appropriated by the city authorities toward purchasing trees for ornamenting the grounds, and from that date the whole appearance of the Hill began to change"—a point that was no small source of pride, as the remainder of the passage makes clear: "Those trees have all been removed, and other, of a more appropriate character, numbering one hundred and eighty, have taken their places, which makes a very agreeable shade to the visitor on a sultry day, as well as the children who come to play. The Hill is visited not only by residents of the city, but by people from all parts of the globe" (MacDonald 1885, 30–31). Within five years "new avenues and walks were laid out; grave stones were removed for that purpose, thus affording opportunities for pleasant promenades" (MacDonald 1885, 31). And at later dates a wrought-iron fence was erected around the graveyard, individual wrought-iron fences were erected around and subsequently removed from some of the plots, and grasses and plants were cultivated to make the Religionist gravescape more aesthetically acceptable to Romanticists.[6]

Not all Americans agreed that these extensive efforts to alter the graveyard's appearance and purpose actually improved it in any sense. Some Religionists felt that removing or altering the position of markers resulted from "mistaken efforts at symmetry" (*Historical Sketch* 1901, 8). Others recognized that the claim that "the danger to health which arises from" burying the dead among the living "has probably been over-rated, if, indeed, it exist at all" (Peabody 1831, 403). "In some cases," B. D. Halsted (1880) noted, the efforts of Romanticists were "met with lukewarmness, in others with prejudice, and in others with direct opposition" (74). In all, a significant segment of the population continued to believe that "it is of little importance where dust returns to dust" (Peabody 1831, 403).

Despite the opposition and objections of others, however, Romanticists were determined to supplant these "unnatural" practices with "natural" practices. As Henry Ward Beecher (1859) proclaimed, it simply was impossible for cultural members not to "be pained at the desolation of these places." "The fences," where there were fences, "are dilapidated, the head-stones broken, or swayed half over, the intervals choked up with briers, elders, and fat-weeds; and the whole place" bears "the impress of the most frigid indifference" (123). This was not simply a matter of graveyards being unattractive, Beecher claimed, "it is a shame and a disgrace that the only places in thrifty New England where weeds are allowed to grow unmolested are graveyards, where the bodies of our sweet children, where father and mother, brother and sister, husband and wife, rest" while "cows and horses are often allowed to pasture on the graves; thus saving the expense of mowing, beside a clear gain in grass!" (124).

Writing in the *North American Review,* William B. O. Peabody (1831) not only echoed Beecher's criticisms, but also saw the dominant gravescape as an insult to human intelligence, a recently developed superstition, and an affront to the emotions and rights of the living and the dead—an interesting twist of advancing an innovation by claiming that the received view is an innovation. "The cold ghastliness of the sculptured marble,—the gray stone sinking, as if weary of bearing unregarded legends of the ancient dead; the various inscriptions showing, sometimes, what the dead were, but still oftener what they ought to have been," Peabody told his readers, "subdue the heart to sadness, not to gloom" (398). Sadness is the theme of the Religionists' graveyard, Peabody continued, because the history of the human race tells us that "man [seeks] to re-assure himself, in the presence of death, that he is not all frailty, by raising monuments, which long after he is gone, may resist the waste of time" (399–400). Throughout history, he reasoned, humans have believed that "the thought of death must be presented in such a manner as makes it welcome" (400). But Peabody lamented that in his time, in his homeland, "the burying place continues to be the most neglected spot" and can be "distinguished from other fields only by its leaning stones and the meanness of its enclosure, without a tree or shrub to take from it the air of utter desolation" (405). All that the Religionist gravescape is, all that it represents, he insisted, "is an invention of comparatively modern times" that seeks to promote the dread of death, which "is not a natural feeling" (403).

Rather than using the dead to promote the dread of death, Romanticists insisted, the living should learn valuable lessons from the burial customs of the ancients. "How many mansions of death remain, when ancient houses of the living are gone! The tombs of Hadrian and Metella have outlasted the palaces of the Caesars; the Egyptian tomb of the kings remain perfect, when the pyramids are nameless ruins" (Peabody 1831, 399). Another lesson citizens should learn from the burial practices of the ancients is that "the grave, in all countries and times, is the place where the best feelings are awakened; the conflicts of passion cease there, and all other feelings are lost in sympathy and concern for those who sleep within its narrow bounds" (402). This is why "the stiff and ungainly head-stone should be banished to give place to the *cippus,* or some simple form suited to resist the elements, and receive inscriptions," and why monuments should "not be such as the elements waste, but such as time only strengthens and repairs" (p. 406).

> Let clean and sufficient fences be made; let the borders and paths be planted with shade trees; let the side paths be lined with roses, vines and free-growing shrubs; let the grass be shorn at least every month; let measures be taken to erect again the drooping head-stones of the ancient dead, and, if needful, retrace the effaced letters; for all these things are within the reach of every village parish. . . . (Beecher 1859, 126–27)

These things and more cultural members sought to accomplish, driven as they were by a strong desire to rid the environment of "the sad spectacle of promiscuous ruins and intermingled graves" and to "cast a cheerful light over the darkness of the grave" (Story 1859a, 160). Yet, try as they might, cultural members could not adequately alter the appearance and purpose of the Religionist gravescape to comport with their view of the world; nor could they adequately incorporate into the graveyard all those things that would fully and naturally afford them "the luxury of grief" (159). This did not prevent cultural members from continuing to try to reform the graveyard, but it did suggest that the majority of their energies and efforts might be better directed toward creating a new, beautiful, natural, serene place for the dead.

Speaking to the Massachusetts Horticultural Society in 1832, Edward Everett noted that many citizens had long felt the need for a new type of burial place. The "chief obstacle to the execution of this project," he noted, has been "the difficulty of finding a proper place" (as quoted in Halsted 1880, 71). Seven years earlier, a young Boston physician by the name of Jacob Bigelow not only had overcome this "chief obstacle," but had also overcome the obstacle of designing a cemetery that would allow Romanticists to effect the union of art and nature. Having become aware of "certain gross abuses in the rites of sepulture as they then existed under churches and in other receptacles of the dead in the city of Boston," Jacob Bigelow (1859) asked several of his friends to meet with him at his home to discuss his proposal for a new "rural cemetery" (1). "This original meeting," Bigelow noted, "was attended by Messrs. John Lowell, William Sturgis, George Bond, Thomas W. Ward, John Tappan, Samuel P. Gardiner, Nathan Hale, and Jacob Bigelow"—all of whom heartily endorsed the proposal (2).

From that initial meeting in 1825 until late in 1830 Bigelow and his friends failed to secure suitable land for the project, due either to "the high prices at which the land was held, or from the reluctance of the owners to acquiesce in the use proposed to be made of the premises." Finally, in 1830 Bigelow (1859) persuaded George W. Brimmer to sell "a tract situated in Cambridge and Watertown, then known as 'Stone's Woods,' and more familiarly to the college students as 'Sweet Auburn'" (3)—a name it had earned through the ribald activities of Harvard's students. Even having overcome this obstacle, however, Bigelow was acutely aware that the notion of a rural cemetery "was new, the public were lukewarm, and, in many cases, the prejudices of the community were strongly opposed to the removal of the dead from the immediate precincts of populous cities and villages to the solitude of a distant wood." Clearly, Religionists continued to exert considerable power in the community. If "these prejudices were to be overcome," Bigelow acknowledged, "it would be best done by enlisting in favor of a change, the co-operation of a young, active, and popular society" (4–5).

As it happened, Bigelow knew of just such a society—the Massachusetts Horticultural Society, which the Massachusetts legislature had recently incorporated in 1829. Among its members were some of the most socially and politically influential people in Boston, including Joseph Story, Daniel Webster, H. A. S. Dearborn, Charles Lowell, Samuel Appleton, Edward Everett, George W. Brimmer, George Bond, A. H. Everett, Abbott Lawrence, James T. Austin, Franklin Dexter, Joseph P. Bradlee, Charles Tappan, Charles P. Curtis, Zebedee Cook, John Pierpont, L. M. Sargent, and George W. Pratt. As the "Corresponding Secretary," Jacob Bigelow knew well that he was in a position to call for a meeting of the Society to discuss his proposition (Bigelow 1859, 7–8; see also Dearborn 1859; Manning 1880; Story 1859b).

At that meeting, on November 23, 1830, the Society appointed a committee to study the feasibility of combining a cemetery and an experimental garden. On June 8, 1831, the committee reported its findings to the Society, "and it was voted expedient to purchase the estate offered by Mr. Brimmer,—containing about seventy-two acres,—at six thousand dollars, in behalf of the Horticultural Society, as soon as one hundred subscribers for cemetery lots, at sixty dollars each, should be obtained" (Bigelow 1859, 7). By August 3, the requisite one hundred lots had been sold. By September 24, cultural members were anxiously prepared to consecrate their first beautiful, natural, rural cemetery.

At the consecration ceremonies Joseph Story delivered an address that gave a strong, clear voice to the ethos and worldview that had impelled cultural members to alter the appearance and purpose of the graveyard, to develop different iconographic forms, and to create a radically different cemeterial form. Part of the justification for such things, Story (1859a) remarked, is that "it is in vain, that Philosophy has informed us, that the whole earth is but a point in the eyes of its Creator,—nay, of his own creation; that, wherever we are,—abroad or at home,—on the restless ocean, or the solid land,—we are still under the protection of his providence,"

> and safe, as it were, in the hollow of his hand. It is in vain that Religion has instructed us, that we are but dust, and to dust we shall return, . . . Dust as we are, the frail tenements, which enclose our spirits but for a season, are dear, are inexpressibly dear to us. We derive solace, nay, pleasure from the reflection, that when the hour of separation comes, these earthly remains will still retain the tender regard of those whom we leave behind;—that the spot where they shall lie, will be remembered with a fond and soothing reverence;—that our children will visit in the midst of their sorrows; and our kindred in remote generations feel that a local inspiration hovers round it. (145-146)

Places of the dead, Story proclaimed, ought to be places from which the living can derive pleasure, emotional satisfaction, and instruction on how best to live their lives. If this were true of present burying-grounds, then, sitting by the graves of loved ones, citizens would be able "to hear the tone of their affection, whispering in our ears." The dead would speak to the living there "in the depths of our souls." There, the living could shed their tears—not "the tears of burning agony," but the tears of relief that would allow the living to "return to the world," where they could feel themselves "purer, and better, and wiser, from this communion with the dead" (148-149).

All of the ancient civilizations, Story continued, have understood the lessons of the rural cemetery. "The aboriginal Germans," who "buried their dead in groves consecrated by their priests"; the Egyptians, who "satisfied their pride and soothed their grief, by interring" their dead "in their Elysian fields"; the Hebrews, who buried their dead in "ornamented gardens and deep forests, and fertile valleys, and lofty mountains"; the "ancient Asiatics," who "lined the approaches to their cities with sculptured sarcophagi, and masoleums, and other ornaments, embowered in shrubbery"; the Greeks, who "exhausted the resources of their exquisite art in adorning the habitation of the dead," who "consigned their relics to shady groves, in the neighborhood of murmuring streams and mossy fountains, close by the favorite resorts of those who were engaged in the study of philosophy and nature," and who called their places of the dead, "with the elegant expressiveness of their own beautiful language, CEMETERIES, or 'Places of Repose'"; the Romans, who "erected the monuments to the dead in the suburbs of the eternal city, (as they proudly denominated it,) on the sides of their spacious roads, in the midst of trees and ornamental walks, and ever-varying flowers"—all of these ancient civilizations have provided ample evidence of the value of the rural cemetery (149–51). Why, then, Story asked, have citizens refused to listen to the lessons of the dead? "Why should we deposit the remains of our friends in loathsome vaults, or beneath the gloomy crypts and cells of our churches . . . ?" "Why should we measure out a narrow portion of earth for our graveyards in the midst of our cities, and heap the dead upon each other with a cold, calculating parsimony,"

> disturbing their ashes, and wounding the sensibilities of the living? Why should we expose our burying-grounds to the broad glare of day, to the unfeeling gaze of the idler, to the noisy press of business, to the discordant shouts of merriment, or the baleful visitations of the dissolute? . . . Why all this unnatural restraint

upon our sympathies and sorrows, which confines the
visit to the grave to the only time, in which it must be
utterly useless—when the heart is bleeding with fresh
anguish, and is, too weak to feel, and too desolate to
desire consolation? (154–55)

Cultural members need not answer such questions, Story
insisted, for the consecration of Mount Auburn on this day
announced to the world the arrival of a much needed, purer, more
beautiful relationship between the dead and the living. With the
consecration of this shinning example of art and nature and emotions combined, all the world would realize that "our cemeteries
rightly selected, and properly arranged," will "preach lessons, to
which none may refuse to listen, and which all, that live, must hear,"
for in the midst of Nature, with time to contemplate and to feel, the
living will understand beyond all doubt that "the grave hath a voice
of eloquence, nay, of superhuman eloquence" (156). At long last,
mourners will be able to "revisit these shades with a secret, though
melancholy pleasure. The hand of friendship will delight to cherish
the flowers, and the shrubs, that fringe the lowly grave, or the sculptured monument." At long last, "Spring will invite thither the foot-
steps of the young by its opening foliage; the Autumn detain the
contemplative by its latest bloom" (165). At long last, cultural members can banish "the thought, that this is to be the abode of a
gloom, which will haunt the imagination by its terrors, or chill the
heart by its solitude." At long last, citizens can "erect the memorials
of our love, and our gratitude, and our glory," for here individuals
may "let youth and beauty, blighted by premature decay, drop, like
tender blossoms, into the virgin earth; and here let age retire,
ripened for the harvest" (166–67).

Judging from the rapid emergence of rural cemeteries subsequent to the establishment of Mount Auburn, as well as Mount
Auburn's immediate popularity, this new cemeterial form quickly
lived up to Joseph Story's rhetorical epiphany (see figure 3.10). As

"America's most influential writer on gardening and rural architecture" (Tatum 1974, v), Andrew Jackson Downing, pointed out in
1849, "no sooner was attention generally raised to the charms of the
first American cemetery, than the idea took the public mind by
storm." Within a matter of months travellers from near and far
began to make "pilgrimages to the Athens of New England, solely to
see the realization of their long cherished dream of a resting place
for the dead, at once sacred from profanation, dear to the memory,
and captivating to the imagination" (Downing 1974, 154). Part of
the reason for Mount Auburn's immediate popularity, perhaps, was
due to the novelty of a beautiful cemetery. Yet, as Stanley French
(1974) has observed, Mount Auburn was still being "proudly dis-
played to foreign and native visitors in the decades before the Civil
War" (69), long after its novelty had worn away.

More than that, if Mount Auburn's popularity had been
due primarily to its novelty, it is unlikely that it would have been
"rapidly imitated in all parts of the United States" (Bigelow 1859,
vi). Yet, by 1836 Philadelphians marveled at the pleasures of Laurel
Hill Cemetery. By 1837 New Yorkers strolled through the sylvan
scenes of Brooklyn's Greenwood Cemetery. In 1838 Massachusetts
(Worcester Rural Cemetery), Kentucky (Cave Hill Cemetery),
Rochester, New York (Mount Hope), and Baltimore (Greenmount)
boasted new rural cemeteries. Pittsburgh in 1844 (Allegheny),
Cincinnati in 1845 (Spring Grove), and Louisville in 1848 added
their voices to a growing chorus. And by 1849 Downing (1974) was
able to observe with due pride that "there is scarcely a city of note
in the whole country that has not its rural cemetery." Philadelphia
alone, he continued, has "nearly twenty rural cemeteries at the present moment—several of them belonging to distinct societies, sects
or associations, while others are open to all" (154–55).

In addition to providing cultural members with numerous
occasions to echo Story's sentiments in their consecration addresses,
the continual consecration of rural cemeteries also provided ample
opportunities to articulate the best ways to appreciate rural ceme-

teries.[7] Seemingly every rural cemetery fostered one or more guide-books, each of which provided prospective visitors with a detailed description of the cemetery and "a walking tour" designed to conduct visitors "within every occupied spot, and every object of interest" (Cleaveland 1850, 4).[8] Very likely, these efforts were not wasted, since rural cemeteries are not only generally large and complex by design, but also because cultural members made certain that visitors would continually confront things that would be "dear to the memory, and captivating to the imagination." "In their mid-century heyday, before the creation of public parks," as Blanche Linden-Ward (1989b) very well understands, "these green pastoral places also functioned as 'pleasure grounds' for the general public" (293). Mount Auburn, like so many other Romanticist cemeteries, "presented [and still presents] visitors with a programmed sequence of sensory experiences, primarily visual, intended to elicit specific emotions, especially the so-called pleasures of melancholy that particularly appealed to contemporary romantic sensibilities" (295).[9]

The owners of rural cemeteries played a significant roll in the effort to capture the hearts and imaginations of visitors. Diligently, they sought to ensure that visitors confronted Nature's many splendors not only by taking great care to select sites that would reveal "Nature's own easy and graceful outline" (Cleaveland 1850, 250), but also by purchasing and importing wide varieties of exotic shrubs, bushes, flowers, and trees. At Laurel Hill in Philadelphia, for example, the owners immediately purchased and planted "almost every procurable species of hardy tree and shrub" to make it "a better *arboretum* than can easily be found elsewhere in the country" (Downing 1974, 155–56). Both from within the gravescape and from a distance, rural cemeteries thus frequently appear to be lush, carefully constructed forests (see figure 3.10).

Promoting a love of Nature, however, was only a portion of what cultural members sought to accomplish in their cemeteries. "The true secret of the attraction," Downing (1974) insisted, lies not only "in the natural beauty of the sites," but also "in the tasteful and harmonious embellishment of these sites by art." Thus, "a visit to one of these spots has the united charm of nature and art,—the double wealth of rural and moral association. It awakens at the same moment, the feeling of human sympathy and the love of natural beauty, implanted in every heart" (155). To effect this union of nature and art cemetery owners went to great lengths—and often enormous costs—to commission and obtain aesthetically appealing objects to adorn the cemetery and to set a standard for those wishing to erect memorials to their deceased friends and relatives.

Almost immediately following the consecration ceremonies owners of Mount Auburn commissioned M. P. Brazee to build a wooden entrance gate "for $1,366. This wooden gate, painted in imitation of granite, stood until 1842," when it was replaced by a granite gate created "in the Egyptian style." Shortly thereafter the owners commissioned Leonard Stone to construct a temporary wooden fence for the sum of $2,636.65 (Bigelow 1859, 24–26). This, too, was replaced, in 1844, by a "curved iron fence which forms a part of the design of the gateway extending from the lodges to the obelisks," all of which "are essentially Egyptian in their character. The constituent parts are selected from among the emblems and trophies, which are sculptured on various structures extant on the banks of the Nile" (Bigelow 1859, 48).

During the same year (1844) the cemetery owners voted to commission the building of a granite chapel "of a Gothic design" (figure 3.11) to be used as "a suitable place for funeral services, and for the reception of statues and other pieces of delicate sculpture unfit to bear exposure to the air of our variable climate" (King 1883, 40). The owners later named the chapel after Jacob Bigelow, who had inspired the creation of Mount Auburn and who designed Mount Auburn's most prominent structure—a sixty-two foot tower (figure 3.12) "built on the general plan of some of the round towers of the feudal ages" (Bigelow 1859, 60). Soon afterward, the cemetery owners commissioned Richard Greenough to sculpt a marble statue of John Winthrop, Thomas Crawford to sculpt a marble statue of

James Otis, and Randolph Rogers to sculpt a marble statue of John Adams (Bigelow 1859, 72–73). In effect, cemetery owners were resolutely suggesting by example that "memorials are, or ought to be, works of art" (Bigelow 1859, 64). Even the smallest rural cemeteries suggested this much by creating, at the very least, elaborate entrance gates to greet visitors (see, for example, figure 3.13) so that their cemeteries would help to create "a distinct resonance between the landscape design of the 'rurual' cemetery and recurring themes in much of the literary and material culture of that era. . . . The popular taste for the new cemetery echoed cultural trends and tastes shared by many Americans" (Linden-Ward 1989b, 295).

What is perhaps even more important—and what constitutes one of the most striking features of the rural cemetery—is the consistency with which cultural members manifested their worldview through their cemeterial iconography. This much was already becoming clear when their memorials began to emerge in Religionist's graveyards. But with the introduction of a cemeterial form that actually *encouraged* lot owners to create memorials designed as works of art that praised Nature and promoted pathetic responses, cultural members had the requisite social positioning to work diligently to create a gallery of art embraced by Nature.

With so much freedom at their disposal, Romanticists created an enormous variety of memorials to express their worldview and ethos. For purposes of analysis, however, we might say that such memorials fall into two categories or strains. The first strain abides principally by the creed that "memorials are, or ought to be, works of art" insofar as they serve primarily to draw attention either to the memorial as a work of art or to the work of art as a memorial. In either case, what is most immediately notable about these memorials is that someone was wealthy enough and cared enough about the deceased (or about their status in the community) to commission a work of art to their memory. Given the extent to which cultural members relied on the "rural" burial practices of "ancient civilizations" to justify the need for a new cemeterial form, and given the prominence of Egyptian, Greek, Gothic, and Roman influences in the efforts of cemetery owners, it is not at all unexpected that the most common art memorials also borrow heavily from these same sources.[10]

The Grecian pelike jars that surmount the entrance gate of the Confederate Section of the Old City Cemetery in Lynchburg, Virginia (figure 3.14) are illustrative. Pelike jars are not necessarily associated with death. Nevertheless, their memorializing purpose here is a reflection of the inscription carved on the gate's arch, which is to say that the jars and the gate were both created "IN MEMORY / OF THE CONFEDERATE DEAD / WHO ARE BURIED HERE."

The memorial of James Lawrence (figure 3.15) features a less ornate, but considerably larger Grecian amphora, which is mounted on an unadorned pedestal. The memorial of William Perkins Walker (figure 3.16), on the other hand, features a finely polished granite orb, apparently Egyptian in design. Mounted on a marble pedestal, ornate braces hold the orb in place. And the memorial created by Martin Milmore (figure 3.17) to commemorate "the preservation of the Union," as noted in the inscription, features an enormous sphinx resting on a granite base.

The Martin memorial (figure 3.18) and the A. D. Harris memorial (figure 3.19) do not rely so obviously on borrowed burial symbols, but more explicitly draw attention to the union of art and Nature. The Martin memorial, for example, is a granite tree stump whose "bark" has been removed to provide room for the inscription. The A. D. Harris memorial presents viewers with a slightly more ornate version of the tree stump image.

A second strain of memorials, which we might term pathetically evocative works of art, draws attention not only to the work of art as a memorial (or to the memorial as a work of art), but also to pathetic sentiments. One of the more common focal points for such memorials is the faithful animal—a significant connection with

Nature. The Schluter memorial (figure 3.20), for example, features a lamb "resting" in the tympanum, which surmounts the inscription: "INFANT SON OF / H. & A. SCHLUTER / BORN & DIED / NOV. 18, 1916 / Gone so soon." Similarly, the memorial of Warren Cone (figure 3.21) features a marble Irish Setter placidly "resting" on a two-tiered marble base. In the dog's mouth is a lily symbolizing, one might suppose, either the deceased's immortality or the dog's eternal love of its master. And the memorial of William Frederick Harden (figure 3.22), features a large, gabled structure supported by four granite columns. Under the protection of the structure is a large, marble amphora, which rests on a granite pedestal. Inscribed on a marble plaque that is recessed into the face of the pedestal is the following inscription: "WILLIAM FREDERICK / HARDEN / FOUNDER / OF / THE EXPRESS BUSINESS / IN / AMERICA / DIED IN JANUARY 1943 / AGED 31 YEARS." As though waiting patiently for its master's return, a large marble dog attentively rests directly in front of the plaque.

Another common focal point for pathetically evocative memorials is the angel. The Chickering memorial (figure 3.23), for example, features the archangel Gabriel either placing a funeral shroud on or lifting it from a female figure, who is reverently kneeling and clutching a cross to her breast. Carved in relief on the pedestal of the memorial is another female figure, who is sitting on a rock with her head bowed. In her left hand she holds a lyre. More simply, the Emmert Hamilton memorial (figure 3.24) presents viewers with a female angel mounted on a marble pedestal. The inscription notes that this memorial was erected "In memory of / Our little darling / EMMERT HAMILTON / Son of / Emmert & Teresa Jefferson. / Born July 23, 1907. / Died July 3, 1909. / Another little angel, / Before the heavenly throne." The memorial of Nathan and Isabel Sargent (figure 3.25) presents viewers with a similar, but rather more elaborate image. Poised on the bow of a ship, a finely sculpted female angel succumbs to the ravages of turbulent waves. In the angel's right hand is a trumpet, which is positioned near her lips, suggesting, perhaps, that she is preparing to announce the deceased's arrival in heaven. Yet another angel is the focal point for the Thomas and Nancy McKee memorial (figure 3.26). Here, however, a finely sculpted female angel stands next to a huge, roughly hewn cross. With her head bowed in grief, the angel holds a bunch of flowers in her left hand, and gently brushes the plaque bearing the inscription with her right hand. A similar, but more complex arrangement of icons accompany the male angel featured on the Cottrell memorial (figure 3.27). Standing on top of a small obelisk, the angel is pointing to the sky with his right hand and is either depositing or removing a cluster of fruit, which is positioned just above the mouth of a pelike jar. Just below the angel and the jar is the face of a child carved in relief on the face of the obelisk. To the left and right of the obelisk are hydra jars, each partially covered by a funeral shroud.

Poised women and children, being "inherently" closer to Nature, constitute a third major focal point of pathetically evocative memorials. The Annie E. Mallory memorial (figure 3.28), for example, features a marble female figure mounted on a marble pedestal. Standing with her left knee slightly bent, as if frozen in motion, the figure's left hand is positioned across her breast, and in her right hand is what appears to be a walking stick.

The memorial of Eliza Smull (figure 3.29) on the other hand, presents viewers with a sculptured marble infant "asleep" in its cradle, which rests on top of a small pedestal that bears the following inscription: "ELIZA SMULL / INFANT DAUGHTER OF / J.B. AND A.E. SMULL. / BORN JULY 20, 1864 / DIED JULY 23, 1864." Similarly, the memorial of Mary R. Swain (figure 3.30) features a small marble child bowing her head and sitting on a rock. The rock and child are positioned on top of a pedestal, and on the face of the pedestal an inscription notes that this memorial was erected in memory of "OUR / LITTLE MAY."

Slightly beyond (but clearly related to) this strain are memorials that seek to preserve some significant association or set of associations that serve to keep the deceased's life somehow alive in a manner reminiscent of mummification. Graceland (figures 3.30 and 3.31), for example, presents visitors with an estate filled with artifacts that seek to preserve and perpetuate memories of Elvis Presley.[11] Throughout visitors find live and recorded stories (as well as rooms that have been meticulously preserved, suggesting that the deceased left very recently and might well return in a matter of moments) detailing not only the individual's achievements, but also (and especially) the preservation of literally hundreds of moments of endearment—all of which preserve slices of time that persistently return the visitor's focus to emotions that (from this perspective) swirl around images of the deceased.

Near the location where Martin Luther King, Jr. was assassinated outside room 308 in the Lorraine Motel in Memphis, Tennessee, by contrast, we find a single wreath (figure 3.33). Inside, visitors may view the room which preserves that tragically violent moment in time. Rather than a single image or set of images that draw attention homeopathically to the deceased, however, the object of memory here shifts through transculturation. A plaque below the wreath draws attention away from homeopathy and toward achievement and external association (characteristic of Heroism, as we see in the next chapter), thus suggesting that we are to remember the man for whom the wreath was created primarily (perhaps exclusively) because he was the "Founding President [of the] Southern Christian Leadership Conference." That the deceased's memorialization is surrounded and engulfed by a second, much more spatially and temporally expansive object of memory (the Civil Rights Movement, as commemorated by the the plaque featured in figure 3.33 and by the National Civil Rights Museum that occupies the motel), miniaturizes and marginalizes the location as a memorial for Martin Luther King, Jr. and heroically foregrounds the achievements of a collective in which, within this rhetorically specified context, the deceased was but a part.

I do not mean to suggest that these few instances exhaust the kinds of memorials that Romanticists have produced or might yet produce. Nor do I mean to suggest that this way of grouping constitutes a prolegomenon to any future discussion of Romanticist memorials. On the contrary, the point I wish to make is far simpler. Regardless of particular design, and despite the impressive and difficult to comprehend array of designs, Romanticist memorials manifest, in one way or another, a very particular worldview and ethos.

## NATURE AND THE UNNATURAL

Within that particularity, confrontation with death for cultural members is far less a struggle against chaos than an opportunity to understand the unity and universality within a seemingly specific disunity, which focuses attention and experience both on living in the moment and on the dichotomy between the "natural" and the "unnatural." As with the Religionist dichotomy between body and soul, the Romanticist dichotomy between the "natural" and the "unnatural" serves as a synecdoche for primary cultural principles, values, and beliefs (where "natural" equates with "good," and where "unnatural" equates with "bad" or "evil") and as the axial mode for identifying and expressing cultural realities that constitute this worldview.

Memorials thus serve not as a means of reminding cultural members of their urgent need to bring order out of chaos in order to prepare religiously for death, but as a means of encouraging others to live in the moment, "naturally." Like Lincoln, cultural members who adopt an ethos that emerges from living within the moment will be native, aboriginal, perfectly fitted to their time and place, immersed and content with being immersed in the inevitable process of being, happy in the sight of Nature and art, imaginative, guileless, in touch with their feelings, sublime, prepared to found charitable institutions and build monuments to art and Nature, and, above all else, appreciative of the unity and universality of all things. Moreover, because living in the moment is a "natural" expression of the past, just as the future is a "natural" expression of the present, emotions (the most obvious and immediate manifestations of lived experience, from this perspective) both identify the "authenticity" of the individual's lived experience and promote "authentic" experience (Koestenbaum 1964, 1971), thereby freeing the individual by encouraging them to cast off the burdens of the past and the anxieties of the future (Heidegger 1962).

At the level of the cultural community, this horizontality so positions the collectivity that the insistence on unity dissolves difference, which simultaneously makes interpretation an apparently open-ended but clearly constrained matter. Ostensibly, that is, any interpretation is permissable, yet only "authentic" (that is, Romanticist) interpretations are acceptable, which makes worldview the boundary that restrains and disciplines the freedoms of ethos. No less than Religionists, then, "authentic" Romanticists must restrict the interpretations and alternatives of those outside the community both for their own sake and for the sake of their obligation to the community.

At the social level, memorializing thus authenticates the individual and perpetuates the community. Individually, to be memorialized by/within the community is to be authenticated, to be "present" in memory; collectively, controlling (or, at least, contributing significant elements to) public memory perpetuates cultural principles, values, and beliefs by keeping cultural memory ever-present. Further, because the past and the future live in and through the present, maintaining hegemony in the moment of Lincoln's death was not a matter of turning chaos into order but a matter of encouraging social utilization of all things "natural" that defined the moment.

Here, the possibilities of cultural transformation surrounding Lincoln's death became immediately problematic. On one front, Religionists saw and responded to the opportunity to regain their lost hegemony by focusing attention on the need to restore order amidst the chaos. On another front, as the next chapter details, members of a third cultural group would press for a markedly different orientation that challenged and eventually displaced the Romanticist hegemony.

Fig. 2.1.  Religionist gravescape. Old Colony Burying Ground; Norfolk, Connecticut

Fig. 2.2.  Headstone of Richard More, 1692. The Burying Place; Salem, Massachusetts

Fig. 2.3.   Headstone of Jane Second, 1686. The Burying Place;
Salem, Massachusetts

Fig. 2.4.   Headstone of Roger Hooker, 1698. Ancient Cemetery;
Hartford, Connecticut

Fig. 2.5.   Headstone of Josiah
Hayward, 1736. South Burying
Place; Concord, Massachusetts

Fig. 2.6.   Headstone of
John Haynes, 1895. Eakins
Cemetery; Ponder, Texas

Fig. 2.7. Headstone of
Elizabeth Mockridge, 1940.
Woodlands Cemetery;
Philadelphia, Pennsylvania

Fig. 2.8. Headstone of Ella
Brock Sinkler, 1960.
Woodlands Cemetery;
Philadelphia, Pennsylvania

Fig. 2.9. Headstone of
Lowell M. Clucas III, 1986.
Woodlands Cemetery;
Philadelphia, Pennsylvania

Fig. 2.10. Memorial of
Nathanael Mather, 1688.
The Burying Point; Salem,
Massachusetts

Fig. 2.11. Headstone of Doraty Cromwell, 1673. The Burying Point, Salem, Massachusetts

Fig. 2.12. Headstone of Joseph Barrett, 1763. South Burying Place; Concord, Massachusetts

*Fig. 2.13. Sideplate of Robert Rad sarcophagus, 1753. Church Burying Ground; Williamsburg, Virginia*

*Fig. 2.14. Detail of Samuel Adams headstone, 1728. King's Chapel Burying Ground; Boston, Massachusetts*

*Fig. 2.15. Detail of George Ropes' headstone, 1755. The Burying Point, Salem, Massachusetts*

*Fig. 2.16. Memorial of Humphrey Barrett, 1783. South Burying Place; Concord, Massachusetts*

*Fig. 2.17. Memorial of Jonathan Melven, 1737. Old Hill Burying Ground;
Concord, Massachusetts*

*Fig. 2.18. Detail of James Barrett memorial, 1779. Old Hill Burying Ground;
Concord, Massachusetts*

*Fig. 2.19. Purves memorial, 1931. Woodlands Cemetery; Philadelphia, Pennsylvania*

*Fig. 2.20. Brewster memorial, 1888. Woodlands Cemetery, Philadelphia, Pennsylvania*

*Fig. 2.21. Webb memorial, 1980. Woodlands Cemetery; Philadelphia, Pennsylvania*

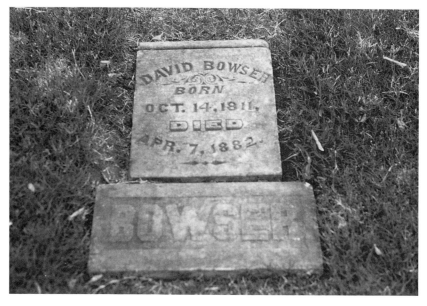

*Fig. 2.22. Bowser memorial, 1882. Restland Memorial Park; Dallas, Texas*

*Fig. 2.23. Memorial of Alice Jones, 1792. South Burying Place; Concord, Massachusetts*

Fig. 3.1. *Headstone of Ephraim Jones, 1756. South Burying Place; Concord, Massachusetts*

Fig. 3.2. *Headstone of Catherrine Conant, 1780. South Burying Place, Concord, Massachusetts*

Fig. 3.3. Headstone of Joseph Watson, 1806. Ancient Cemetery; Hartford, Connecticut

Fig. 3.4. Headstone of Andrew Conant, 1813. South Burying Place; Concord, Massachusetts

Fig. 3.5. Headstone of Abigail Dudley, 1812. Old Hill Burying Ground; Concord, Massachusetts

Fig. 3.6. Headstone of Judith Archer, 1801. The Burying Point; Salem, Massachusetts

Fig. 3.7. Headstone of Paul Reed, 1799. The Burying Point; Salem, Massachusetts

Fig. 3.8. Headstone of Luke Roberts, 1780. King's Chapel; Boston, Massachusetts

Fig. 3.9.  Granery Burial Ground subsequent to reorganization and
beautification efforts. Boston, Massachusetts

Fig. 3.10.  Romanticist gravescape. Mount Auburn Cemetery; Cambridge,
Massachusetts

Fig. 3.11.   Bigelow Chapel. Mount Auburn Cemetery; Cambridge,
Massachusetts

Fig. 3.12.   The Tower. Mount
Auburn Cemetery; Cambridge,
Massachusetts

*Fig. 3.13.  Entrance. Elm Grove Cemetery; Mystic, Connecticut*

*Fig. 3.14.  Entrance gate of the Confederate Section of the Old City Cemetery in Lynchburg, Virginia*

Fig. 3.15. James Lawrence
memorial, 1855. Mount
Auburn Cemetery,
Cambridge, Massachusetts

Fig. 3.16. William Perkins Walker memorial, 1892. Mount Auburn Cemetery;
Cambridge, Massachusetts

*Fig. 3.17. Memorial for the Preservation of the Union, Mount Auburn Cemetery; Cambridge, Massachusetts*

*Fig. 3.18. Martin memorial, 1876. Woodlands Cemetery; Philadelphia, Pennsylvania*

Fig. 3.19. A. D. Harris
memorial, 1917. Eakins
Cemetery; Ponder, Texas

Fig. 3.20. Schluter memorial,
1916. Eakins Cemetery;
Ponder, Texas

Fig. 3.21. Warren Cone memorial, 1856. Old Colony Burying Ground;
Norfolk, Connecticut

Fig. 3.22. William Frederick
Harden memorial, 1845.
Mount Auburn Cemetery;
Cambridge, Massachusetts

Fig. 3.23. Chickering memorial, ND. Mount Auburn Cemetery; Cambridge, Massachusetts.

Fig. 3.24. Emmert Hamilton memorial, 1909. Church Burying Ground; Williamsburg, Virginia

Fig. 3.25. Nathan and Isabel Sargent memorial, 1907. Arlington National Cemetery; Arlington, Virginia

Fig. 3.26. Thomas and Nancy McKee memorial, 1924. Arlington National Cemetery; Arlington, Virginia

Fig. 3.27.  Cottrell memorial, 1865.
Elm Grove Cemetery; Mystic,
Connecticut

Fig. 3.28.  Annie E. Mallory memorial,
1864. Elm Grove Cemetery; Mystic,
Connecticut

Fig. 3.29.  Eliza Smull
memorial, 1864. Elm
Grove Cemetery; Mystic,
Connecticut

Fig. 3.30. *Mary R. Swain memorial, 1877. Old Colony Burying Ground; Norfolk, Connecticut*

Fig. 3.31. *Front view of Graceland. Memphis, Tennessee*

*Fig. 3.32. Memorial wall outside Graceland. Memphis, Tennessee*

*Fig. 3.33. Memorial to Dr. Martin Luther King, Jr. and plaque outside the Lorraine Hotel. Memphis, Tennessee*

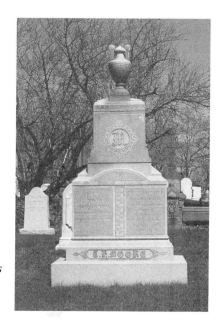

Fig. 4.1. Albin Thomas and Mary Moore memorial, c. 1879. Woodlands Cemetery; Philadelphia, Pennsylvania

Fig. 4.2. Nathaniel and Lucy Tucker memorial, c. 1865. Church Burying Ground; Williamsburg, Virginia

Fig. 4.3. William Worth
Belknap memorial, 1890.
Arlington National Cemetery;
Arlington, Virginia

Fig. 4.4. Memorial for Confederate soldiers of La Fayette County;
Oxford, Mississippi

*Fig. 4.5. Andrew Dunlap memorial, 1914. Arlington National Cemetery; Arlington, Virginia*

*Fig. 4.6. Heroist memorials in a Romanticist gravescape. Mount Auburn Cemetery; Cambridge, Massachusetts*

Fig. 4.7. Washington
Monument, 1848–1884.
Washington, D. C.

Fig. 4.8. The Jefferson memorial, 1943. Washington, D. C.

Fig. 4.9. Memorial statue of Thomas Jefferson, 1943. Washington, D. C.

Fig. 4.10. Ulysses S. Grant memorial. Washington, D. C.

*Fig. 4.11. Civil War memorial. Washington, D. C.*

*Fig. 4.12. Marine Corps memorial, 1954. Arlington, Virginia*

*Fig. 4.13. Ironwork fencing with gate. Mount Auburn Cemetery; Cambridge, Massachusetts*

*Fig. 4.14. Ironwork enclosure. Rosehill Cemetery; Concord, California*

*Fig. 4.15. Heroist gravescape. Princeton Memorial Park; Princeton, New Jersey*

*Fig. 4.16. Heroist gravescape. Oaklawn Memorial Park; Washington, New Jersey*

*Fig. 4.17. Arlington National Cemetery. Arlington, Virginia*

*Fig. 4.18. Price memorial, 1989. Eakins Cemetery; Ponder, Texas*

*Fig. 4.19. Milton C. Broad memorial, 1939. Restland Memorial Park; Dallas, Texas*

*Fig. 4.20. Joseph H. Kelly memorial, 1985. Princeton Memorial Park; Princeton, New Jersey*

Fig. 4.21. William H. Buchanan memorial. Oaklawn Memorial Park;
Washington, New Jersey

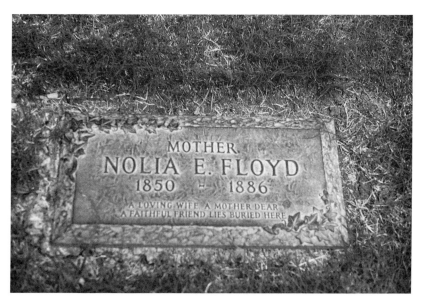

Fig. 4.22. Nolia E. Floyd memorial, 1886. Restland Memorial Park;
Dallas, Texas

*Fig. 4.23. Funerary art in the Heroist gravescape. Princeton Memorial Park; Princeton, New Jersey*

# 4

## HEROES

*Properly, then, he will be called brave who is
fearless in the face of a noble death, and of
all emergencies that involve death; and the
emergencies of war are in the highest degree
of this kind.*

—Aristotle, *Nicomachean Ethics*

Struggling without much obvious success to obtain a voice throughout the Religionist and Romanticist hegemonies, Heroists, I think it
is fair to say, were the greatest beneficiaries of the cultural chasm created by Lincoln's death. Here was an opportunity unlike any before
for Heroists to take control of the cultural scene—much as they succeeded in taking control of the death-bed scene by bringing in physicians who were clearly antithetical to homeopathic (Romanticist)
medicine, by maginalizing Mary Lincoln whose genuine grief clearly
was too emotional (too Romanticist) for Seward and others, and by
seizing every opportunity to install their own cultural members in
key positions over the next four years. The Rev. A. A. Miner (1865),
like so many other cultural members, understood the opportunity
very well: "Called from us at the culmination of his fame, he may be
more to us in the coming years, than he could have been had he still
tarried in the flesh. He died as a martyr dies." Therefore, "Especially

115

should you, young men, and particularly those of you, who, through liberal education, are seeking fields of widest influence, enter in at the open door of opportunity, which the new order of things proffers you" (291). As Religionists turned the minds of their auditors inward in an effort to move them to "*suppress or modify all natural impulses by the controlling power of religious feeling*," and as Romanticists turned their attention to the enormous tasks of beautifying and naturalizing not only Lincoln's death, but also the deaths and the social, political, emotional, cultural, and physical devastation wrought by the Civil War, Heroists focused their attention on taking action. And it was against just such a backdrop that Lincoln was for them perfectly memorable.


## LINCOLN AS A HEROIST

Like other cultural groups, Heroists were quick to focus on Lincoln's humble origins—but not because they illustrated how "God was giving him an iron frame" (Simpson 1865, 233), and not because Lincoln's origins illustrated how, "despite all that, he preserved every fine fibre of his nature" (White 1865, 95). Rather, Lincoln's disadvantaged early life loomed large because his rise from a lowly birth to the presidency was an integral part of the story of how Lincoln *heroically* had triumphed over adversity. Lincoln was most remarkable, most admirable, most worthy of emulation, and most memorable, cultural members insisted, because his life and death so well illustrated their ethos and worldview.

"In 1809, in a little village in Kentucky, beneath the thatched roof of a poor man's cottage," George Hepworth (1865) reminded his Boston audience, "was born a child whose prospects for the future seemed very limited. He received from his parents nothing but poverty and a good name" (111). Yet, through his own efforts Lincoln overcame the disadvantages to which he was born. Having "spent the first thirty years of his life upon that monotonous plane on which every poor farmer's boy lives," having "given his services in the Black Hawk war" in which he showed "no lack of courage, but rather a quiet persistency and fearlessness," and having "served his constituents faithfully in a minor position, he began that slow and toilsome journey of promotion, which is marked at every stop by honesty of purpose; and which ended, when, obedient to the will of the North, he assumed the position of the President of the United States" (112). In New York Representative Weaver (1865) similarly reminded his colleagues that Lincoln's mind, "rescuing itself by its own native strength and vigor from the relationships of its early and humble career, won for its possessor promotion to the highest civil and political position in the land" (23). Contrary to what others might say, George Chaney (1865) intoned, Lincoln "had a working religion, which believed that God helped those who helped themselves to right ends. . . . He had not profited so little by his pioneer life, as to wait for the lightening to plough his land or the whirlwind to fell his trees; but he took the instruments that were at hand, the plough and the axe" (330).

Beyond these early heroic achievements, cultural members contended, was the remarkable heroism of Lincoln, the President. He did not succumb or pander to Nature but dominated and controlled it: "If he must plunge into the depth of the forest, he took care to trace his path by blazing the trees with his mark; and if sometimes he seemed slow emerging from the wilderness, it was because, when a boy, he had learned to halloo till he was out of the woods" (Thompson 1865, 181). More, as George Bancroft (1865), the "father of American history," declared before the thousands of Americans who had gathered at Union Square in New York City to witness the city's tribute to Lincoln, history will decide how much of Lincoln's success was due to circumstance and how much to "his own good common sense, his shrewd sagacity, readiness of wit, quick interpretation of the public mind; his rare combination of fixedness and pliancy; his steady tendency of purpose" (199; see also Bancroft 1866). Still, history cannot and will not deny that the accomplishments of his administration were largely, if not wholly, cultural members insisted, the consequence of Lincoln's own efforts; for,

> after every allowance, it will remain that members of the government which preceded his administration opened the gates to treason, and he closed them; that when he went to Washington the ground on which he trod shook under his feet, and he left the republic on a solid foundation; that traitors had seized public forts and arsenals, and he recovered them for the United States, to whom they belonged; that the capital which he found the abode of slaves, is now only the home of the free; that the boundless public domain which was grasped at, and, in a great measure, held for the diffusion of slavery, is now irrevocably devoted to freedom; that then men talked a jargon of a balance of power in a republic between Slave States and Free States, and now the foolish words are blown away forever by the breath of Maryland, Missouri, and Tennessee; that a terrible cloud of political heresy rose from the abyss threatening to hide the light of the sun, and under its darkness a rebellion was rising to indefinable proportions. (199–200)

While the triumph over his humble beginnings and such remarkable achievements helped cultural members illustrate Lincoln's heroic ethos, they did not fully explain what truly made Lincoln heroic. For this, cultural members repeatedly turned to evidence of Lincoln's inner qualities; for "The great man is the controlling power, and he cannot be anticipated" (Chaney 1865, 325). In part, they urged, it was because of Lincoln's "honesty of purpose" that he was memorable, for it "inspired him with true moral heroism. Abraham Lincoln always met his duty as calmly as he met his death" (Thompson 1865, 198). The "remarkable self-control of Mr.

Lincoln was an element in his character which contributed largely to his success." Although the "waves of faction and the tumult of civil war beat wildly and fiercely about him, yet his serenity was never disturbed. Anxiety might cloud his brow, doubt and apprehension oppress his heart," John Albion Andrew (1865) announced, "but his calm judgment and clear perceptions were never swayed or obscured" (90). He acted "boldly and fearlessly," he "stood firm and unshaken," "calm and self-possessed, with a strong heart and a firm hand, steering for that haven which his mind's eye so distinctly saw" (Schlesinger 1927, 107). During the heat of war, "when failure after failure tended to discourage the stoutest hearts, Lincoln never failed and never quailed." He "stood firm, immovable, hopeful, trying and trying again until his firmness and his hope inspired the whole nation, the hecatombs of blood and treasure were offered willingly and unsparingly" (Lilienthal 1927b, 128). "How he grew under pressure. How often did his patient heroism in the earlier years of the war serve us in the stead of victories. He carried our mighty sorrows, while he never knew rest, nor the enjoyment of office" (Thompson 1865, 203). For Philip Joachimsen (1927), as for so many other cultural members, Lincoln succeeded "solely by force of his own native intelligence, industry, and, above all, his purity of character. . . . Unaided by worldly fortune or powerful friends, he attained to the fame of the most eminent patriots and statesmen—aye, even of Washington, the Father of his Country" (31). These things cultural members knew beyond doubt because "manners are an index of the mind" (Putnam 1865, 313). Just so, for A.N. Littlejohn (1865), Lincoln satisfied all the key criteria of Heroism:

> There are certain tests—certain properties of character which, whenever they are found, assert the presence of true greatness, and secure for it, in the critical estimate of the world, the attribute of immortality. . . .
>
> 1st. It is a proof of greatness to discharge immense responsibilities in times of change and peril,

and to hand over a trust of extraordinary power without even the suspicion of failure or abuse. There can be no question that Mr. Lincoln met his test as completely as any ruler of ancient or modern times. . . .

2nd. It is an evidence of greatness to lead and to fashion, amid all possible elements of hazard and convulsion, an era of transcendent success in the life of empires or republics. Without controversy, we find this in the character and administration of this man. . . .

3rd. It belongs to the highest order of mind and character to mold and govern the opinions of a free people. This, Abraham Lincoln did as few have done before him. . . .

4th. It is a quality of greatness to win and to hold in high station and amid days of change and peril the confidence of millions. In this Mr. Lincoln was pre-eminent. . . .

5th. It has always been reckoned a mark of greatness to preserve an original, uncorrupted individuality amid the frictions and abrasions of a rulership which makes the incumbent the depository of all men's notions, the prey of flatterers, deceivers and parasites, the victim of the menace or the blandishments of a dominant party. Who has shown this mark of greatness more clearly than this man? . . .

6th. It is the effort of a great man's life to enrich by character, deeds, and sufferings, the annals of a people, and to multiply their traditions of endurance, heroism and triumph. In this our late President, by general consent, will rank second only to Washington. . . .

7th, and finally. The sovereign and unchallenged test of greatness, as adjudged by all nations and ages, is to complete service by sacrifice; to attest by death what was toiled and fought for in life; to add the martyr's crown to the patriot's work. This alone was needed to round out and immortalize Abraham Lincoln. (153–56)

Here is the quintessence of the matter. Lincoln was memorable within this worldview not only because he *acted* heroically, garnering achievements along the way, but primordially because success figured prominently into his scheme of things. Lincoln was not "a mere sentimentalist," but had a remarkable "ability to grasp a great subject" and "strip it of all mystery" (Bailey 1865, 100–101). What he was able to accomplish and the way that he acted were not circumstantial, matters of good advice, of good advisors, or of fortune. Rather, his heroism came out of him despite, some believed, his many flaws: he who was "artless," with no military reputation, with no brilliant oratory, with no winning grace of manners," with an "unpolished style," "pithy in his sentences" (Webb 1865, 149). His actions and accomplishments, even so, were the results of a hero *being* heroic, of acting well beyond himself. Just so, Henry Foote (1865) approvingly announced, "the thought of what he *did*, or had a part in,—of what he *was*,—and of what he *will* be in the influence of example, is in all our hearts" (181). That is why and how Lincoln ought to be remembered: "as an heroic martyr for his country's good, he will live in all eternity" (Schlesinger 1927, 108). And this is why he is worthy of emulation: "You can point him out to your children as one of the men worthy of emulation, as a pattern and as an example" (Joachimsen 1927, 31).

This is also the center of the Heroist ethos and worldview. Lincoln's heroism—his attitudes and his actions—"inspired the whole nation." The living *ought* to profit by Lincoln's example, *ought* to be heroic. "Truly do 'we live in deeds, not years' for centuries of life could not more indelibly have written his name among the illustrious ones of history" (Jones 1865, 154–55). "Abraham Lincoln was a 'self-made man'; but in just the sense in which any man of marked individuality is self-made" (Thompson 1865, 176). To be heroic is to rise above circumstances by one's own efforts; to show "no lack of courage, but rather a quiet persistency and fear-lessness"; to adhere to an "honesty of purpose"; to rely on one's own "strength and vigor"; to possess "courage," "justice," an "even temper," "humanity," "self-control," "calm judgment and clear perceptions"; to act "boldly and fearlessly"; to stand "firm and unshaken," "calm and self-possessed, with a strong heart and a firm hand"; to be "firm, immovable, hopeful, trying again and again." The message translates for the audience: If heroes react to the world heroically (actively, aggressively, as agents of action and change), if a strong belief that one's own efforts will result in success is a necessary component of anyone who would be a hero, and if one assumes that the fact of an intimate's death cannot be altered, then auditors who would don the mantle of Heroism will respond not to death, but to the things surrounding death that action can change.

Here is one of the main reasons why cultural members agreed that saying anything at all about Lincoln's death was inutile (despite the fact that they spoke no less frequently nor at any less length than anyone else). From this point of view language simply cannot convey the gravity and solemnity of their experiences—thus prefiguring the abandonment of metaphysics. The emotions sponsored by death produce not a reason to be still, not a deeper appreciation of Nature, but "an unutterable woe" (Joachimsen 1865, 36). Language fails so the individual need not take responsibility for failure. As E. B. Webb (1865) observed before his audience in Boston, "citizens meet, and shake hands, and part in silence. Words express nothing when uttered" (145–46). In New York Frank Brockholst Cutting (1865), speaking to the House of Representatives, similarly insisted that "words, however sincere or eloquent, are wholly inadequate to express what every one of us would so deeply feel, and the silent cunning with our own hearts would but enable us to read, as we ought, the great lesson which is now so solemnly taught us" (30). In St. Louis, Henry Vidaver (1927) simply placed the meaning of such experiences beyond "the power of a human tongue" (52). And in Washington City FH. Morgan, JC. Tasker, and Major W. H. H. Allen

(1865) spoke heroically for the citizens of New Hampshire: "Resolved, ... We are lifted above the capacities of common speech by emotions born of such a terrible and unlooked-for calamity" (123).

In adhering to this cultural logic many, like Charles Folger (1865), insisted that they would "have preferred to have been silent. For what can one utter, that is not already in the throbbing heart of the nation? What is the word of any one, but the fond, vain attempt to voice the dumb agony of this afflicted people" (73–74). Major Alfred Avery Burnham (1865) insisted that words fail "to express or even indicate one thousandth part of the emotions which rise in our breasts and struggle for utterance," and "we feel the poverty of language to body forth the fullness of our hearts" (119). Emotion thus "breaks down our confidence and stuns the public heart. It distracts and confuses the public mind. It produces a chaotic state of feeling incompatible with the duties of the hour, and unfavorable to the unity of effort" (Miner 1865, 284).

The dichotomy between mind and body emerges in full rhetorical force: emotions block heroic action; and language, so much the servant of emotion, is useless and petty when only action can speak louder than words. Speaking to his colleagues in the U.S. Court of Claims in Washington, D.C., the Assistant Solicitor alluded to this key dichotomy: "not only here, but reaching across the continent, you find everywhere" the "fitting emblems" of mourning, "speaking more eloquently than words of the deep personal and public grief of a whole people" (Weed 1865, 145). Another cultural member insisted that "acts are enduing memorials of men, words are evanescent" (Cook 1865, 86). Lincoln's actions spoke vociferously, and through his actions he *earned* his immortality—not the otherworldly immortality of Religionism, not the natural immortality of Romanticism, but the immortality of the meritist:

> He lives in all that can eternize the memory of man on earth; he lives in those glorious actions he executed in order to rescue his country from peril, shame, and dis-

> grace; he lives and will live forever in those grand and
> sterling principles which he displayed and maintained
> with an unparalleled moral force—principles which not
> only helped to uphold the power of our Union, but
> which likewise wiped out the blackest spot which stig-
> matized our splendid star-spangled banner. Yes,
> Abraham Lincoln still lives, and will live forever, and "a
> double portion of his spirit" will rest upon us, the peo-
> ple of the United States, who will strive to follow his
> examples, and live in his spirit of liberty, justice, and
> love, and thus he will live in his people eternally.
> (Vidaver 1937, 50)

Immortality clearly is neither granted nor inherited in this worldview; it is merited through action. Lincoln will live forever in the
hearts of a nation, in the memories of the living, because immortality finds its locus in the *collective memory* of the living. Here, then,
is a "species immortality": "But not to dwell upon this [that is, death
and emotions], I remark, that we have here a lesson presented to us
that we may do well to learn, and that gives us hope and trust. We
see that this government of ours, no matter what wicked schemes
may be brought to assail it, will live and is destined to endure
throughout all time" (Pitts 1865, 47). Heroic actions beget immortality: "Honor, honor, honor, eternal honor to their names" (Foote
1865, 188); "the brave and good die first" (Williams 1865, 109); "It is
trial that gives us strength, suffering that gives us fortitude, conflict
that lends us courage, blood that consecrates the cause of truth, and
patriot martyrdom that gives it life eternal" (Low 1865, 107); "whenever such an individual [as Lincoln] is transferred to that list which
makes up the record of the distinguished dead, just in proportion to
the extent of his influence while living will be the respect paid his
memory by those who shall come after him" (Walbridge 1865, 288).
Although such a notion no doubt might seem strange to people who
are outside this perspective, it is perfectly reasonable from within. As

James Carse (1980) has pointed out, "we can imagine a great many states and locations in which the dead might exist, but if we do think of them existing there they are not truly dead for us" (vii).

Cultural members celebrate and seek to emulate those who are agents of action and change; and words and emotions are inadequate; private and public demonstrations of emotion, however deeply felt, are superfluous. Individuals must demonstrate cultural membership through their agency if they are to insure they will be recognized and remembered by the collectivity. No friend of Lincoln, George Bancroft (1865) nevertheless spoke directly to the matter: "How shall the nation most completely show its sorrow at Mr. Lincoln's death? How shall it best honor his memory? There can be but one answer. . . . Grief must take the character of action, and breathe itself forth in the assertion of the policy to which he fell a sacrifice" (200).

But to focus attention on the cultural membership of the deceased serves to accomplish much more than to recognize the need to place that individual in cultural or collective memory.[1] As the following analyses demonstrate, such a focus serves also to bring to light the ethos and worldview that others must embrace if they, too, are to be or become worthy of remembrance.

*"The Assassination of Lincoln"*
On April 22, 1865, the Broadway Synagogue in Cincinnati, Ohio, was curried with people anxiously waiting to hear the words of Max Lilienthal, "one of the best known Jewish leaders" in America during the nineteenth century (Philipson 1915, 48). Taking his place at the front of the room beside a mourning-draped bust of Lincoln, he begins his address. He speaks neither of the need to prepare for death nor of Nature's unity, but, initially, of the causes of the confusion and emotional distress people experienced upon hearing of Lincoln's assassination. Only "a few days ago," he observes, "a grateful and victorious people" were celebrating "with the intensest national pride and national joy" (Lilienthal 1927a,

110).² But today the people are "ashamed and frightened to look up to" the "mild and good feature" of "this bust." The suddenness of this radical shift from intense joy to intense sorrow clearly contributed to the magnitude of the confusion and emotional disarray Americans experienced on that day—already the moment is in the past.

Yet, there is another, perhaps even more significant cause, for the character of this occasion is unprecedented: "From the dawn of American history up to this mournful hour, such an assemblage has never been convened." True, "we have buried our Washington and our Jefferson, our Franklin and our Jackson," but these and other American patriots died "full of years and full of honors," according to "the stern laws of nature," which enabled the American people to accompany "them quietly to their resting place." But today emotions "are aroused as never before" because "a new crime has made its way into our Republic, and murder! murder! is the agonizing cry that echoes from the Atlantic to the shores of the Pacific" (110). Coupled with joyful expectations, Lilienthal asserts, the unprecedented murder of an American patriot predictably produced extraordinary confusion and disorientation:

> We hurried to the telegraphic dispatches—what letters are these? What do they mean? We were unwilling to trust our senses; we thought in the dizziness of yesterday's feast we had forgotten our letters, had unlearned our spelling; we could at first not realize the stern truth. But when we recovered from our first shock—when we became convinced of the terrible reality—then the heart of the nation stood still, breathless, lifeless, paralyzed! And when tears began to relieve our stupefaction, the lips were quivering and shivering with the heart-rending exclamation: O God, our good President has been assassinated! That was a terrible

morning, indeed! People were running to and fro, rest-less, comfortless, pursued in all streets by the same bewildering uneasiness, void of speech, void of thought—for we had not yet learned to read and to understand a page of American history written by the dagger of an Assassin. (110–11)

Having quickly, but carefully described confusion and emo-tional turmoil as a momentary experience belonging to the past, Lilienthal immediately shifts his auditors' attention to the reasons that they should be mindful of Lincoln. "There never sat in the Presidential chair of this country," Lilienthal intoned, "a man, who, by his life, as well as by his death, so fully demonstrated the progress of modern ideas and the greatness and glory of our institutions." This is why the nation stands "at the shrine of the assassinated body," why she "offers prayers and thanks for having witnessed the example of such a man's life," and why she "thinks herself especially indebted to him and to his memory, and mourns so much the deeper for his loss" (111).

Even more important, Abraham Lincoln was "the first laborer-President! Of his antecedents nothing could be said, but that he had risen by his own energies from the lowest sphere of life." Throughout his life he had heroically "battled with all kinds of per-sonal difficulties, and had overcome them; and by his sagacity, energy and unsophisticated honesty, he succeeded to be elected to fill the greatest office in the hands of the people." Because of his character and efforts, and because the nation recognized and rewarded his efforts by electing him President, "the people, the laboring classes all over the world, were now emancipated indeed; their rights were not a mere dead letter, they were now sealed and signed by the majestic hand of history, they were, in Abraham Lincoln, the workman, raised to the full acquisition of the infinite rights of man (111). Here is a great and valuable lesson Lincoln has willed to the people:

Do not give up the work, says his example, because you were born in an obscure station; do not get disheartened, because you have to wrestle with the disadvantages of a want of education—life is the best school, energy and perseverance the best teacher, honesty of purpose the best means for obtaining success; follow his example, and we shall finally, and in fact, establish the equality of mankind. He has achieved this triumph, and a whole world stands there, first amazed and then admiring the man, who, by his own indomitable energy, proved the greatness and glory of our institutions. (111–12)

Dear because he rose by his own efforts from a log cabin in the wilderness to become "the first laborer-President," thereby providing an example of how individuals ought to live their lives, Lilienthal continues, Lincoln became dearer still "by being the truest representative of our unlimited and invincible love for the Union and our flag." Throughout the years of war, confusion and doubt assailed others; yet clear-minded cultural members were increasingly aware and confident that he would stand strong against the dangers, "that he would not surrender the Union cost what it may," that "the Union must, and shall, be saved, was the unwavering motto of his administration," that "he was the true interpreter of our feelings toward the South," that "for the Union he stood, immovable as the North Star." And thus the people rewarded his efforts by electing him for a second time, knowing that "his sincerity, the simplicity of his heart, and the homely shrewdness of his mind were, to the people, the best guarantees against the intrigues of diplomacy, or the connivances of party passions." As payment for the people's confidence "the Union was saved under his administration—established upon a platform broader and finer than under either Washington or Jackson." Lincoln was "the incarnation of our Union," and this is why "we revered him, we loved him, we regarded him as a man of superior destiny, and intrusted willingly and thankfully to him the helm of our ship" (112–13).

Having inherited a lesson of inestimable value from Lincoln's example, Lilienthal assures, cultural members have inherited a lesson of equal value from his death. "If he had lingered on his sickbed, and died a natural death, the calamity then, too, would have been a national one, but it would not have taught us a new and important lesson." Despite the confusion, the disorientation, and the dangers promoted by the war and by Lincoln's assassination, citizens witnessed "no revolution, no anarchy, no outbreak, but everywhere respect for the law, willing submission to the constituted authority, the machinery of Government neither interrupted nor out of order." Lincoln's death thus provided a lesson, Lilienthal proffers, that "fills us with a new reverence for our almost superhuman institutions; makes the Republic still more precious, in our estimation, than ever before" (113–14).

At this point, Lilienthal shifts focus yet again. People must "turn away," he maintains, from "the object to whom our love and affection were devoted"; for "the sight is too overwhelming; the meaning of such a life and death overawes our innermost soul." Instead, auditors must turn their attention to Lincoln's inner qualities, qualities that unquestionably identified him as an exemplary cultural member. And in this the living may yet speak of Lincoln in the present tense, for these qualities still live inside the people and their institutions. Inside Lincoln, the President, "the hero and the patriot," is a man "without pride and ostentation, with a smile for everyone and everything, with the welcoming grasp and winning word." Beyond his "homely appearance beats a heart full of faith, love and charity." Inside "this heart thrones an integrity that escaped suspicion in the most corrupt time." However they might try,

> his enemies and his opponents could excite in him neither anger, nor hatred; his good humor assists him in overcoming the onerous duties of his office, or the malice of his assailants; he often enlivens the consultation by an apt anecdote; he indulges in sallies of wit, but they leave no sting behind. His heart is as good as

his conscience is just and clear. He can do no harm; he can not mistrust; he can not punish; he can only love and forgive; he is bent on grace and reconciliation. Stern to himself, he is lenient towards others; faithful to his trust and his duties, he can not mistrust others; knowing the obstacles he himself has to overcome, he has an excuse for the tardiness and shortcomings of others; when every one points to faults and mistakes, he is still hopeful and waits for improvement; when everyone desponds and despairs, he still has faith in the sacred cause of his mission; and then, and only then, when the success of his sacred charge is at stake, then he strikes the blow, which others would have dealt long ago. (114–15)

Lincoln's deeds and actions—his heroism, his agency—were not the denouements of divine providence, of Nature, or of accident; they were the results of his efforts and correct attitudes—of a man knowing when and how to act, of a man standing larger than life, heroic. The "sacred cause of his mission" and his "sacred charge" were not dictated by anyone or anything, save his conscience. With such inner qualities one need not wonder why or how Lincoln won "the love and respect of all those who knew him," that he "at last won the respect even of the rebel press in Richmond," that "this combination of firm, unselfish patriotism with such a kindness of heart and shrewdness of mind obtained for him the admiration of Europe," or that "his words became as full of influence as any of the sovereigns of the great powers" (115). Lincoln yet lives because his heroism yet lives in the people and their institutions.

To be sure, Lilienthal reminds his auditors, Lincoln's assassination and the dangers that his assassination appeared to pose to the people and their institutions initially caused confusion, emotionalism, and disorientation. Now, however, "the first, wild excitement, that so justly aroused all, has passed away; consideration, stern, calm and impassionate, takes its place, and we do not know which shall we more condemn—the atrocity of the crime, or the folly and madness of the murder." As to the atrocity of the crime, there can be no question. To any who wonder about the folly of the crime, cultural members may say without doubt that "Lincoln was no Caesar, no Henry IV, no William of Orange, no Louis XIV." Neither "the military genius of this war, that by his death our armies were deprived of their leader," nor "a concentrated power like Louis XIV," Lincoln, the President, "was nothing but the elected executive of the people's Government; nothing but the representative of the ideal of universal freedom." The crime was folly because it could never have achieved the desired effect: "You may kill a man, but you can not kill a nation. You may kill the temporary executive, but you can not assassinate the Government" (115–16).

Nor can there be any question about the madness of this crime, Lilienthal continues, because Lincoln "was willing to forgive and to pardon" the South, and because, having murdered their "best" and "truest friend," the South has caused the world to pass an irrevocable judgment. Even now, "all sympathy is lost for her, all pity with the vanquished is gone for her." Even now, "the nations despise her," and inevitably "the princes will hate her for having given such an example; her negroes will exult in having obtained license for murder and assassination" (116).

Yet, all of these things belong to the unchangeable past; they are beyond the influence of actions. Lincoln is dead. Confusion, emotionalism, and disorientation have already given way to "consideration, stern, calm and impassionate." The world has rendered its judgment of the South; and the South has purchased a dim future for herself through cowardly actions. What remains, Lilienthal insists, is the present; for the future will be determined by the quality of present attitudes and actions. Americans have "assembled to pay homage to [Lincoln's] memory; we have come to do honor to his great and good name; let us not desecrate this solemn hour by thoughts of vengeance and outbursts of indignation," which would not befit "the calm and magnanimous character of a great, free and victorious nation" (116–17).

What remains, in other words, is to put the lessons inherited from Lincoln's life and death into action, to shape the future by shaping attitudes and actions:

> Do you wish to honor his memory indeed; do you intend to hand down to posterity his name in all its grandeur and glory, unstained by passions and untarnished by violence!—consider the legacy he has left you, execute it in the sense he was willing to finish his great work. To finish the work he has begun; to do it with that spirit of justice and firmness he has taught and shown us; to perform our duties with that sincere aspiration for universal happiness, without any desire of satisfying a momentary passion or impulse, however justifiable it may be—this is the only way in which we can honor the departed, and celebrate their hour in a manner becoming the great man who is gathered to his predecessors. Be men, before, and above all, cool, calm, and dispassionate. He has set us the example, and by following his teachings, we will honor his memory. His disposition was not turned to passion by the bloodiness of the time. . . . Let us profit by his almost divine example. The arm of the law is strong; the eye of justice is sharp and watchful; the constituted authorities will do their duty fully and solemnly, to bring the criminals and their abettors to light, and to the bar of punishment. Let us not take justice into our hands. No mob and no anarchy! (117)

Here is the crux of Lilienthal's effort and, again, of the this worldview. In the struggle with the confusion, disorientation, and emotionalism necessarily occasioned by the death of an intimate, cultural members must be "before, and above all, cool, calm, and dispassionate." But thinking alone is insufficient. Thinking too soon becomes contemplation, and contemplation is not the stuff of which authentic cultural members are made. Thinking from this perspective is rather a means to an end: heroic action. Beyond thinking for purposes of orientation, of assessing circumstances and future actions, individuals must "honor his memory indeed." To honor Lincoln's memory is to follow his example. To follow his example is to be heroic. Thus, to honor Lincoln's memory, citizens must be Heroists.

Like Lincoln, cultural members must overcome "personal difficulties," must possess "a heart full of faith, love, and charity," a heart "as good as [our] conscience is just and clear." They must rely on their own "sagacity, energy and unsophisticated honesty," on "life [as] the best school, energy and perseverance [as] the best teacher, honesty of purpose [as] the best means for obtaining success." They must conduct themselves "without pride and ostentation, with a smile for everyone and everything, with the welcoming grasp and winning word." They must stand "immovable as the North Star," with "faith in the sacred cause of our mission" to demonstrate by their lives as well as by their deaths "the progress of modern ideas and the greatness and glory of our institutions." Above all, they must be "cool, calm, and dispassionate."

Throughout this discourse Lilienthal has been preparing his audience for just this point. Consider, for example, the opening paragraphs. Ostensibly directed at identifying the nature of the occasion, the clearer, more significant emphasis there is on the audience's overly *emotional* response to Lincoln's assassination. Emotions, brought to the fore by an outside agency, incapacitate people, make them "unwilling to trust [their] senses," cause them to run "to and fro, restless, comfortless, . . . void of speech, void of thought," and force them to stand "still, breathless, lifeless, paralyzed!" Since cultural members cannot function as agents of action and change while they are in this condition, they must not allow themselves to be possessed by emotionalism. They must be entirely under their own control—taciturn in the face of adversity so that they may turn death into a fighting chance to live. This is why

Lilienthal insists that the audience de facto immediately recovered from the "first shock" and, equally important, why he directly focuses attention on Lincoln's cultural membership. Having told his auditors that they are no longer possessed by emotionalism, Lilienthal fills the void by providing them with an example of how they ought to feel, think, and act. Lincoln weathered hardships from birth to death; yet, he was *not* a man possessed by emotionalism. Lincoln was a man completely under his own control; in the midst of the most difficult circumstances Lincoln was "cool, calm, and dispassionate," and this, in no small measure, is why Lincoln is memorable, why he is immortal, why his ethos is the ethos of Heroism.

Cast in this light, the consequences of failing to be heroic are significant and severe. Lilienthal has repeatedly reminded auditors that failing to follow Lincoln's example—failing to be an authentic cultural member, that is—would stain and tarnish his name. The name of Lincoln—thus: Lincoln's immortality—depends on auditors' attitudes and actions. Failing to be heroic would also reveal that cultural members have not been strengthened by the hardships they have endured, that they have neither been heroic nor become even more heroic by standing larger than life before their circumstances. Moreover, failing to be heroic tarnishes "the calm and magnanimous character of a great, free, and victorious nation." Finally, failing to follow Lincoln's "almost divine example" (117) calls into question the nation's "almost superhuman institutions," which amounts to calling immortality itself into question.

Had Lincoln not been a remarkable cultural member, he would not be memorable; and if he were not memorable, he would not be immortal. But there is an important link missing here. To whom is Lincoln memorable? To "the people," obviously; and if "the people" fail to remember Lincoln's "almost divine example," his heroism will have been in vain. Immortality in this worldview necessarily depends on merit and memory. If the memory—hence: the immortality—of such an obvious cultural member is called into question, what must that mean for the immortality of those whose lives and deaths are less impressive than Lincoln's? In fact, the immortality of everyone who would be a cultural member becomes extraordinarily provisional if cultural memory fails. This may well help to explain why the "log cabin to the White House" element figures so strongly into the Lincoln myth. Lincoln's transformation—brought about not by deity's plan or Nature's goodness, but by Lincoln's heroic efforts—is not only a synecdoche for Lincoln's cultural membership, but is also a perpetuated token of the people's immortality. Given the logic at work here, cultural members must perpetuate their institutions and their heroes if they, too, are to have an opportunity to merit immortality.

But the matter goes still further, for Heroism implicitly casts the notion of dying "full of years and full of honors" in the form of a moral imperative. Had Lincoln died "full of years and full of honors," as other American patriots did, then "a grateful people" could have resigned themselves "to the stern laws of nature" and "accompanied" him "quietly" to his "resting place." But Lincoln's sudden death has violated the moral imperative dictated by "the stern laws of nature." This is clearly reminiscent of the view of sudden death disclosed by the Religionist worldview, but there is an important difference. Lincoln's sudden death within this worldview is not a matter of ignominy that must be explained and justified by appealing to divine omniscience or omnipotence, by looking to instrumental nature for the communicative signs of an angry deity. Heroists need not "acquiesce in heaven's decrees." On the contrary, they are justifiably indignant because a law of nature has been violated.

The underlying assumption here is that cultural members have a *right* to expect to live long lives so that they can obtain honors—an essential ingredient of this perspective. How this came about historically is not entirely clear. Certainly nineteenth-century citizens had little substantive basis for believing that their lives were any less fragile than those who had lived before them. Epidemics were still quite commonplace, and infant mortality was still high.[3] "Modern" medical practice was still in its infancy—indeed, still struggling to eliminate the primary competition—namely, homeopathic physicians, who, along with ministers, had long controlled the medical scene.[4] And the newly emerged field of statistics, which would later provide people with the hope of living longer, had not yet offered evidence that citizens were living longer or that they *ought* to live longer (Farrell 1980; Tyng 1881, 1893). It is more a peculiarity of modern times that people are willing to believe that medicine has extended life, given the fact that even requesting such entirely private information was unthinkable until the middle of the nineteenth century, at the very earliest.

Rather than a cognitive transformation that suddenly gave people greater facility with (or concern for) numbers, what we witness here, then, is another moment of cultural ascendance indicative of the influence that cultural members were beginning to have on how society conceptualized disease and death. This is why, as James Farrell (1980) has observed, "during the nineteenth century, hereditarian theories of disease were being superseded by ideas of diseases as discrete microbial entities invading the human body to wreak destruction and death. This new definition of disease encouraged naturalists to consider old age and death as outside agents as well. . . . In effect, the conceptual elimination of natural death offered the possibility of physical immortality" (60–61).

This is not to say that all cultural members necessarily believed in the microbial theory of disease or that such a belief is requisite to cultural membership. Yet, the view that death is controlled by the *laws* that govern nature—rather than by deity or Nature (neither of which can be altered fundamentally by human beings)—is entirely consonant with the general tenor of the Heroist worldview. To believe that nature is governed by laws is to open wide an avenue for believing that one can understand, manipulate, control, circumvent, and overcome those laws. It opens, in other words, an avenue for cultural members to act heroically by conquering nature and, therefore, death. One might well have reason, then, to insist that cultural members ought to die "full of years and full of honors." Whatever the explanation, immortality from this perspective necessarily depends on the species itself; for without the species there can be no memory, and without memory there can be no immortality—all of which reasonably explains why this world-view encourages cultural members to remember the deceased hero-ically and why public memory is so ultimately important.

Self-preservation is a strong motive. To cultural members, the dead are most admirable as individuals whose lives were led heroically; and what most matters, given this starting point, is that people put the significance of death in proper perspective, that cul-tural members not permit death to disrupt the flow of life, that they fill the social or personal or political void that death creates quickly and efficiently. Life must go on because Heroism must go on, because life is action. Because reflection is inconsistent with action, the burden for dealing with one's grief and anxiety thus shifts away from the community, which invariably fills the void, to the individ-ual. Individuals who respond heroically to death act with self-con-trol, knowing as they do that death is a past fact that no amount of contemplation or action can alter. The main task of the living in matters of death, then, is to focus attention on something heroic, to adopt appropriately *heroic* attitudes, and to take action. For Heroists living in the moment so dramatically framed by Abraham Lincoln's death, the primary task at hand was to press forward, to take actions that would assist in the construction of a hegemonic ascendance already well under way in the cemeterial landscape.

## HEROISM'S ESCAPE

As Romanticists formerly had introduced similar yet divergent memorials in the Religionist gravescape by producing and erecting markers that ambiguously or vaguely redefined the object of mem-ory, so Heroists initially borrowed obelisks, *cippi*, and other Romanticist forms to memorialize their deceased in ways more con-sistent with their ethos and worldview—in part, a matter of tran-sculturation; perhaps in larger part a practical matter, given that Religionists controlled gravescapes until the turn of the nineteenth century and given that Romanticism created and maintained a hegemonic hold on the scene throughout much of the nineteenth century. Consider the subtle contrast between the Moore (figure 4.1) and Tucker memorials (figure 4.2).

The Moore memorial is a relatively unadorned structure, where the work of art—in this case a Grecian pelike jar at the crown—draws attention to the memorial as a work of art (or to the work of art as a memorial). The inscription carved on the back of the memorial serves to inform viewers that the objects of passionate memory here are three "dearly loved and cherished" individuals. In the presence of such artistry, according to the Romanticist perspective, one may sit to contemplate natural beauty and serenely listen while the dead speak to us "in the depths of our souls." The Tucker memorial, by contrast, neither accompanies nor presents itself as a work of art. Stripped of the adornments that are so characteristic of Romanticist memorials, this stark white shaft suggests nothing about "finer sentiments" and even less about artistic effort. Nor does it invite viewers to contemplate the beauty and harmony of art and Nature. Nevertheless, this memorial is not completely outside the Romanticist tradition, for the inscription informs viewers that this memorial is "SACRED TO THE MEMORY / OF / JUDGE NATHL BEVERLY TUCKER / . . . / And of his Wife / LUCY ANN TUCKER /. . ." And the discourse on the other three sides of the base reminds us that these dear deceased friends were greatly loved and cherished by the members of their community. On one hand, then, the inscription allies the memorial's purpose with the Romanticist memorial tradition by drawing attention to typical Romanticist themes. On the other hand, the memorial eschews Romanticist themes, such as the need for contemplation or affective homeopathy by insinuating the Heroist view regarding the inutility of works and the impropriety of public affective displays.

Rather than presenting viewers with ambiguity, the memorial of William Worth Belknap (figure 4.3) presents viewers with purposive vagueness. Its membership in Heroist culture is articulated both by the silence of its form and by the epitaph, which explicitly draws attention to the deceased's heroic achievements:

"WILLIAM WORTH BELKNAP / BORN 1828-DIED 1890 / COLONEL 15TH IOWA VOL. INFANTRY / BRIGADIER & BREVET MAJOR GENERAL U.S. VOLS. / SECRETARY OF WAR 1869-1876 / ERECTED BY HIS COMRADES OF THE / CROCKER IOWA BRIGADE / 11TH, 13TH, 15TH AND 16TH IOWA VOL. INFANTRY / ARMY OF THE TENNESSEE, / COMPANIONS OF THE MILITARY ORDER OF THE / LOYAL LEGION OF THE UNITED STATES / AND OTHER FRIENDS." Taken together, the silence of this memorial's form and the attitudes identified by the epitaph suggest that what is most memorable about the deceased are his heroic accomplishments: here lies an agent of action and change. Note, however, that the portrait attached to the face of the memorial is vaguely reminiscent of Romanticism. One might reasonably argue that the portrait is not a work of art and that it portrays the deceased stoically (hence: heroically). But the fact that it is a *portrait* of the deceased at the very least allows viewers to remember this individual as an individual, specifically. There is, in other words, room for the viewer to contemplate Romanticist themes.

One method that cultural members have used to eliminate Romanticists themes—an effort widely employed by cultural members in the South—is to mount an agent of action and change at the top of the cippus or obelisk and to use discourse to draw attention to Heroist themes explicitly. The memorial that stands at the entrance of the University of Mississippi is typical (figure 4.4). Here, a statue of a Confederate soldier, surveying all before him, stands proudly at the crown, and the discourse informs viewers that this memorial was erected "TO THE HEROES / OF LA FAYETTE COUNTY / WHOSE VALOR AND DEVOTION / MADE GLORIOUS MANY A / BATTLEFIELD."

A second method, which cultural members across the country have embraced, is to strip obelisks and *cippi* completely of their Romanticist associations. The Andrew Dunlap memorial (figure 4.5) both illustrates this method and manifests three central tendencies or characteristics of the Heroist memorial tradition. First, even more than the presence of discourse that describes the cultural achievements of the deceased, the absence of such discourse on this memorial reflects the rhetorical tendency toward silence in the presence of death. Second, the absence even of Heroist discourse and the effort to promote silence in the presence of death reflect the desire to shift the viewer's focus away from death to action by allowing memorials, like heroic actions, to speak louder than words, to speak for themselves through a Heroist manifestation. Third, this memorial reflects the tendency to equate a memorial's size with the merits and significance of the deceased.

While the introduction of transitional memorials such as these signals the beginning of ascendance, cultural members faced two major obstacles that they would have to overcome in order to pursue the logic of their ethos and worldview with the consistency necessary to establish their tradition as independent of and distinct from the other memorial traditions. Because of the tendency to equate size with the deceased's merits and significance, because such memorials are conspicuously silent with regard to Romanticist themes, because Romanticists strenuously objected to such "barbarous" memorials, and because Romanticists controlled rural cemeteries, there were only infrequent opportunities for Heroists to begin to develop their tradition within the confines of the rural cemetery. To put the matter differently, Romanticists then and now, as Robert Prestiano's (1983) remarks reveal, reject Heroist memorials as repugnant: "The contemporary memorialist is confronted with the challenge to redirect form from the moribund overuse of nineteenth-century stylistic prototypes and the unimaginative, mass-produced slab shape, toward more sculpturally vital expressions of our time" (203). Further, because erecting heroist memorials in rural cemeteries might easily diminish their capacity to establish or evoke memory heroically, and because cultural members objected to certain fundamental characteristics of the rural cemetery (see figure 4.6), Heroists faced the possibility that there would be no gravescape in which they could continue to advance their tradition fully. To overcome these obstacles cultural members developed their memorial tradition in two divergent but complimentary directions.

On the one hand, cultural members took the development of their tradition outside the rural cemetery, erecting their memorials in cities and towns, which afforded the double advantage of allowing them to construct memorials of sufficient size (without having to confront Romanticist cemetery owners) and of dissociating their memorials from Romanticist associations. Thus, whereas memorials had been almost wholly confined to graveyards and cemeteries prior to 1840, we begin to see a spate of exclusively Heroist memorials appear outside of their traditional settings during subsequent decades. That memorials had not appeared outside their traditional settings—despite the fact that that possibility had been pursued successfully outside the United States—is a measure, first, of the fact that Romanticists—and before them Religionists—controlled the memorial scene both inside and outside the gravescape and second, of the marginality of Heroists prior to the beginning of their hegemonic ascendance in the middle of the nineteenth century.

One of the earliest efforts in this direction is a rather larger version of the Dunlap memorial—namely, the Washington Monument (figure 4.7). Here is a prototypical, unadorned obelisk that is formally and functionally silent with regard to Romanticist themes. Measuring more than 555 feet from the ground to its crown, this white marble shaft, which was begun in 1848, does not invite viewers to contemplate nature or art or one's "finer sentiments." Quite the contrary. One need not indulge in fanciful psychologizing about its phallic appearance to recognize that this memorial is an accomplishment of labor rather than of artistic skill, that it equates size with significance, that it asserts its dominance over its environment, over nature—that it speaks of *power over*, of control. Rather than being an expression of a need to live in harmony with that against which all things are measured from the Romanticist perspective, a

structure of such monumental proportions announces both the
dominance of the species over nature and the consequences of
Heroist immortality.

To draw attention to the fact that this structure was begun
in 1848 points not only to the Washington Monument as an early
instance of the effort to move memorials outside of the rural cemetery and into national prominence, but also to the difficulties cultural members faced in attempting to develop their tradition in this
direction. One very significant reason this structure was not completed until 1884 is that cultural members could not acquire the
necessary funding. And one clear reason they could not acquire the
necessary funding is that Romanticists opposed memorials that
substituted size for elegance. More, Romanticists were concurrently
seeking to maintain their hold on collective memory by creating a
memorial for George Washington.

Speaking to the issue on behalf of the Mount Vernon
Association, Richard Owen (1859), a professor at the University of
Nashville, told Tennessee legislators and readers of the *North
American Review* that "size, as an expression of reverence, is barbarous; expense natural, but cockneyish. The moment ideas of size
and expense take the lead in the conception of a reverential structure, the result assumes at once the dignity and satisfaction of a
stone-cutter's bill" (55–56). Citizens do not want a mere "pile,"
Owen insisted, for "if a true conception of greatness fill the soul, a
huge tumulus is to us as a child's garden, over which we tread
unconsciously in gazing at a great, glorious landscape, flooded with
dazzling sunlight" (56). Rather than "a huge tumulus" that would
fail to capture people's hearts and imaginations, Owen continued,
citizens would prefer that "one grand leading idea govern, as it
should, every part of the design" of their memorials, that this "leading idea" demands that "nature, simplicity, and a truly rural grace
will prevail throughout" (60). The nation's memorial to Washington

must, then, be something exquisite,—expressive
rather of thought, feeling, and skill, than of labor;

more suggestive than ambitious; appealing not to criticism, but to love; belonging at once to past, present, and future; meeting universal tastes, whether uncultivated or refined; enduring in its nature, yet susceptible of continual growth in elegance as Time shall unfold new resources; associated so intimately with the idea on which it is founded. . . . (56)

In sum, Owen concluded, citizens would prefer to turn Washington's home, Mount Vernon, into "one grand monument,—majestic, living," where visitors might sit "in some spot made beautiful alike by sun and shade, by nature and art" (61). That this is what citizens want, Owen intoned, is made all the more obvious by the fact that, while others cannot raise the funds to erect their "piles," "money seems the least part of the affair, in this case; feeling carries all before it." Even now, "ladies sitting at home have many hundreds [of dollars] poured into their laps in a day. A school-boy, in his play hours, gathers in less than three weeks, nearly a thousand dollars" (53).

With this sort of resistance facing them, it is not at all extraordinary that Heroists found it difficult to fund their projects. Nevertheless, although memorials outside of the rural cemetery may not have emerged as rapidly as cultural members might have hoped, they did emerge to become some of the most notable monumental landmarks in the nation. In addition to mere size, however, memorials belonging to this tradition increasingly manifested a preference for Heroist dignity and action. The Jefferson memorial, for example, again exemplifies the cultural and rhetorical tendency to equate size with merit and significance. Both the structure (figure 4.8) and the statue (figure 4.9) of Jefferson contained within it are monumental in their proportions. But beyond simply being large, the statue presents viewers with a quiet, dignified, idealized Heroist image of Jefferson. Heroist memorials that do not adhere to the larger-than-life trait, like the Ulysses S. Grant memorial (figure 4.10), nevertheless articulate the same cultural themes.

This brings us to a second option to which cultural members turned with increasing frequency as their tradition outside of the cemetery continued to develop—a type of memorial that portrays its subject in action, thereby explicitly reflecting the view that individuals worthy of remembrance are agents of action and change. The Civil War memorial (figure 4.11), which constitutes a part of the Ulysses S. Grant memorial, for instance, presents viewers with life-sized Union soldiers courageously riding into battle. Similar in character, the Marine Corps memorial (figure 4.12) presents viewers with larger-than-life soldiers heroically planting their flag on Iwo Jima.

Efforts to articulate this ethos and worldview by erecting memorials beyond the gravescape were fecund, but they did not provide very many individuals with opportunities to participate in articulation and ascendance. Nor did efforts outside the gravescape apostrophize what cultural members regarded as the overly sentimental, overly expensive, and overly arrogant features of the Romanticist gravescape. The same cultural logic that led Heroists to strip Romanticist memorials of their "overly sentimental" features again served cultural members well when they turned their attentions to the rural cemetery.

Unknowingly, Romanticists greatly assisted such efforts by being generally willing to acknowledge that they had given lot owners too much latitude in developing their lots. At the same time that Downing (1974) was heaping praise on the rural cemetery for its natural beauty, for example, he complained that that "natural" beauty was severely diminished "by the most violent bad taste; we mean the hideous *ironmongery*, which [rural cemeteries] all more or less display." "Fantastic conceits and gimcracks in iron might be pardonable as adornments of the balustrade of a circus or a temple of Comus," Downing charged, "but how reasonable beings can tolerate them as inclosures to the quiet grave of a family, and in such scenes of sylvan beauty, is mountain high above our comprehension" (see figures 4.13 and 4.14). Worse, "as if to show how far human infirmity can go," Downing continued, "we noticed lately several lots in one of these cemeteries, not only inclosed with a most barbarous piece of irony, but the gate of which was positively ornamented with the coat of arms of the owner, accompanied by a brass door-plate, on which was engraved the owner's name, and city residence!" (156).

Beyond the disruptive character of "hideous *ironmongery*," some Romanticists were also willing to acknowledge the "deforming effect of those little terraces and angular disturbances of the surface, which result from leaving this work to the taste and caprice of individuals" (Cleaveland 1850, 250).[5] Having acknowledged this much, Romanticists found it necessary to institute rules to govern not only what they would permit visitors to the cemetery to do, but also what they would allow lot owners to do by way of "improving" their lots.[6] In turn, instituting rules to govern the behaviors of visitors and lot owners shifted much of the decision-making power from lot owners, who, in many instances, were also part owners of the cemeteries, to a newly created professional position, the cemetery superintendent (Farrell 1980).

One of the most important consequences of the admission that the form of the rural cemetery could be improved by restricting individualism is that it provided Heroists with an opportunity to create their own cemeterial form. And in 1855 they took full advantage of that opportunity. Only ten years after Spring Grove Cemetery in Cincinnati had been developed into a rural cemetery, according to the design of "John Notman, who also planned Laurel Hill Cemetery, near Philadelphia" (Kenny 1875, 318), Adolph Strauch submitted and put into effect a plan to alter its form. Originally, the plan to redesign Spring Grove appears to have been directed primarily at removing the "hideous *ironmongery*" and "little terraces and angular disturbances" that Romanticists admitted were unappealing. But Strauch took the plan several steps further.

Not only did Strauch remove "the numerous and crowded enclosures," he also eliminated burial mounds, hedges, stone fences, numerous trees, and "the innumerable tombs and gravestones," which "break up the surface of the ground, cut it into unsymmetrical sections, destroy the effect of slopes and levels, and chop up what should be the broad and noble features of one great picture into a confused and crowded multitude of what seem like petty yards or pens" (Perkins 1871, 841–42). As John Brinkerhoff Jackson (1972) approvingly remarks,

> It was Strauch who in effect first created what is known as the lawn cemetery; one in which the size and design and placement of the memorials are subject to esthetic control, and where all extraneous ornaments—railings, plantings, cemetery furniture—are forbidden in order to preserve an open and harmonious environment. With Strauch the cemetery became a landscape more spacious and parklike. It ceased to be a motley collection of every style, each enclosed in its own well-defined space, and became instead an integrated composition of lawn and clusters of trees. As a reorganization of a highly traditional kind of space, Spring Grove was a small but significant instance of the rejection of obsolete boundaries and the perception of a larger, more "natural" unity. It remains to this day an extremely beautiful place. (70–71)

"Esthetic control"—the elimination of diversity in favor of homogeneity—came in the form of rigid rules that the owners of Spring Grove Cemetery instituted to prohibit lot owners from altering their lots. Lot owners could still purchase "a single monument" to be "erected in the centre of each lot." But because the lots had been arranged symmetrically to make the best use of the land and to make maintenance more efficient, the cemetery's owners maintained that small markers "rising but a little above the ground" were more than sufficient to say what needed to be said. Spring Grove's owners also encouraged lot owners to plant "a tree," instead of erecting a memorial, and disallowed "small isolated flower-beds and the like, managed by individual proprietors, . . . as they patch and reform the scenery" (843). Finally, for those who felt the need to erect a memorial on their lots, cultural members had this advice: "Quiet and simple memorials sufficiently indicate the places of interment" (843–44).

To cultural members, "the landscape lawn method" or lawn cemetery, as it was later called, possesses several distinct advantages.[7] First, it provides visitors with an open vista, unobstructed by fences, memorials, and trees (see figures 4.15 and 4.16), where "the mind is not disturbed by the obtrusion of bounds and limits that seem to claim superiority and respect, or to assert rights of ownership and contrast of station, even among the dead" (Perkins 1871, 843). Second, it allows cemetery superintendents to make the most efficient use of the land in the cemetery, thereby advancing the view that "individual rights must be subordinated to this general plan." "Civilization," according to Matthew Brazil, "consists in subordinating the will of the individual to the comfort and well-being of all" (as quoted in Farrell 1980, 118). Third, by eliminating fences, hedges, trees, and other things associated with the rural cemetery, and by requiring markers to be small enough to be level or nearly level with the ground, so "they do not appear in the landscape picture," cultural members were able to eliminate "the old graveyard scene" (Weed 1912, 94). Together, Sidney Hare remarked, these "improvements" allowed citizens to eliminate, albeit gradually, "all things that suggest death, sorrow, or pain" (as quoted in Farrell 1980, 120)—clearly a direct and distinctive move away from the worldviews of Religionists and Romanticists.

Perhaps the strongest advantage to which cultural members could point, however, was that their new cemeterial form considerably lowered the cost of burial. When Mount Auburn was first opened for public burials, for example, a single lot of 300 square feet cost $60.00. By the time Adolph Strauch had finished redesigning Spring Grove Cemetery in 1855, the price of a lot at Mount Auburn had increased to $150.00 (Bigelow 1859, 23), and by 1883 lot prices ranged from $225.00 for an "unexceptional lot" to $750.00 for "choice lots" (King 1883, 27). Add to this the cost of an elaborate memorial, of creating a burial mound, of landscaping the lot, of an iron or stone enclosure, as well as the cost of the funeral, and the total was well beyond the modest means of most citizens.

By contrast, as late as 1875 the lot prices at Spring Grove ranged only "from thirty cents to forty to fifty cents per square foot" (Kenny 1875, 319)—in equivalent terms, from $90.00 to $150.00 for a lot of 300 square feet. And, having eliminated elaborate memorials, grave mounds, enclosures of any kind, and the various other things that make burial in the rural cemetery extraordinarily expensive, survivors encountered few costs to add to the price of the funeral itself. As F. B. Perkins (1871) proudly told his readers,

> it is a curious illustration of the power of habit over right reason, to see wealthy proprietors sinking a heavy granite coping around a lot, expending perhaps $2,500 or $3,000 for the sake of making the place look like a magnified city "area," and then placing a monument within it at a cost of say $2,000 more. The result of such an arrangement is, probably, some excellent masonry and a respectable monument. But suppose the bounds of the lot simply defined by durable, unobtrusive posts even with the surface of the earth, and $4,500 or $5,000 expended in a noble central group or symbolic structure. The mere statement of the contrast shows how incomparably superior in solemnity and impressiveness is the landscape lawn plan. (845)

Lawn cemeteries did not take "the public mind by storm," as the rural cemetery had, but they did increase in number nearly as rapidly as rural cemeteries had; and in the years following the Civil War they gradually became the most common type of gravescape—a clear measure of the influence Heroists were beginning to have at the national level. Instead of presenting viewers with markers to remind them of their need to prepare for death or with elaborate memorials nestled in "sylvan scenes," the modern lawn cemetery presents viewers with "a landscape more spacious and parklike" (Jackson 1972, 70) and with memorials that suggest very little in the way of artistic skill, particularity, or death.

Typically, when Heroist memorials appear in non-Heroist gravescapes, the lack of cemeterial restrictions result in memorials that are overtly expressive of Heroist sentiments (see figure 4.16). True to the mandates of the first Heroist gravescape, however, ceme-terial rules and regulations in lawn cemeteries require markers to be small and, in the vast majority of instances (military gravescapes like Arlington serving as exceptions; see figure 4.17), flush with the ground. The size and position of the markers thus ensure not only that cultural members will be able to erect memorials in an envi-ronment that is clearly indicative of their worldview and ethos, but also that non-cultural members who wish to bury their friends and loved ones in this gravescape will have exceedingly little opportunity to "mar" the scene with their non-Heroist sentiments.

Consider some typical instances. The Milton C. Broad memorial (figure 4.19) is vaguely reminiscent of the inscription-only markers so commonly erected in Religionist gravescapes, but it might as well be understood as expressing the Heroist principle of silence. The Joseph H. Kelly memorial (figure 4.20) bears a cross above the inscription, which might encourage visitors to think of matters religious, but nothing about the memorial insists on an association with Religionism. The William H. Buchanan memorial (figure 4.21) bears a wreath, which might remind viewers of Nature, but, again, the memorial offers no necessary association. The Nolia E. Floyd (figure 4.22) memorial, which provides viewers with a rather larger set of iconographic and discursive indicators, seems more clearly to insinuate a Romanticist perspective; but even here, the tradition to which the memorial belongs is far from obvious. Beyond simply providing citizens with a relatively inexpensive method of burial, beyond providing communities with a cemeterial

form that is extraordinarily easy to develop (one that requires someone who knows how to draw an efficient grid rather than someone
who has an understanding of landscape architecture) and maintain,
the lawn cemetery thus also provides cultural members with an
opportunity to maintain maximum hegemonic control.

These few markers obviously do not exhaust the variations
one might find in the lawn cemetery, but they are representative.
More important, they illustrate two key points. First, in developing
the lawn cemetery cultural members successfully eliminated not
only those things that Romanticists acknowledged were excesses,
but also those things Heroists regarded as excessive—especially
efforts to particularize the gravescape, individual lots, or markers.
Rather than allowing lot owners latitude to "beautify" the cemetery, cemetery owners and superintendents assumed all responsibility for cemeterial aesthetics. Those few "works of art" that do
appear in lawn cemeteries consequently are selected and their locations determined by a select few (see figure 4.23) so that "the will
of the individual" may be subordinated "to the comfort and well
being of all."

Second, by moving their memorials out of the cemetery, by
developing the lawn cemetery as they did, by promoting the kinds of
memorials we have examined, and by eliminating "all things that
suggest death, sorrow, or pain," cultural members not only overcame
the chief obstacles that initially stood in the way of their
being able to develop an independent, distinct memorial tradition
fully, they also gave a clear, strong voice to their ethos and worldview.


## REASON AND EMOTION

Central to that voice is a clear and irrevocable dichotomy between
reason and emotion. Like the dichotomy between body and soul for
Religionists and the dichotomy between "natural" and "unnatural"
for Romanticists, the dichotomy between reason and emotion
serves as a synecdoche for primary cultural principles, values, and
beliefs (where reason defines the "good" and emotion defines the

"bad" or evil) and, in its various manifestations, as a vehicle for expressing primary cultural realities that constitute this worldview.

Among the primary realities from which this culture's memorials emerge and from which they obtain their significance is the view that life is a journey toward success, toward an immortality that individuals must strive to merit through their heroic actions. That view certainly and immediately brings into focus the necessity of providing mechanisms for identifying the means by which cultural members can achieve and measure success.

For individual cultural members, the dichotomy between reason and emotion (as synecdoche and as vehicle for expression) thereby indexes key elements of the ethos they must adopt. Like Lincoln, cultural members must be prepared to triumph over adversity, maintain a quiet persistence and fearlessness, tirelessly advance on the toilsome journey of promotion, maintain an honesty and steadiness of purpose, believe that they possess an intelligence that is able to rescue itself by its own native strength, understand and act on their duty to dominate and control nature, revere and seek to cultivate a shrewd sagacity that provides a quick interpretation of the public mind, discharge their responsibilities even amid times of change and peril, lead and fashion transcendent success, demonstrate their ability to grasp a great subject and strip it of all its mysteries, revere and promote efficiency, recognize and work within the laws of nature, be a person of action. Additionally, cultural members must avoid entanglements with emotion—meet duty calmly and with an even temper that demonstrates their self-control, possess a serenity that is never disturbed, remain firm and unshaken, possess a strong heart and a firm hand, never fail and never quail, grow larger and stronger under pressure, be ever self-possessed, and preserve their uncorrupted individuality.

Within the vertically structured community that meritocracy mandates, such an ethos presses forward both as boundary and as discipline. As boundary, ethos serves the purposes of worldview by restricting and identifying cultural members—for example, by reducing all *topoi* of mode to quantity as the primary principle for determining individual merit (Perlman & Olbrechts-Tyteca 1971), or by insisting on the principle of efficiency as a fundamental measure of success. As discipline, ethos helps to maintain the integrity of the community by promoting individuality yet insisting on uniformity so that measurement and merit remain autonomous of difference. Thus constrained and disciplined, community achieves interpretation uniformly (that is, there can be one and only one "correct" interpretation) and autonomously (that is, because the laws of nature make "reality" transparent), which provides the same ostensibly open but clearly closed result that marks both Religionism and Romanticism.

In the social environment, memorializing reinforces ethos and worldview through the cultivation of homogeneity and fragmentation. Homogeneity, as so clearly demonstrated in the lawn cemetery, publicly announces the group's power and dominance, and fragmentation serves both to sustain the place of the individual and to stifle voices outside the community. Moreover, because efficiency and success (and other similar Heroist values) are outcomes that privilege the future over past and present, judgment is inherently teleological, which focuses cultural memory on becoming.

Given the timing and circumstances of Lincoln's death, the rapid ascendancy of Heroists is not in the least surprising. While Religionists advanced their appeals to return to a lost order, and while Romanticists focused their attentions on living in the moment, Heroists seized a remarkable opportunity to make the future of the nation their own becoming.

# 5

## CONCLUSION

*There can be no such thing as an isolated utterance. It always presupposes utterances that precede and follow it. No one utterance can be either the first or the last. Each is only a link in the chain, and none can be studied outside this chain. Among utterances there exist relations that cannot be defined in either mechanistic or linguistic categories. They have no analogues.*

—Mikhail Bakhtin

Different people memorialize, embrace, and seek to codify through public memory their different images of the memorable not merely because of temporal or spatial or physiological divergences, but because different cultures with different worldviews and *ethoi* require different images of and from their members. That there is a Lincoln myth at all, of course, undoubtedly owes much to circumstances; "reality," however mutable, lives within the possibilities of what is given and of what is conceivable in the midst of what is given. Had Lincoln not signed the *Emancipation Proclamation*, had many of his contemporaries not needed to believe that he publicly and personally identified himself as a religious individual, had he not been President during such an enormous civil crisis that marked an unmistakable moment of cultural transformation, had he not died suddenly and in the midst of intensely emotional expectations,

153

had powerful contemporaries not been so taken with the image of a man whose life began in a log cabin in the American wilderness and who spent his youth splitting rails in the midst of nature, had they not seen in his comportment some measure of a man of passions, had others not seen in him a man who had developed a commanding bearing through his own efforts, had they not believed that he had overcome early disadvantages and later ordeals through his own energies, had they not needed to see him as an agent of action and change, had his assassination not resulted in extreme psychological discomfort—in short, had the circumstances surrounding Lincoln's life and death been substantively other than they were or other than what his contemporaries believed them to be, the memorial responses to his assassination would have been other than they were.

Yet, the struggle to recreate Lincoln reveals a great deal more than the distant sentimentality of nineteenth-century citizens, of some distant past that is only marginally related to the present. At one level of analysis, Lincoln's image as an ongoing site of ideological conflict reveals the contours of three powerful, reasonably distinct cultural groups, each of which continuously has sought to lay claim to the nation's hegemony and public memory. At another level, the disparities among the worldviews and *ethoi* of these three groups helps explain significant past, present, and future multicultural tensions. And at a third level, an understanding of this ongoing struggle provides a perspective whereby we can begin to reframe our understanding of cultural conflict so that resolution (or, at least, the possibility of resolution) emerges out of an understanding of difference rather than from the imposition of homogeneity.

## LINCOLN AS A SITE OF IDEOLOGICAL STRUGGLE

That there are three dominant elements of the Lincoln myth undoubtedly owes much to the efforts of three relatively distinct cultural groups, each of which confronted similar circumstances and yet portrayed and promoted Lincoln quite differently. Clearly having begun with markedly different presuppositions about the world and the place of human beings within that world, each group was differently predisposed to comprehend, reorganize, shape, and lend significance to the circumstances surrounding Lincoln's life and death. As a consequence, the reasons that and the manner in which these groups regarded Lincoln as memorable concomitantly differed to such a degree that Lincoln became and has remained a site of ideological conflict.

Viewing Lincoln's life and death from a perspective in which the individual is a temporarily mixed manifestation of deity and dust whose possibilities are both finite and infinite, and in which human activities, the "progress" of history, and the actions of nature are utterly subordinate to an omniscient, omnipresent, omnipotent, supremely moral, comprehensive, controlling, evaluative, infinite, immediate, personal, and perfect deity, for example, Religionists clearly were (and are) predisposed to attend to Lincoln's inner qualities and to those circumstances that supported and advanced their worldview and ethos. Within this frame, the most immediate problem was to arrive at an acceptable interpretation of the divine message embedded in the manner and circumstances of Lincoln's death. Had Lincoln been bereft of those qualities Religionists believe are necessary for an individual to merit immortality in the eyes of the supreme deity, the ignominious manner of his death, for example, might have been interpreted as deity's way of reminding mortals of the disastrous consequences of living a religiously insalubrious life, which would have produced a radically different set of memorial responses.

Whether particular Religionists portrayed Lincoln as ordinarily or as extraordinarily devoted to the their worldview in part clearly depended on the extent to which they agreed with his policies and actions. Political considerations aside, the logic of this perspective mandates that, if the manner of death cannot sensibly be interpreted as a malediction aimed at the individual, the living can and should regard the individual's life and death as having had a divine purpose; for there can be no purely accidental occurrences in a perspective dominated by a deity that is utterly and in every sense supreme. At the very least, acknowledging that Lincoln's life and death were divinely endowed lent special significance to Lincoln's life and necessarily identified him as a Religionist. At the very best, deity's hand in this matter identified Lincoln's death as akin to the deaths of exemplary cultural figures, which unequivocally identified him as one of the *devoti* whose particular significance Religionists could and did describe in messianic terms. For many cultural members, consequently, Lincoln was memorable because, like Christ and Moses, deity had identified him as a mortal of special significance, who was entirely worthy of immortality—and because claiming him as one of their own might lend credence to their claim on collective memory and to their effort to regain control of the future of the nation. Then, too, many cultural members undoubtedly overlooked what they regarded as Lincoln's non-Religionist qualities not only out of respect for the dead, but also because his death signaled a tremendous opportunity for cultural transformation.

By contrast, Romanticists viewed the circumstances surrounding Lincoln's life and death from a perspective in which the individual is a natural being striving to comprehend and live in harmony with Nature, which is regenerative, eternal, omnipresent, calm, friendly, beautiful, unified, infinite, passionate, and all of everything. From this perspective the most pressing matter was not to arrive at an acceptable interpretation of a deity's message, but to comprehend and appreciate the beauty and unity of Nature. To be sure, the manner of Lincoln's death was no less shocking to Romanticists than it was to Religionists. Rather than recognizing therein justification for mortification, humiliation, and supplication, however, Romanticists were impelled by the logic of their worldview to regard the occasion as deserving of extraordinary emotions and to regard even this manner of death as beautiful.

If Nature is unified and all of everything, then it is the metric against which all things are measured. This being so, the beauty of a thing must depend on the extent to which it is "natural." Though cultural members acknowledged that Lincoln's death was not natural in the usual sense, they nevertheless insisted that it was natural insofar as it provided a poignantly natural conclusion to Lincoln's life and insofar as death itself is inevitably natural. Thus having reframed Lincoln's death as beautiful, cultural members could justifiably turn their attention and energies toward the aesthetic dimensions of Lincoln's life, growth, and death. From their hands and imaginations flowed a richly adorned pageant of death that focused the nation on images of the harmony of life and death through art.

Like Religionists, however, Romanticists were not uniformly enthusiastic in endorsing Lincoln as a member of their group. More than the other two cultural groups we have considered, for example, Romanticists were disturbed by Lincoln's lack of refinement. Despite their dissatisfaction with his inelegance, however, cultural members generally were willing to acknowledge that, beneath the rough exterior, Lincoln was essentially a passionate man of Nature. To identify Lincoln either as a passionate man or as a man of Nature was, at the very least, to identify him as an individual who understood and lived in accordance with the "appropriate" worldview. At the very best, to identify Lincoln as both a passionate man and a man of Nature was to identify him as "authentic," as having manifested the "appropriate" ethos and as having lived according to the "appropriate" worldview. In either case, Lincoln was most memorable as "the rail-splitter" from this perspective because that image symbolized his adherence to and, to some, his personification of the Romanticist perspective, which served to identify him as an exemplary cultural member and allowed Romanticists to lay claim to his legacy and to public memory.

Viewing the circumstances surrounding Lincoln's life and death from a perspective in which genuine cultural members are agents of action and change, inventors and managers of destiny, dis-coverers and manipulators of nature, perpetuators of the immortal species, Heroists clearly were predisposed to attend to those things they believed Lincoln had done to advance the species and, thus, to merit immortality. Within this worldview, cultural members were most immediately concerned to assess Lincoln's inner strengths in order to determine if his accomplishments could sensibly be imputed to his own efforts. Had Lincoln not manifested those inner strengths Heroists regard as necessary to success, they might well have attributed his accomplishments to mere chance, circumstance, accident, or able assistance. Yet, in considering Lincoln's life many cultural members found ample evidence to substantiate his mem-bership in their group—even if not all cultural members were equally ebullient in countenancing Lincoln's status in the ranks of the truly heroic. Even given the misgivings that some cultural mem-bers had about the magnitude or source of Lincoln's inner strengths, they were at least willing to grant that his inner strengths were ade-quate to ensure that some of his accomplishments were the result of his own energies. For those who were very doubtful of Lincoln, this implied only that he should be identified as a rather ordinary member of the group, who, through various forms of external assis-tance, had been elevated to an heroic status that would not other-wise have been possible. For those who articulated few or no doubts, Lincoln's status as one of the greatest heroes of his age was beyond question. Regardless of the degree of fervor with which par-ticular cultural members accepted Lincoln as a member of the group, then, the group as a whole endorsed him as a man who deserved to be remembered because he had succeeded by his own energies. To most cultural members that success and the inner strengths that such success presupposes were (and are) most acutely symbolized by Lincoln's rise "from a log cabin to the White House."

To put the conjunction of perspective and circumstance in slightly different light, Heroists organized and shaped circumstances as they did because their worldview presupposes a deity that is distant, dispassionate, unknowable, and ostensibly unattached to human affairs; a nature that is limited, law-governed, mechanical, and subordinate and susceptible to human understanding, control, and manipulation; a role for the individual as a member of the species, who possesses the possibilities of achievement and success, but must struggle continuously to overcome individual weaknesses and life's obstacles; a dichotomy between effete and virile emotions, which removes the former from the public to the personal domain, thereby eliminating public displays of vulnerability; and a type of immortality that is predicated on merit, which is determined by the manner in which the individual confronts the world and by the extent to which the individual has contributed to the perpetuation and advancement of the species. Romanticists organized and shaped circumstances as they did because their perspective presupposes that deity is passionate, unified, infinitely forgiving and patient, regenerative, and synonymous with Nature; that Nature is a passionate, infinitely forgiving and patient, regenerative, omnipresent, eternal, aesthetically exhilarating, and unified continuum of experience; that the individual is a wholly unified and natural being whose primary aim is to explore and contemplate the wonders, beauties, mysteries, and unity of Nature; that emotions are primordial and serve as a principle mode of coming to appreciate harmony of every variety; and that immortality is natural and inevitable. Finally, Religionists organized and shaped circumstances as they did because their perspective presupposes an infinitely powerful deity, who takes a personal and active interest in every occurrence; a morally neutral nature, which functions as the scene in which human actions take place and as a vague, but interpretable unidirectional channel of communication between deity and mortals; a morally responsible role for mortals, who are part deity and part nature, frail yet eternal, and destined to choose continuously between right and wrong; a dichotomy between morally salubrious and insalubrious emotions, which constitute the calculus of human choice, of merit, and of deity's judgment; and a type of immortality that requires the individual to accept the challenge of living a morally responsible life, and to live up to that challenge within the time allotted or suffer eternal horror and pain.

Cast against the backdrop of memorializing, Lincoln's death moves well beyond a momentary ideological struggle. It is difficult, at best, to know exactly how much Lincoln's death served to facilitate cultural transformation in nineteenth-century America, but it is clear that the same three cultural groups that sought to lay claim to his legacies as a means of laying claim to hegemonic status and public memory have executed the same struggle, the same conflict of worldviews and *ethoi*, the same conflict of pasts and presents and futures countless times in the graveyard and beyond. Having established their hegemonic status early on in the years of colonization, Religionists successfully held at bay the efforts of others to announce their presence and advance their futures through denial, through brute force, through social control, through the implementation of laws, through the maintenance of educational mechanisms—all of which served to communicate, perpetuate, and develop their worldview and ethos, often at the expense of others. In a moment of cultural transformation that we as yet little understand, Romanticists found or created an opening that moved them toward and into a hegemonic posture that they were able to maintain in the garden of graves and beyond—albeit, sometimes tenuously—throughout much of the nineteenth century. And in the tremendous opportunity for cultural transformation so clearly marked by Lincoln's assassination, Heroists secured for themselves a position of power that, with momentary lapses, they appear to have maintained since the latter years of the nineteenth century.

## THREE VARIATIONS ON SIX THEMES

That Lincoln served and continues to serve as a site of ideological conflict is, in this sense, an illustration. Beneath the details live much larger conflicts that have emerged and continue to emerge in everyday life. And it is at that level that we find an extensive, substantive, lived explanation for Alasdair MacIntyre's (1981) observation that "The most striking feature of contemporary moral utterance is that so much of it is used to express disagreements that are expressed in their interminable character. I do not mean by this just that such debates go on and on and on—although they do—but also that they apparently can find no terminus" (6). For MacIntyre this is a philosophical matter precisely because "There seems to be no rational way of securing moral agreement in our culture" (6). Viewed against the background of memorializing, however, this feature of contemporary life emerges less as a philosophical problem—and not at all as a problem of "our culture"—than as a struggle among cultures that embrace radically different worldviews and *ethoi*. The reason that there is no terminus, to put the matter in a different light, is that cultural members cannot compromise their principles, values, and beliefs—the stuff of which worldviews and *ethoi* are made—without a significant loss of integrity that inherently and necessarily places cultures and their members at risk. To understand this matter more fully, consider how dramatically the three cultures examined here differ on six key themes—time, space/place, mode, nature, emotion, and death.

*Time*
As so well illustrated by the Samuel Adams memorial (figure 2.14), time for Religionists generally has a dual character. On the one hand, "time is death" serves as a guiding metaphor that characterizes temporality as an enemy against which cultural members must struggle continuously. Time in this sense is the representative of body, which is ephemeral, all-too-human, and even pornographic because time/body is always the opposite of eternality, which refigures deity within the self. Therein emerges a second sense of time as goad and friend; for eternality—curiously, it would seem, ever

stretching forward but not backward—is timelessness, which is to say, within this perspective, deity's time. The duality of time as death and time as deity participates in a hierarchy of values wherein cultural members come to value the present and the past only to the extent that they illuminate the future because human time can only point toward some future moment when mortals can join with deity in an understanding and appreciation of eternality.

By contrast, Romanticists operate within the parameters of the metaphor "time is cyclical." In the most obvious sense, this equation seemingly places a premium on living within the moment because, as isochronal, the present contains past and future. This comports well with the emphasis on emotions as essential to well-being that is so central to the homeopathic impulse. And yet the memorial tradition that emerges from this worldview seems to make the present a submission to the past. To place images of the memorable at the forefront of memory is necessarily to make the present subordinate to the past because the present derives its character from the past. No doubt, this is partly a consequence of the temporal position of the memorable; but it is also largely a consequence of a worldview that encourages its members to define themselves in terms of the past—for example, by borrowing from ancient Rome and Greece and Egypt to create and justify their memorial tradition.

At the opposite end, seemingly, are Heroists for whom time's greatest significance is as a measure of exchange—as expressed, for example, in the metaphor "time is money," which served both as justification for and celebration of a cemeterial form that substantially reduced the cost of death by increasing efficiency. This creates a temporal relationship that subordinates the past and present to the future—not because eternality is a goad, but because exchange, which is to say merit, occurs moment-to-moment. One therefore lives in (but not for) the moment, lying in wait for the next opportunity to exchange time for immortality, which makes the future entirely immediate rather than eternal and timeless.

*Space/Place*

As with time, space/place for Religionists has a dual character. One part of its dual character derives from the relationship between the place of humans and the place of deity, which lends to sanctified space/place the qualities of mind, thought, and spirit. A second sense derives from the relationship between the location of humans and the location of absolute evil, which lends to space/place the qualities of intellect, instinct, and body. This duality explains the significance of maintaining sanctified spaces/places as sanctuaries (graveyards and churches) within strictly human spaces/places (towns and cities), as well as the need to place deceased cultural members inside the boundaries of sanctified space. Sanctified space recapitulates the relationship between deity and human-as-deity (soul/spirit), provides specific locations where cultural members may feel closer to deity, and sets aside sanctuaries where the living may retreat from the temptations of ephemeral space/time and where the dead may begin the final stage of their journey toward judgment. In contemporary terms, the dual character of space/place explains Religionist actions that are designed to increase sanctified space/place such as exists within the impulse to construct missions among unbelievers, to spiritualize the political arena, to mandate the adoption of a specific set of "family values," and even to require prayer in schools.

Here, again, the Romanticist worldview provides an interesting contrast; for space/place (as necessarily "natural") is always already sanctified. What remains is for humans to recognize their place within a preexisting harmony so that they may better protect Nature from the "unnatural" acts and actions of those who fail to understand the "natural" sanctity of space/place. Yet, as the rural cemetery makes entirely clear, preservation as an impulse and motive carries with it a responsibility to create a harmonious relationship between humans and Nature through the production of art. Space/place thus becomes a medium through which individuals may actualize their potential to achieve a harmonious relationship with Nature by protecting Nature from the "unnatural" (seemingly the underlying motive of the environmental movement, for example) or by joining Nature in the production of beauty through human creativity.

Perhaps the most significant meaning of space/place for Heroists is that it serves the function of witnessing. Since Heroists cannot be heroic (and, thus, cannot merit immortality) without being witnessed (and since self-reporting fails to satisfy the necessary conditions of Heroism), Heroism must provide spaces/places in which members may be witnessed. This goes a long way toward explaining, for example, how and why athletic contests have continuously emerged so completely throughout Heroism's hegemonic sway and why, not incidentally, athletic contests occur within spaces that are designed to surround the potential heroes with witnesses (spectators). If witnessing were not such an enormously significant part of this worldview, as it is not in either of the other worldviews we have examined, it seems extremely unlikely that athletic contests would have emerged as they did (formally) or as significantly as they did (functionally). This also helps to explain how and why this century has witnessed a tremendous increase both in the quantity of athletic contests and in the creation of more and more kinds of athletic contests (perhaps even in the emergence of other similar activities—for example, graffiti) whereby individuals may be witnessed as a means of meriting Heroist immortality. In all, the significance of space/place within the Heroist lexicon produces a rhetoric of exhibitionism.


*Mode*
Intimately related to time and space/place, mode for Religionists emerges from and reinforces the journey-toward-judgment metaphor by recapitulating the vertical structure of the moral universe. Within this scheme, cultural members are expected to adopt a method or mode of conduct and attitude that "moves" them ever

"upward" away from the absolute evil that threatens their immortal souls by pulling them "down." Since some individuals may be more "up" (hence: more deitylike) or "down" (hence: less deitylike) than others, mode also serves as an expression of worth and authority through hierarchical differentiation, which makes this largely (but not wholly) a qualitative matter because judgment assesses the quality of human existence. As already noted, mode thus expresses itself through an evangelical impulse that presupposes cultural members have a duty (derived from the requirement that they demonstrate worth) and a right (derived from authority) to require others to adopt their worldview and ethos—as in the creation of laws that discipline moral action, for example.

This is where Romanticists potentially diverge most radically from Religionists; for theirs is a world in which all "natural" things presumably are horizontally related. Implicitly, mode becomes an expression not of hierarchy but of equality and similitude where difference dissolves into universality. Because some things within this worldview may be more "natural" than others, that is, there is always at least the potential for the implementation of a hierarchy that generates and sustains a vertical mode of conduct and attitude within a supposedly horizontal, egalitarian environment. Among cultural members, such a hierarchy may constitute grounds for disagreement over elements and degrees of "authenticity" (for example, the kinds of "natural" activities in which one engages and the degree to which one engages such activities), which index the quality of one's cultural membership. Between cultural members and those clearly outside the boundaries of Romanticism, mode further generates hierarchy by separating, at a minimum, the "natural" from the "unnatural" (the debate over whether old-growth forests ought to be preserved because they are "natural" or destroyed because they are resources and sources of employment is illustrative).

Although proceeding from very different cultural premises, the primary mode for Heroists is also clearly vertical. Rather than indexing deity and absolute evil (despite a similar cast), mode here indexes success and failure, which, in contrast to both Religionism and Romanticism, emerge as quantities rather than qualities. Relating back to the size-equals-significance motif that is so obvious in many of the memorials that participate in this worldview, one conceivably might merit immortality on the basis of a single act or action, but the accumulation of acts and/or actions across time seems a far more common basis of celebration. At any rate, the privileging of quantification over and against other modes of being immediately and directly results in the need for identifying the "best"—fastest, largest, most, and so forth—as the primary means of determining worth. Without this mechanism of competition (along with the quantitative means of measuring outcomes and the witnesses who verify such outcomes), cultural members would have no method of achieving immortality through the accumulation of merit.

*Nature*

To the extent that it serves as a conduit for deity's desires, nature is something to which Religionists are obligated to pay attention, but they are not thereby obligated to preserve, emulate, or protect things natural. Except when functioning as deity's medium of displeasure (through catastrophes, for example) or as a testing ground for human worth, such a view ascribes to nature a uniquely neutral role in a universe that is entirely driven by the contest between good and evil. Such neutrality is what makes possible the conversion of space/place from human to divine, thereby affording mortals a means of traversing the void between the ephemeral and the eternal. To believe otherwise, within this perspective, too readily leads individuals to focus their attentions on the secular world, which immediately and directly places their immortality in jeopardy. Objecting to artistic renderings that focus on nudity, for example, proceed for the most part from the possibility that cultural members (and others for whom Religionists feel a moral responsibility) will be tempted to enjoin the temporal world at the expense of their immortal well-being.

Such a neutral role for Nature within the worldview of Romanticists clearly is unthinkable since Nature is itself goodness. Yet, the belief that human efforts can somehow improve Nature seems to insinuate that goodness is a human product. No doubt, this is due in part to the view that human beings are "natural" and that, therefore, their efforts are concomitantly "natural." Yet, the equally central belief that some actions and/or acts and some individuals are more "natural" (qualitatively) attenuates this belief by introducing the distinct possibility that human actions are not necessarily "natural." Nature thus serves not only as the metric by which all things are measured, but also functions to create and justify hierarchy.

Well away from this point of view, Heroists see nature as mechanical, law-governed, and fundamentally subject to the desires and manipulations of humans. This is similar to the Religionist point of view, of course, since nature within both worldviews is formally instrumental. The instrumentality here, however, is not that of a communication medium between deity and mortals, but that of a commodity (or set of resources) that cultural members can use to advance their individual cases for immortality. The creation of a large memorial, for instance, announces the individual's worth not simply because such a memorial dominates nature, but also because it demonstrates the individual's command of the resources that nature has to offer. In this sense, the introduction of skyscrapers, massive modes of transportation, and the general commodification of nature stand as tributes not only to their creators, but also to the principles of Heroism.

*Emotion*
Given the view that body and soul serve as moral coordinates within a vertically structured universe driven by good and evil, emotions

serve either to perpetuate or negate the principles of Religionism. This is so not because human beings are extensions of a morally neutral nature, but because they are an uneasy composite of mortality and immortality. Employed in the "wrong" way, emotions lead human beings to focus their attention on their bodily selves at the expense of their spiritual well-being. Employed "correctly," emotions lead individuals to attend assiduously to their preparation for judgment *qua* immortality. Becoming "too attached" to the rights of women (clearly a temporal concern) over and against the preservation of the immortal soul of a fetus, for example, employs emotions that perpetuate attachment to the here-and-now rather than to the ever-after.

Perhaps nothing save Nature itself is as central to Romanticists as emotions, which serve as media through which cultural members sustain their attachment to Nature, as the means by which cultural members establish and perpetuate their relationships with others, and as the primary vehicle for attending to one's physical and spiritual well-being. As media, emotions both articulate Nature and provide members with a lens through which Nature's mysteries are revealed, which helps explain why cultural members so often employ pathos as a means of expression and as a means of evoking pathetic response. As relational conduit, emotions provide the basis on which cultural members believe they conjoin with one another and, more, with the world-at-large. And as vehicle emotions serve to move cultural members into harmony with themselves so that they might be in greater harmony with Nature. Numerous self-help groups, for example, serve to conjoin individuals who are similar in their needs and states of being by seeking collectively to explore the mysteries of Nature that will unburden them of their problematic situations, thereby restoring them to physical and/or spiritual well-being.

Far from seeing emotions as a key source of harmony, Heroists, like Religionists, divide emotions into two sorts—namely, those that perpetuate and those that impede cultural ends. Those that perpetuate cultural ends (bravery, courage, and the like) often play the role of motive and function much like nature—which is to say, as natural resources that are valuable for their instrumentality. Those that impede cultural ends by distracting cultural members from their journey toward success, on the other hand, are much more likely to be subject to harsh discipline. This is why, for example, Heroists had so little patience with Mary Lincoln, who "refused" to discipline her emotions in order to attend to the "successful" completion of the work that resulted from Lincoln's death.

### Death

For Religionists death unquestionably is an ideological centerpiece that informs memorializing and life more generally. Within the context of memorializing, death is a constant reminder to avoid the temptations of secular life and attend assiduously, tenaciously to the cultural dictates that will insure deity's affirmative judgment and, thus, will underwrite immortal bliss. Within the larger life-context, death is the bond of community, the common adversary and friend; it is a corporeal visitation of the eternal that ever reminds devoted and simple cultural members of duty, responsibility, right conduct, right attitudes, and, most important, the possibility of mortal transcendence. As in the case of Lincoln's assassination, death is an opportunity for cultural members to come together to reaffirm their worldview and ethos, to struggle together collectively and individually to restore order, to exert collective and individual power against the darkness, to bring new members into the fold to increase the collectivity's power. The significance of death, therefore, cannot be underestimated without irreparable damage to the underlying cultural logic.

Within the cultural logic of Romanticism, death is "natural," eternal, regenerative. Far from being a negativity that members of the cultural group must combat to restore order, death is an expression of the natural order of things. Still, here, too, death serves significant cultural ends. For death provides cultural members with an opportunity to gather together, to blend their voices and emotions, to reinforce cultural values, to heal themselves and one another homeopathically, to celebrate the circle of Being, to embrace and become even more intimately harmonious, to produce and elicit creative responses that will enhance and extend Nature through artistic means. Death thus is that which cultural members embrace as a means of living more "authentically" in and for the moment, that which makes life so much more meaningful and opulent.

For Heroists, on the other hand, death is both nothing more than a disease to be conquered and an opportunity to turn crisis into a fighting chance to live. As a disease, death is a subject to be investigated, understood, explained, manipulated, predicted, controlled, eliminated. This is why Heroists have persistently insisted and continue to insist that "we" are living longer than our ancestral counterparts—despite the obvious fact that our ancestral counterparts kept no such statistics (indeed, were explicitly opposed to the collection of such private information) and despite the equally obvious fact that efforts to extrapolate such data from extant sources (such as cemeteries) are destined to produce woefully biased results since those extant sources are both remarkably incomplete and unrepresentative. As an opportunity, death becomes one among many potentially powerful antagonists—but not so powerful that human effort cannot prove itself superior.

Even so briefly considered, these three variations on six themes highlight numerous points of potential conflict. Such differences—often radical—easily generate tensions that are irresolvable at fundamental levels—a point all too well illustrated by many of the tensions that have come to define contemporary life. Heroists and Romanticists are unlikely to find common ground when dealing with issues of nature/Nature, for example, unless what seems "natural" to the latter seems also "efficient" or a good use of resources to the former. Religionists and Romanticists are just as unlikely to resolve differences in their interpretations of space/place because their principles and values in this area differ too radically. And Religionists and Heroists are unlikely to reach accord when addressing issues of death for the same reason. At the same time, there is also the distinct possibility of cooperation and coalition formation among and/or between the members of these three cultural groups—for example, between Religionists and Heroists, who are likely to find sufficient common ground when addressing matters of mode.

Unless and until we begin to understand and treat cultural conflict as a consequence of conflicting worldviews and *ethoi* that cannot be compromised without placing cultural members at risk, however, we will continue to perpetuate views that address themselves to matters that are fundamentally meaningless to the very individuals and groups for whom they ought to be most meaningful. Thus, we turn finally to a brief consideration of cultural conflict.

## A NOTE ON CULTURAL CONFLICT

The temptation to see "America" as a singularity—as emerging, developing, moving, "evolving," progressing like a great, giant millipede across time and place—is strong, sometimes overwhelming, irresistible. Libraries, conversations, personal diaries, textbooks, scholarly works, and popular media are filled with accounts of how this dimension or that signals this or that dimension of *the* American conscience, spirit, feeling, destiny, motif, principle, belief, value, worldview, ethos—culture. What those in the moment so clearly experience as a struggle, a contest, an opportunity, transforms alterity into sameness through the lens of singularity. This is far from accidental, but not so determined as one might imagine.

The ascensions and declines of cultures into and out of a hegemonic position are surrounded with undulations of power—

those places and moments wherein we both witness, looking backward, and experience, looking slightly forward, the contest for place. Movement into that place carries with it the burden of stability—sometimes a ruse, sometimes a project, but always a necessity. The second order of stability is to reassure the minions, but the first order is to insure one's own future, the future of hegemony for one's own. As with the succession of monarchs, cultural ascension to place—and therewith a nod toward stability—requires legitimacy. Here, at this very moment, is the first interplay of the new/old order and public memory *qua* cultural memory.

What is at stake in such moments is far more than simple stories about how societal members might remember distant figures or events; for public memory is inexorably a particularly designed cultural record of how things ought to be remembered as well as a proscription for how societal members ought to live their lives. Under some circumstances (for example, in monocultural societies or within certain totalitarian environments) cultures ascending to hegemony can simply install cultural memory as public memory without conflict or contest such that their cultural logic—always more ordered and coherent than the world—can maintain its curious symmetry. Under other circumstances, however, public memory is inherently and necessarily a site of cultural conflict, a place where cultures struggle to install images that reflect their worldview and ethos over and against all others.

What invariably is at issue in the installation and maintenance of public memory, then, is the matter of which set/sets of principles, values, and beliefs will control the past and shape the future. Especially in this moment in the United States (and elsewhere), the cultural character of this conflict is difficult to detect—not because its undulations are not everywhere visible or because we are too close to the conflict to understand its dimensions and features, but because the nature and origin of cultural conflict has been so redefined that worldview and ethos are no longer pertinent to the analysis of that conflict. Rather, as I suggested in the introduction, cultural conflict has come to mean conflict between and among ethnic groups, nations, sexes, races, and so forth.

What seems to go unnoticed in this redefinition is that the endless divisions of society into demographic categories is a Heroist tactic—though perhaps not a conscious tactic—that serves to protect hegemonic authority by continually pitting groups against one another. Given a visually (or geographically) obvious "enemy," people both unwittingly and wittingly use their already limited resources to create and recreate and fight against finer and finer artificially created and often quite meaningless fragmentations, thereby depleting resources and having little left either for working to find and unite themselves with other cultural members (whose ethos and worldview are neither visible nor immediately obvious) or to join in any kind of unified effort to engage in cultural preservation or transformation.

This tactic, of course, is a trick of mind that often hides itself inside a generalization where cognitive slippage is not always easy to detect. Consider from among a great many possibilities involving ethnicity, nationality, and so forth an everyday example concerning the fragmentation of sex. To argue, for example, that "men are visual, while women are auditory," as many people have and do, not only distorts the generalization's meaning but also exaggerates a tendency or correlation into a trait or characteristic. Suppose we have just concluded a study, the results of which state that 63 of the 100 women in the study identified themselves as being more auditory than visual and that 75 of the 100 men identified themselves as being more visual than auditory. Assuming that our study was conducted rigorously and well and leaving out of consideration the fact that such a formulation ignores other equally intriguing senses, to conclude that "men are visual, while women are auditory" clearly distorts the study's results; for it fails to account for 37 of the 100 women and 25 of the 100 men, or 31 percent of the total. Significantly, the women and men who "fail" to fit the profiles just identified now have sufficient reason to feel that they are "abnormal."

Even more significantly, men and women now have an issue over which they can divide themselves, about which they can argue and struggle, and through which they can erect barriers to coalition formation and the possibilities of any unified effort to work collectively to advance common goals. Multiply this times the countless generalizations that proceed from similar assumptions and produce similar results, and we have a remarkably potent tactic for urging people to feel "abnormal," alone, alienated, and with few remaining resources for the work of cultural unity or cultural transformation.

On the other hand, by reframing our understanding of cultural conflict so that it comprehends differences among and between worldviews and *ethoi,* we can begin to address the cultural sources that generate tensions among and between cultures and, perhaps, begin to identify conflicts that we cannot resolve as well as tensions that we can in some measure relieve. As we edge ever closer to the twenty-first century, no project seems more worthy of our collective efforts.

# NOTES

PREFACE

1. Namely, Alabama, Arizona, Arkansas, California, Colorado, Connecticut, Delaware, Illinois, Indiana, Iowa, Kansas, Kentucky, Louisiana, Maryland, Massachusetts, Michigan, Minnesota, Mississippi, Missouri, Montana, Nebraska, Nevada, New Jersey, New Mexico, New York, North Carolina, Ohio, Oklahoma, Oregon, Pennsylvania, Rhode Island, South Dakota, Tennessee, Texas, Utah, Virginia, Washington, West Virginia, Wisconsin, and Wyoming.

CHAPTER ONE

1. Previous iterations of arguments presented here appear in Morris 1985, 1986a, 1986b, 1987, 1990, and 1995.

2. Use of the term "America" is problematic, at best. I use the term and its cognates here and throughout strictly as a matter of convenience.

3. See Bigelow 1831; Blake 1959; Boller 1969; Brieger 1972; Clebsch 1973; Daniels 1971, 1976; Dillenberger 1960; Dixon 1855; Ekirch 1944, 1963;

Farrell 1980; Gaustaud 1982; Haller 1981; Huth 1972; Jackson 1972; Kett 1980; Marsden 1970; Mead 1963; Nye 1974; Parker 1972, 1973; Rosenberg 1974, 1976; Scott 1978; Scudder 1979; Smith, Handy, and Loetsher 1960; Welter 1974; White 1968; Williams 1970; Wood 1973.

4. Dr. E. W. Abbott (1865b, 70) noted two occasions—one at 1:45 A.M. and one at 2:55 A.M.—and Maunsell Field (1865, 71) noted a third occasion at 7:00 A.M.

5. For a slightly different account of the embalming see Morris 1865, 41-42, and Williamson 1865, 204. The casket was walnut, not mahogany.

6. Randall (1953) infers that this letter, which was not dated, refers to destruction rather than construction, which seems peculiar since one typically does not drive nails at this time.

7. I have qualified this remark because Holmes does not cite the source of his information regarding Mary Lincoln's opinion on this matter, because other sources maintain that Mary Lincoln did not leave the White House on any occasion during this time, and because there is no record of the committee having consulted her between noon, when the committee convened, and 4:00 P.M., when it issued its resolution. Further, the record is not clear about Richard Oglesby's presence at this meeting. However, because Mary Lincoln's initial opposition to having her husband's remains interred in Springfield are obvious from her correspondence with Oglesby, and because she threatened in that correspondence to have her husband's remains interred in the vault that had been prepared for George Washington if her demands were not met, it is at least accurate to say that she favored other places over Springfield.

Concerning Mary Lincoln's whereabouts, see Helm 1923, 261-63; Randall 1953, 384-89; Raymond 1865; and Turner and Turner 1972, 223-28. Regarding the composition and actions of the committee, see "Appendix" in Bancroft 1866, esp. 55-57. For Mary Lincoln's correspondence with Oglesby, see "Request for Agreement" and "To Richard J. Oglesby" in Turner and Turner 1972, 243-45. See also Conkling 1860; Ross 1973.

8. For a more detailed account of the ceremonies in Washington, D.C., see Williamson 1865, 216-30.

9. Lincoln's remains were left in this temporary receiving vault until December 21, 1865, when the officials moved them to a second temporary vault; there they remained until September 19, 1871, when officials

removed them to a vault inside the Lincoln Monument, which was finally dedicated on October 15, 1874.

10. Originally, the date set aside for this purpose was May 25. Due to pressure from various Christian groups, however, Andrew Johnson changed the date to June 1 (Morris 1865, 261–62).

11. John Qunicy Adams received the lowest (30.5 percent) in the election of 1824.

12. See Andrews 1865, 90–91; Joachimsen 1927, 36; Manning 1865, 60–64; Vidaver 1927, 53; Webb 1865, 152.

13. See Beecher 1887, 702; Daggett 1865, 13; Deleeuw 1927a, 162 and 1927b, 176–77; Low 1865, 105; Morgan 1865c, 40.

14. See Cook 1865, 86, Gurley 1865a, 20; Hague 1865, 120; Lilienthal 1927b, 123–24; Pitts 1865, 49; Vidaver 1927, 50–51; Wilbur 1865, 54.

15. On Harrison's death, see Cleaves 1939; and Goebel 1926. On Taylor's death, see Bauer 1985; and Dyer 1946.

16. See Aries 1974, 1975, 1982; Augustine and Kalish 1975; Becker 1975; Blauner 1966; Bowman 1959, 1977; Brandon 1967; Campbell 1969; Carse 1980; Charmaz 1975, 1980; Choron 1963, 1967, 1973; Coffin 1976; Cutler 1966; Diggory and Rothman 1961; Dumont and Foss 1972; Fabian 1973; Feifel 1959, 1974, 1979a, 1979b; Feifel and Branscomb 1973; Gorer 1965; Jackson 1957, 1959; Jung 1959; Kastenbaum 1977; Kastenbaum and Miller 1972; Koestenbaum 1964, 1971; Kroeber 1972; Lindemann 1977; Mitford 1963; Pine 1975; Pine et al. 1976; Pine and Phillips 1970; Rakoff 1973; Sheskin and Wallace 1976; Sudnow 1967; Tillich 1959; and Vernon 1970.

17. For an alternative explanation see Schwartz 1990.

18. For an excellent account of these three elements of the Lincoln myth see Warner 1959, esp. 270–89; for a masterful analysis of five themes that have dominated discussion of Lincoln's place in history, see Peterson 1994.

19. Two points need clarification. First, I noticed these distinctions before encountering *Habits of the Heart*, but this work clearly enhanced my understanding of several key matters. Second, Bellah et al. do not suggest that these are cultural groups.

20. See Cassell 1973; Coffin 1976; Dempsey 1975; Dumont and Foss 1972; Farrell 1980; Fromm 1973; Geddes 1981; Goody 1974; Gordon 1970; Gorer 1965; Harris 1971; Irion 1954, 1977; Jackson 1957, 1959; Kubler-Ross

1969, 1974, 1975; Lamm 1969; Lamm and Eskreis 1966; McCarthy 1979, 1980; Mack 1973; May 1969, 1973; Mills 1969; Morgan 1980; Morgenthau 1961; Natanson 1966; Pine 1976; Puckle 1926; Saum 1975; Smart 1968a, 1968b; Stannard 1975a, 1975b, 1977; Tillich 1959; U.S. Department of Health, Education, and Welfare 1970; Wilcox and Sutton 1977; Williams 1973; Zilboorg 1943.

21. See Agosta 1985; Deetz 1977, 1989; George and Nelson 1983; Ludwig 1966; Norris 1988; Tashjian and Tashjian 1974; and Wright 1988.

22. See Agosta 1985; Benes 1973a, 1973b, 1973c, 1975, 1976, 1977a, 1977b, 1978, 1985; Bergengren 1983; Briggs 1990; Chase and Gabel 1985, 1988; Clark 1989; Cornish 1983; Crowell 1983; Crowell and Mackie 1990; Darnall 1983; Duval and Rigby 1978, 1979/80; Edgette 1989; Forbes 1927, 1990; Foster 1977; Francaviglia 1971; George and Nelson 1979/80, 1982, 1983; Gosnell and Gott 1989; Graves 1988; Harding 1977; Howett 1977; Jeane 1987, 1989; Jones 1979/80; Jordan 1982; Kallas 1983; Kelly and Williams 1983; Levine 1978; Linden 1979/80; Linden-Ward 1986, 1989a, 1989b, 1990; Lucas 1990; Ludwig 1966, 1977; Luti 1983; McDannell 1987; McDowell 1989; McGrath 1987; Margot 1990; Mayer 1978; Meyer 1989a, 1989b, 1989c, 1989d; Milmoe 1979/80; Norris 1988; Oring 1982; Patterson 1989; Prestiano 1983; Roberts 1990; Rotunda 1973, 1989; Sanborn 1989; Scharf 1961; Slater 1977; Slater, Tucker, and Farber 1977; Smith 1987; Snyder 1989; Sweeney 1985; Sweet 1945; Tashjian 1978; Tasjhian and Tashjian 1974; Trask 1978; Vidutis and Lowe 1980; Vinovskis 1973; Walsh 1975; Warren 1987; Watters 1979/80, 1983; Welsh 1987; West 1989; Williams  and Williams 1988; Willshire 1983; Wright 1988; and Zaniello 1977.

23. See also Dethlefsen 1969, 1972; and Dethlefsen and James 1969a, 1969b.

24. See Buckeye 1977; Combs 1972; Crowell 1983; Deetz 1977, 1989; Deetz and Dethlefsen 1967; Dethlefsen 1969, 1972, 1981; Dethlefsen and Deetz 1966, 1969; Dethlefsen and Jensen 1969; Gorman and DiBlasi 1977; Hannon 1989; Hosley 1978; Levine 1978; Richardson and Carlisle 1979/80; Slater 1977; Watters 1979/80; and Young 1960.

25. See Deetz 1989, xiii-xiv; Foster 1977, 40; Graves 1988, 90; Meyer 1989, 106; Slater 1977, 11; Smith 1987, 85.

26. See Aries 1974, 1975, 1982; Bendann 1930; Brandon 1967; Carse 1980; Choron, 1963, 1967, 1973; Diggory and Rothman 1961, Koestenbaum 1964, 1971; Kroeber 1927; Tillich 1959; Toynbee 1968a, 1968b.

CHAPTER TWO

1. See Bigelow 1831; Blake 1959; Boller 1969; Brieger 1973; Clebsch 1973; Daniels 1971, 1976; Demos 1970; Dillenberger 1960; Dixon 1855; Douglas 1975, 1977; Ekirch 1944; Farrell 1980; Garrett et al. 1969; Gaustaud 1982; Griswold 1842; Haller 1981; Harris 1966; Howe 1970; Huth 1972; Jackson 1972; Kett 1980; Kolodny 1975; Marsden 1970; Massachusetts Medical Society 1831; Mead 1963; Nye 1974; Parker 1973; Rosenberg, 1974; Rothstein 1972; Scott 1978; Scudder 1879; Smith 1967, 1971; Smith, Handy, and Loetsher 1960; Somkin 1967; Stamp 1956; Takaki 1993; Welter 1974; White 1968; White 1972; Williams 1970; Wood 1973; Zuckerman 1970.

2. See Barnes 1868; Bentley 1962; Bushnell 1860, 1869; Channing 1827, 1843; *Christian Examiner* 1861; Clarke 1889; *Constitution of the Presbyterian Church, in the United States of America* 1842; Coxe 1865; *Doctrines and disciplines of the Methodist Episcopal Church* 1836; *Doctrines and disciplines of the Methodist Episcopal Church, South* 1846; Edwards 1962; Finney 1835; Frederic 1865; Hall 1865; Keck 1969; Mather ND, 1693, 1970; Post 1856; Potter 1865; Reed 1865; Robbins 1886; Sewell 1967; Spalding 1865; Spear 1865; Sprague 1832, 1857-69, 1865; Stewart et al. 1865; Williams 1865.

3. See Adams 1865; Allen 1865; Banks 1865; Bellows 1865; Buckingham 1865; Burchard 1865; Burr and Hacker 1865; Eells 1865; Ellis 1865; Fenton 1865a, 1865b; Goodrich 1865; Gurley 1865b, 1865c, 1865d, 1865e; Halley 1865; Isaacs 1927; Lesser 1927; McIlvaine 1865; Poor et al. 1865; Raphall 1927; Reed 1865; Sargent et al. 1865; Spear 1865; Studley 1865; Todd 1865; Tyng 1865b.

4. Unless otherwise noted, all references in this section are to this text.

5. See Coffin 1976, esp. 120-30; Farrell 1980, esp. 16-98; French 1975, esp. 69-75; Geddes 1981; Ludwig 1966; Stannard 1977; and Tashjian and Tashjian 1974.

6. See Coffin 1976, Crowell 1983; Farrell 1980; Forbes 1927; French 1974; Ludwig 1966; Ludwig and Hall 1978; Tashjian 1978; Tashjian and Tashjian 1974; and Vinovskis 1973.

CHAPTER THREE

1. Consider Adams 1834; Allen 1936; Angel 1960; Baldwin 1849; Basler 1960, 1962; Beecher 1875; Bigelow 1831, 1859; Bloom 1973;

Bridgeman 1890; Bryant 1865a, 1865b; Carlisle 1973; Clarke 1889, 1891; Cleaveland 1847, 1850, 1866, 1873; Douglas 1977; Downing 1974; Eddy 1855; Emerson 1878, 1882, 1883; Flagg 1861; Garrison 1865; Goodrich 1865; Grice 1982; *Guide to Laurel Hill Cemetery, near Philadelphia, with a list of lotholders* c. 1860; Gunther 1949; Howe 1970; King 1883; Kubler-Ross 1969, 1974, 1975; Lowenfels 1960; Macdonald 1885; Manning 1880; Morford 1865; Meyer 1927; Peabody 1831; *Picturesque pocket companion and visitor's guide through Mt. Auburn* 1829; Pierpont 1841; Pittman 1865; Sandburg 1960; Sandburg and Angle 1960; Simons 1979; Stoddard 1865; Story 1859a, 1859b; Tatum 1951; Temes 1980; Tuckerman 1865; Wakeley 1856; Walter 1850; Whitman 1960a, 1960b, 1962; Whitney 1850.

2. See Dawes and Root 1865; A. Hale 1865; E. Hale 1865; Havens 1865; W. F. Morgan 1865a, 1865b; White 1865.

3. Unless otherwise noted, all references in this section refer to this text.

4. See Adams 1834; Allen 1936; Bender 1974; Darnall 1983; Douglas 1975; Farrell 1980; French 1974; Linden 1979/80; Linden-Ward 1986, 1989, 1990; Morris 1986a, 1987, 1995; Rotunda 1973.

5. According to MacDonald (1885), the first superintendent of Old Copp's Hill Burying-Ground, this fence was removed around 1855, when Well's graveyard became part of the main graveyard on the Hill (28).

6. In 1832 Old Copp's Hill was again expanded to meet the need for additional space. But in 1853 use of this new extension was discontinued and "the bodies it contained [were] removed to Mt. Hope in February, 1861" (*Historical Sketch* 1901, 8; see also MacDonald 1885, 27; *Old Copps Hill and Burying Ground; with Historical Sketches* 1885; Smith 1901).

7. Consider Baldwin 1849; Crittenden 1855; Fraser 1850; Humphrey 1848; Lincoln 1838; Marshall 1855; O'Hara 1855; Powell 1855; Tucker 1948; and Whitney 1850.

8. See also Cleaveland 1847, 1866, 1873; Flagg 1861; *Guide to Laurel Hill Cemetery, near Philadelphia, with a list of lotholders* c. 1860; Gunther 1949; King 1883; Midgley 1856; *Picturesque pocket companion and visitor's guide through Mt. Auburn* 1829; Pierpont 1841; Simons 1979; Temes 1980; and Walter 1850.

9. See also Bender 1974; Darnall 1983; Douglas 1975; Farrell 1980; French 1974; Linden 1979/80; Linden-Ward 1986, 1989a, 1990; and Rotunda 1989.

10. Throughout this discussion I have relied heavily on the informative works of Budge (1967) and Vermeule (1981).

11. All photographs of Graceland were taken from public property with a telephoto lens to honor the request of the executors that visitors not take photographs while visiting the estate.

CHAPTER FOUR

1. Consider Aiken et al. 1865; Bulter 1865; Casey 1865; Clark et al. 1865; Curtain 1865; Dickinson 1865; Dixon et al. 1865; Ekin et al. 1865; McCloskey 1865a, 1865b; Morton 1865; Pierce 1865; Porter 1865; Sargent et al. 1865; Shepard 1865; Stevenson 1865; W. M. Stone 1865; Van Buren 1865; Waldo et al. 1865; Williams 1865.

2. Unless otherwise noted, all references in this section are to this text.

3. See Blake 1959; Brieger 1972; Osler 1904; and Rosenberg 1974.

4. See Haller 1981; Kett 1980; and Rothstein 1972.

5. Strict cemetery regulations eventually led Romanticists to abandon their decorative uses of iron in the cemetery. However, as founder and president of the Friends of Cast Iron Architecture and author of five books on ironwork, Margot Gayle notes, "panels, balustrades, and pickets . . . can be bought to this day from a few foundries, most of them in the deep south" (as quoted in Chase 1990, iv). This, along with my own observations in southern cemeteries, seems to suggest that much of the public power that Romanticists wielded was embedded in and, after the Civil War, migrated more conclusively to southern states. See also Gayle 1990.

6. See Bigelow 1859, 221–54 and Cleaveland 1850, 255–71.

7. Consider Bergman 1988, Branch 1962; Browne 1874; Cist 1851; Commager 1960; Dowd 1921; Draper 1873; Farmar 1897; Grant 1960; Habinstein and Lamars 1955, 1960; Hamill 1865; Hinkel 1970; Hunt 1865; Huntington 1865; Kenny 1875; Raether 1971; Rather and Slater 1974, 1977; Strauch 1869; Strong 1865; Thomas and Dixon 1973; Walsh 1975; Weed 1912.

# REFERENCES

Abbott, E. W. (1865a). Notes of the physician when dying. In B. F. Morris, ed., *Memorial record of the nation's tribute to Abraham Lincoln* (p. 39). Washington, DC: Morrison.

Abbott, E. W. (1865b). Minutes. In J. G. Shea, ed., *The Lincoln memorial: A record of the life, assassination and obsequies of the martyred president* (p. 70). NY: Bunce & Huntington.

Abbott, E. W. (1865c). Letter. In J. G. Shea, ed., *The Lincoln memorial: A record of the life, assassination and obsequies of the martyred president* (p. 71). NY: Bunce & Huntington.

Adams, N. (1834). Mount Auburn. *American Quarterly Observer* 3, 149-72.

Adams, W. (1865). Sermon. In *Our martyr president, Abraham Lincoln* (pp. 329-40). NY: Tibbals & Whiting, 1865.

Agosta, L. L. (1985). Speaking stones: New England grave carvings and the emblematic tradition. *Markers III*, 47-70.

Aiken, F. A., J. W. Clampitt, D. C. Lawrence, W. J. Miller, and C. Allen. (1865). Resolutions [of the National Democratic Association]. In B. F. Morris, ed, *Memorial record of the nation's tribute to Abraham Lincoln* (pp. 151–52). Washington, DC: Morrison.

Allen, Rev. (1865). Springfield's welcome to Lincoln. In B. F. Morris, ed., *Memorial record of the nation's tribute to Abraham Lincoln* (pp. 220–21). Washington, DC: Morrison.

Allen, V. W. (1936). Winged skull and weeping willow. *Antiques 29,* 250–53.

Andrew, J. A. (1865). Message to the Massachusetts legislature. In B. F. Morris, ed, *Memorial record of the nation's tribute to Abraham Lincoln* (p. 126). Washington, DC: Morrison.

Andrews, Mr. (1865). Remarks of Mr. Andrews. In J. B. Cushman, comp., *Legislative honors to the memory of President Lincoln* (pp. 89–92). Albany, NY: Weed, Parsons & Co.

Angel, Mr. (1865). Remarks of Mr. Angel. In J. B. Cushman, comp., *Legislative honors to the memory of President Lincoln* (pp. 36–41). Albany, NY: Weed, Parsons & Co.

Angle, P. M. (1960). Lincoln in New Salem. In R. G. Newman, ed., *Lincoln for the ages* (pp. 58–62). NY: Doubleday.

Aries, P. (1974). *Western attitudes toward death from the Middle Ages to the present.* Trans. Patricia M. Ranum. Baltimore: Johns Hopkins University Press.

Aries, P. (1975). The reversal of death: Changes in attitudes toward death in Western societies. In D. E. Stannard, ed., *Death in America.* (pp. 134–58). Philadelphia: University of Pennsylvania Press.

Aries, P. (1982). *The hour of our death.* Trans. Helen Weaver. New York: Vintage.

Augustine, M. J. and R. A. Kalish (1975). Religion, transcendence, and appropriate death. *Journal of Transpersonal Psychology 7,* 1–13.

Bailey, Mr. (1865). Remarks of Mr. Bailey. In J. B. Cushman, comp.,

*Legislative honors to the memory of President Lincoln* (pp. 98–104). Albany, NY: Weed, Parsons & Co.

Bakhtin, M. M. (1990; 1986). *Speech genres and other essays.* Trans. V. W. McGee, eds., C. Emerson and M. Holquist. Austin: University of Texas Press.

Baldwin, O. P. (1849). *Address delivered at the dedication of Hollywood Cemetery, 25th of June, 1849.* Richmond, VA: MacFarlane & Ferguson.

Bancroft, G. (1865). Oration by the Hon. Geo. Bancroft. In J. G. Shea, ed., *The Lincoln memorial: A record of the life, assassination and obsequies of the martyred president* (pp. 199–204). NY: Bunce & Huntington.

Bancroft, G. (1866). *Memorial address on the life and character of Abraham Lincoln, delivered, at the request of both houses of the Congress of America, before them, in the House of Representatives at Washington, on the 12th of February, 1866.* Washington, DC: GPO.

Banks, N. P. (1865). Address. In J. G. Shea, ed., *The Lincoln memorial: A record of the life, assassination and obsequies of the martyred president* (pp. 156–60). NY: Bunce & Huntington.

Barnes, A. (1868). *Lectures on the evidences of Christianity in the nineteenth century.* NY: Harper & Brothers.

Barnes, J. K. (1865). Post-mortem. In J. G. Shea, ed., *The Lincoln memorial: A record of the life, assassination and obsequies of the martyred president* (pp. 71–72). NY: Bunce & Huntington.

Bartol, C. A. (1865). Address. In J. E. Tilton. comp., *Sermons preached in Boston on the death of Abraham Lincoln* (pp. 51–56). Boston: Tilton & Co.

Basler, R. P. (1960). Lincoln as a man of letters. In R. G. Newman, ed., *Lincoln for the ages* (pp. 367–71). NY: Doubleday.

Basler, R. P., ed. (1962). *Walt Whitman's 'Memoranda during the Civil War [&] Death of Abraham Lincoln.'* Bloomington: Indiana University Press.

Bauer, K. J. (1985). *Zachary Taylor: Soldier, planter, statesman of the old Southwest.* Baton Rouge: Louisiana State University Press.

Becker, E. (1975). *The denial of death.* NY: Free Press.

Beecher, H. W. (1859). *Star papers, or, experiences of art and nature.* NY: Derby & Jackson.

Beecher, H. W. (1875). *The sermons of Henry Ward Beecher, in Plymouth Church, Brooklyn.* NY: Ford & Co.

Beecher, H. W. (1887). Abraham Lincoln. In J. R. Howard, ed., *Patriotic addresses in America and England, from 1850-1885, on slavery, the Civil War, and the development of civil liberty in the United States by Henry Ward Beecher* (pp. 701-12). NY: Fords, Howard & Hulbert.

Bellah, R. N., R. Madsen, W. M. Sullivan, A. Swindler, and S. M. Stipton. (1985). *Habits of the heart: Individualism and commitment in American life.* New York: Harper & Row.

Bellows, H. W. (1865). Sermon by Rev. Henry W. Bellows. In J. G. Shea, ed., *The Lincoln memorial: A record of the life, assassination and obsequies of the martyred president* (pp. 90-98). NY: Bunce & Huntington.

Bendann, E. (1930). *Death customs: An analytical study of burial rites.* NY: Knopf.

Bender, T. (1974). The rural cemetery movement: Urban travail and the appeal of nature. *New England Quarterly 47,* 196-211.

Benes, P. (1973a). Abel Webster, pioneer, patriot, and stonecutter. *Historical New Hampshire 28,* 221-40.

Benes, P. (1973b). John Wright: The hieroglyph carver of Londonderry. *Old-Time New England 64,* 31-41.

Benes, P. (1973c). Lt. John Hartshorn: Gravestone maker of Haverhill and Norwich. *Essex Institute Historical Collections 109,* 152-64.

Benes, P. (1975). Additional light on wooden grave markers. *Essex Institute Historical Collections 111,* 53-64.

Benes, P., ed. (1976). *Puritan gravestone art.* Boston: Boston University Press, 1977. Proc. of the Dublin seminar for New England folklife.

Benes, P. (1977a). The caricature hypothesis re-examined: The animated skull as a Puritan folklore image. In P. Benes, ed., *Puritan gravestone art* (pp. 57–67). Boston: Boston University Press.

Benes, P. (1977b). *The masks of orthodoxy: Folk gravestone carving in Plymouth County, Massachusetts, 1689–1805.* Amherst, MA: University of Massachusetts Press.

Benes, P., ed. (1978). *Puritan gravestone art II.* Boston: Boston University Press, 1978. Proc. of the Dublin seminar for New England folklife.

Benes, P. (1985). A particular sense of doom: Skeletal 'revivals' in northern Essex County, Massachusetts, 1737–84. *Markers III,* 71–92.

Bentley, W. (1905/1962). *The diary of William Bentley, D.D., pastor of the East Church, Salem, Massachusetts.* 4 vols. Ed. P. Smith. Gloucester, MA: Essex Institute.

Bergman, E. F. (1988). *Woodlawn remembers: Cemetery of American history.* Utica, NY: North Country Books.

Bergengren, C. (1983). Folk art on gravestones: The glorious contrast. *Markers, II,* 171–85.

Berkovitch, S. (1993). *The rites of assent: Transformations in the symbolic construction of America.* NY: Routledge.

Bigelow, J. (1824/1831). *Elements of technology,* 2nd ed. Boston: Hilliard, Gray, Little & Wilkins.

Bigelow, J. (1859). *A history of the cemetery of Mount Auburn.* Boston: Munroe & Brothers.

Blake, J. B. (1959). *Public health in the town of Boston, 1630–1822.* Cambridge: Harvard University Press.

Blauner, R. (1966). Death and social structure. *Psychiatry, 29,* 378–94.

Bloom, H. (1973). Death and the native strain in American poetry. In A. Mack, ed, *Death in American experience* (pp. 83–96). NY: Schocken.

Bodnar, J. (1992). *Remaking America: Public memory, commemoration, and patriotism in the twentieth century.* Princeton, NJ: Princeton University Press.

Boller, P. F., Jr. (1969). *American thought in transition: The impact of evolutionary naturalism, 1865-1900.* Chicago: Rand-McNally.

Bowman, L. (1959). *The American funeral: A study in guilt, extravagance, and sublimity.* Washington, DC: Public Affairs Press.

Bowman, L. (1977). Group behavior at funeral gatherings. In A. Wilcox and M. Sutton, eds., *Understanding death and dying: An interdisciplinary approach* (pp. 182-94). Dominguez Hills, CA: Alfred.

Branch, E. D. (1934/1962). *The sentimental years, 1836-1860.* NY: Hill & Wang.

Brandon, S. G. F. (1967). *The judgment of the dead: The idea of life after death in the major religions.* NY: Scribner.

Brieger, G. H. (1972). *Medical America in the nineteenth century: Readings from the literature.* Baltimore: Johns Hopkins University Press.

Briggs, M. W. (1990). Charles Miller Walsh: A master carver of gravestones in Virginia, 1865-1901. *Markers VII,* 139-71.

Browne, J. H. (1874). The silent majority. *Harper's Monthly 49,* 468-86.

Bryant, W. C. (1865a). Ode for the funeral of Abraham Lincoln. In J. G. Shea, ed., *The Lincoln memorial: A record of the life, assassination and obsequies of the martyred president* (p. 205). NY: Bunce & Huntington.

Bryant, W. C. (1865b). Thou hast put all things under his feet. In J. G. Shea, ed., *The Lincoln memorial: A record of the life, assassination and obsequies of the martyred president* (pp. 205-6). NY: Bunce & Huntington.

Buckeye, N. (1977). Early American gravestone studies: The structure of the literature. In P. Benes, ed., *Puritan gravestone art* (pp. 130-36). Boston: Boston University Press.

Budge, E. A. W. (1967). *The Egyptian book of the dead.* NY: Dover.

Budington, W. I. (1865). Sermon. In *Our martyr president, Abraham Lincoln* (pp. 111-27). NY: Tibbals & Whiting.

Burchard, S. D. (1865). Sermon. In *Our martyr president, Abraham Lincoln* (pp. 255-72). NY: Tibbals & Whiting.

Burnham, A. A. (1865). Address. In B. F. Morris, ed., *Memorial record of the nation's tribute to Abraham Lincoln* (pp. 118–19). Washington, DC: Morrison.

Burr, J. F. and I. Hakcer (1865). Resolutions [of the citizens of New Jersey in Washington City]. In B. F. Morris, ed., *Memorial record of the nation's tribute to Abraham Lincoln* (p. 131). Washington, DC: Morrison.

Bushnell, H. (1860). *Nature and the supernatural, as together constituting the one system of God*, 5th ed. NY: Scribner.

Bushnell, H. (1869). *Woman's suffrage: The reform against nature.* NY: Scribner.

Butler, B. F. (1865). Speech of Gen. Butler. In J. G. Shea, ed., *The Lincoln memorial: A record of the life, assassination and obsequies of the martyred president* (pp. 81–83). NY: Bunce & Huntington.

Campbell, E. (1969). Death as a social practice. In L. O. Mills, ed., *Perspectives on death* (pp. 209–30). NY: Abington Press.

Campbell, J. (1973). *The hero with a thousand faces.* Princeton University Press.

Carlisle, E. F. (1973). *The uncertain self: Whitman's drama of identity.* East Lansing: Michigan State University Press.

Carrington, E. C., J. H. Bradley, P. R. Fendall, G. A. Bohrer, J. Y. Davis, and H. Baron (1865). Resolutions [of the Washington City Bar and Grand Jury]. In B. F. Morris, ed., *Memorial record of the nation's tribute to Abraham Lincoln* (pp. 148–49). Washington, DC: Morrison.

Carse, J. P. (1980). *Death and existence: A conceptual history of human mortality.* NY: Wiley.

Casey, J. (1865). Announcement [to the U.S. Court of Claims]. In B. F. Morris, ed., *Memorial record of the nation's tribute to Abraham Lincoln* (pp. 146–47). Washington, DC: Morrison.

Cassell, E. J. (1973). Being and becoming dead. In A. Mack, ed., *Death in American experience* (pp. 162–76). NY: Schocken.

Chaney, G. L. (1865). Sermon. In J. E. Tilton, comp., *Sermons preached in Boston on the death of Abraham Linoln* (pp. 325–34). Boston: Tilton & Co.

Channing, W. E. (1827). *A discourse, preached at the dedication of the second Congregational Unitarian Church, New York, December 7, 1826.* NY: Second Congregational Unitarian Church.

Channing, W. E. (1843). *Works.* Boston: Munroe.

Charmaz, K. C. (1975). The coroner's strategy for announcing death. *Urban life 4,* 296–316.

Charmaz, K. C. (1980). *The social reality of death: Death in contemporary America.* Menlo Park, CA: Addison-Wesley.

Chase, T. and L. K. Gabel (1985). The Colburn connections: Hollis, New Hampshire, stonecarvers, 1780–1820. *Markers III:* 93–146.

Chase, T. and L. K. Gabel (1988). Seven initial carvers of Boston, 1700–25. *Markers V,* 211–32.

Choron, J. (1963). *Death and Western thought.* NY: Macmillan.

Choron, J. (1967). Death as a motive of philosophic thought. In E. S. Shneidman, ed., *Essays in self-destruction* (pp. 59–77). NY: Science House.

Choron, J. (1973). *Death and modern man.* NY: Collier.

*Christian Examiner* (1861). The theory of a personal devil. LXXI, 157–80.

Cist, C. (1851). *Sketches and statistics of Cincinnati in 1851.* Cincinnati: Moore & Co.

Clark, E. W. (1989). The Bigham carvers of the Carolina Piedmont: Stone images of an emerging sense of American identity. In R. E. Meyer, ed., *Cemeteries and gravemarkers: Voices of American culture* (pp. 31–59). Ann Arbor: University of Michigan Research Press.

Clarke, J. F. (1865). Who hath abolished death. In J. E. Tilton, comp., *Sermons preached in Boston on the death of Abraham Lincoln* (pp. 91–106). Boston: Tilton & Co.

Clarke, J. F. (1889). *Manual of Unitarian beliefs,* 13th ed. Boston: Unitarian Sunday-School Society.

Clarke, J. F. (1891). *Autobiography, diary and correspondence.* Ed., E. E. Hale. Boston: Houghton-Mifflin.

Clarke, S. and H. C. Fields (1865). Sentiments [of the citizens of

Kansas in Washington City]. In B. F. Morris, ed., *Memorial record of the nation's tribute to Abraham Lincoln* (pp. 140–41). Washington, DC: Morrison.

Cleaveland, N. (1847). *Green-Wood illustrated.* NY: Martin.

Cleaveland, N. (1850). *Green-Wood: A directory for visitors.* NY: Green-Wood.

Cleaveland, N. (1866). *Green-Wood cemetery: A history of the institution from 1838–1864.* NY: Anderson & Archer.

Cleaveland, N. (1873). *A Hand-book for Green-Wood.* NY: Tripp.

Cleaves, F. (1939). *Old Tippecanoe: William Henry Harrison and his time.* NY: Scribner.

Clebsch, W. A. (1973). *American religious thought: A history.* Chicago: University of Chicago Press.

Coffin, M. M. (1976). *Death in early America: The history and folklore of customs and superstitions of early medicine, funerals, burials, and mourning.* Nashville, TN: Nelson.

Cole, D. B. (1986). *Handbook of American history.* NY: Harcourt Brace Javonovich.

Colfax, S. (1865). Funeral oration. In B. F. Morris, ed., *Memorial record of the nation's tribute to Abraham Lincoln* (pp. 204–18). Washington, DC: Morrison.

Combs, J. D. (1972). Ethnography, archaeology, and burial practices among costal Southern Carolina Blacks. *Conference on historic site archaeology, Papers, 7,* 52–61.

Commager, H. S. (1960). Lincoln and the whole nation. In R. G. Newman, ed., *Lincoln for the ages* (pp. 362–66). NY: Doubleday.

Conkling, M. C. (1860). *Memoirs of the mother and wife of Washington.* Auburn, NY: Derby, Miller & Co.

*Constitution of the Presbyterian Church, in the United States of America.* (1842). Philadelphia: Presbyterian Board of Publication.

Cook, J. M. (1865). Remarks of Mr. Cook. In J. B. Cushman, comp., *Legislative honors to the memory of President Lincoln* (pp. 84–89). Albany, NY: Weed, Parsons & Co.

Cornish, M. (1983). Joseph Barbur, Jr.: The frond carver of West Medway. *Markers II*, 133–47.

Coxe, A. C. (1865). [Letter] To the reverend clergy of the diocese of Western New York. In J. G. Shea, ed., *The Lincoln memorial: A record of the life, assassination and obsequies of the martyred president* (pp. 142–43). NY: Bunce & Huntington.

Crittenden, T. L. (1855). Address of Col. Crittenden upon the life and character of Gen. Chas. Scott. In *Obituary addresses delivered upon the occasion of the re-interment of the remains of Gen. Chas. Scott, Maj. Wm. T. Barry, and Capt. Bland Ballard and wife, in the cemetery, at Frankfort, November 8, 1854* (pp. 11–21). Frankfort, KY: Hodges.

Crowell, E. A. (1983). Migratory monuments and missing motifs: Archaelogical analysis of mortuary art in Cape May County, New Jersey, 1740–1810. Diss. University of Pennsylvania.

Crowell, E. A. and N. V. Mackie, III (1990). The funerary monuments and burial practices of colonial Tidewater Virginia, 1607–1776. *Markers VII*, 103–38.

Cudworth, W. H. (1865). Sermon. In J. E. Tilton, comp., *Sermons preached in Boston in memory of Abraham Lincoln* (pp. 199–212). Boston: Tilton & Co.

Curtin, A. G. (1865). A proclamation. In B. F. Morris, ed., *Memorial record of the nation's tribute to Abraham Lincoln* (p. 159). Washington, DC: Morrison.

Cutler, D. R. (1966). Death and responsibility: A minister's view. *Psychiatric opinion 3:* 8–12.

Cutting, F. B. (1865). Remarks of Mr. Cutting. In J. B. Cushman, comp., *Legislative honors to the memory of President Lincoln* (pp. 30–36). Albany, NY: Weed, Parsons & Co.

Cuyler, T. L. (1865). Sermon. In *Our martyr President, Abraham Lincoln* (pp. 159–72). NY: Tibbals & Whiting.

Daggett, O. E. (1865). *A sermon on the death of Abraham Lincoln, April 15th, 1865, preached in the First Congregational Church, Canadaigua, N.Y., Sunday morning, April 16th, 1865, and again, by request, the following Wednesday evening.* Canadaigua, NY: Milliken.

Daniels, G. H. (1971). *Science in American society: A social history.* NY: Knopf.

Daniels, G. H. (1976). *Nineteenth-Century American science: A reappraisal.* Evanston, IL: Northwestern University Press.

Darnall, M. J. (1983). The American cemetery as picturesque landscape: Belefontaine Cemetery, St. Louis. *Winterthur Portfolio 18,* 249–69.

Dawes, L. M. and G. F. Root (1865). Dirge. In B. F. Morris, ed., *Memorial record of the nation's tribute to Abraham Lincoln* (p. 227). Washington, DC: Morrison.

Dearborn, H. A. S. (1859). A report on the garden and cemetery. In Jacob Bigelow, *A history of the cemetery of Mount Auburn* (pp. 168–74). Boston: Munroe & Co.

Deetz, J. (1977). *In Small things forgotten: The archaeology of early American life.* NY: Anchor.

Deetz, J. (1989). Foreword. In R. E. Meyer, ed., *Cemeteries and gravemarkers: Voices of American culture* (pp. ix–xiv). Ann Arbor: University of Michigan Research Press.

Deetz, J. and E. S. Dethlefsen (1967). Death's heads, cherub, urn and willow. *Natural History 76,* 28–37.

Deleeuw, M. R. (1927a). Abraham Lincoln. In E. Hertz, ed., *Abraham Lincoln: The tribute of the synagogue* (pp. 160–77). NY: Bloch.

Deleeuw, M. R. (1927b). Abraham Lincoln. In E. Hertz, ed., *Abraham Lincoln: The tribute of the synagogue* (pp. 176–77). NY: Bloch.

Demos, J. (1970). *A little commonwealth: Family life in Plymouth Colony.* NY: Oxford University Press.

Dempsey, D. (1975). *The way we die: An investigation of death and dying in America today.* NY: McGraw-Hill.

Dethlefsen, E. S. (1969). Colonial gravestones and demography. *American Journal of Physical Anthropology 31,* 321–34.

Dethlefsen, E. S. (1972). Life and death in colonial New England. Diss. Harvard University.

Dethlefsen, E S. (1981). The cemetery and culture change: Archaeological focus and ethnographic perspective. In R. Gould and M. Schiffer, eds., *Modern material culture: The archaeology of us* (pp. 137–59). NY: Academic Press.

Dethlefsen, E. S. and J. Deetz (1966). Death's heads, cherubs, and willow trees: Experimental archaeology in colonial cemeteries. *American Antiquity 31,* 502–10.

Dethlefsen, E. S. and J. Deetz (1969a). Eighteenth century cemeteries: A demographic view. *Historical Archaeology 1,* 40–42.

Dethlefsen, E. S. and K. Jensen (1969b). Social commentary from the cemetery. *Natural History 86,* 32–39.

Dickinson, D. S. (1865). Speech of Hon. Daniel S. Dickinson. In J. G. Shea, ed., *The Lincoln memorial: A record of the life, assasination and obsequies of the martyred president* (pp. 83–85). NY: Bunce & Huntington.

Diggory, J. C. and D. Z. Rothman (1961). Values destroyed by death. *Journal of Abnormal Social Psychology 30,* 11–17.

Dillenberger, J. (1952/1960). *Protestant thought and natural science: A historical interpretation.* Garden City, NJ: Doubleday.

Dixon, E. H. (1855). *Scenes in the practice of a New York surgeon.* NY: DeWitt & Davenport.

Dixon, J., W. A. Thompson, H. H. Osgood, J. A. Wheelock, and W. H. Almy (1865). Resolutions [of the citizens of Connecticut in Washington City]. In B. F. Morris, ed., *Memorial record of the nation's tribute to Abraham Lincoln* (pp. 127–28). Washington, DC: Morrison.

*Doctrines and discipline of the Methodist Episcopal Church.* (1836). NY: Mason & Land.

*Doctrines and discipline of the Methodist Episcopal Church, South.* (1846). Charleston, SC: Early.

Douglas, A. (1975). Heaven our home: Consolation literature in the Northern United States, 1830–1880. In D. E. Stannard, ed., *Death in America* (pp. 49–68). Philadelphia: University of Pennsylvania Press.

Douglas, A. (1977). *The feminization of American culture.* NY: Knopf.

Dowd, Quincy L. (1921). *Funeral management and costs.* Chicago: University of Chicago Press.

Downing, A. J. (1974). Public cemeteries and public gardens. In G. W. Curtis, ed., *Rural Essays by Andrew Jackson Downing.* Ed. G. W. Curtis. NY: Da Capo.

Draper, H. (1873). Delusions of medicine: Charms, talismans, amulets, astrology, and mesmerism. *Harper's Monthly 46,* 385–95.

Dumont, R. G. and D. C. Foss (1972). *The American view of death: Acceptance or denial?* Cambridge: Schenkman.

Duval, F. Y. and I. Rigby (1978). *Early American gravestone art in photographs.* NY: Dover.

Duval, F. Y. and I. Rigby (1979/80). Openwork memorials of North Carolina. *Markers I,* 63–75.

Dyer, B. (1946). *Zachary Taylor.* Baton Rouge: Louisiana State University Press.

Eddy, D. C. (1855). *Angel whispers; or, the echo of spirit voices: Designed to comfort those who mourn.* Boston: Dayton & Wentworth.

Edgette, J. J. (1989). The epitaph and personal revelation. In R. E. Meyer, ed., *Cemeteries and gravemarkers: Voices of American culture* (pp. 87–102). Ann Arbor: University of Michigan Research Press.

Edwards, J. (1935/1962). The Christian pilgrim. In C. H. Faust and T. H. Johnson, eds., *Jonathan Edwards: Representative selections, with introduction, bibliography, and notes* (pp. 130–51). NY: Hill & Wang. 1962 [1935].

Eells, J. (1865). Sermon. In *Our martyr president, Abraham Lincoln* (pp. 219–32). NY: Tibbals & Whiting.

Ekin, J. F., J. Covade, J. J. Lewis, E. McPherson, W. A. Cook, J. M. Sullivan, J. E. Brady, D. L. Eaton, and S. W. Pearson (1865). Resolutions [of the citizens of Pennsylvania in Washington City]. In B. F. Morris, ed., *Memorial record of the nation's tribute to Abraham Lincoln* (pp. 132–33). Washington, DC: Morrison.

Ekirch, A. A. (1944). *The idea of progress in America, 1815–60.* NY: Columbia University Press.

Ekirch, A. A. (1963). *Man and nature in America.* NY: Columbia University Press.

Ellis, R. (1865). Sermon. In J. E. Tilton, comp., *Sermons preached in Boston on the death of Abraham Lincoln* (pp. 235-242). Boston: Tilton & Co.

Emerson, R. W. (1855/1878). Abraham Lincoln: Remarks at the funeral services held in Concord, April 19, 1865. *Miscellanies.* Vol. XI of *Emerson's complete works* (pp. 307-15). Boston: Houghton, Mifflin & Co.

Emerson, R. W. (1882). *Letters and social aims.* Vol. IV of *Works of Ralph Waldo Emerson.* Boston: Houghton, Mifflin & Co.

Emerson, R. W. (1876/1883). *Essays, first and second series.* Vol. I of *Works of Ralph Waldo Emerson.* Boston: Houghton, Mifflin & Co.

Fabian, J. (1973). How others die—Reflections on the anthropology of death. In A. Mack, ed., *Death in American experience* (pp. 177-201). NY: Schocken.

Farmar, A. (1897). The modern cemetery: The perpetual care lawn plan. *Overland Monthly 29,* 440-47.

Farrell, J. J. (1980). *Inventing the American way of death.* Philadelphia: Temple University Press.

Farrer, C. R. (1991). *Living life's circle: Mescalero Apache cosmovision.* Albuquerque: Univ. of New Mexico Press.

Feifel, H., ed. (1959). *The meaning of death.* NY: McGraw-Hill.

Feifel, H. (1974). Religious conviction and the fear of death among the healthy and terminally ill. *Journal for the Scientific Study of Religion 13,* 353-60.

Feifel, H, ed. (1977a). *New meanings of death.* NY: McGraw-Hill.

Feifel, H. (1977b). Death in contemporary America. In H. Feifel, ed., *New meanings of death* (pp. 4-12). NY: McGraw-Hill.

Feifel, H. and A. Branscomb (1973). Who's afraid of death? *Journal of Abnormal Psychology 81,* 282-88.

Field, M. B. (1865). Letter. In J. G. Shea, comp., *The Lincoln memorial: A record of the life, assassination and obsequies of the martyred president* (pp. 207-10). NY: Bunce & Huntington.

Field, M. B. (1865). Letter. In J.G. Shea, ed., *The Lincoln memorial: A record of the life, assassination and obsequies of the martyred president* (pp. 69-70). NY: Bunce & Huntington.

Fenton, R. E. (1865a). A proclamation. In B. F. Morris, ed., *Memorial record of the nation's tribute to Abraham Lincoln* (p. 130). Washington, D.C.: Morrison.

Fenton, R. E. (1865b). Message to the legislature [of New York]. In J. B. Cushman, comp., *Legislative honors to the memory of President Lincoln* (pp. 3-4). Albany, NH: Weed, Parsons & Co.

Finney, C. G. (1835). *Lectures on revivals of religion*, 6th ed. NY: Leavitt, Lord & Co.

Flagg, T. W. (1861). *Mount Auburn: Its scenes, its beauties, and its lessons.* Boston: Munroe.

Folger, C. J. (1865). Remarks of Mr. Folger. In J. B. Cushman, comp., *Legislative honors to the memory of President Lincoln* (pp. 73-80). Albany, NY: Weed, Parsons & Co.

Foote, H. W. (1865). Address spoken at King's Chapel. In J. E. Tilton, comp., *Sermons preached in Boston on the death of Abraham Lincoln* (pp. 179-90). Boston: Tilton & Co.

Forbes, H. M. (1927). *Gravestones of early New England and the men who made them, 1653-1800.* Boston: Houghton-Mifflin.

Forbes, H. M. (1990). Symbolic cemetery gates in New England. *Markers VII*, 3-8. Reprinted from *Old-Time New England XXIV* (Oct. 1933).

Foster, S. C. (1977). From significant incompetence to insignificant competence. In P. Benes, ed., *Puritan gravestone art* (pp. 33-40). Boston: Boston University Press.

Fox, H. J. (1865). Sermon. In *Our martyr president, Abraham Lincoln* (pp. 341-57). NY: Tibbals & Whiting.

Francaviglia, R. V. (1971). The cemetery as an evolving cultural landscape. *Annals, Association of American Geographers 61*, 501-9.

Fraser, C. (1850). *Address delivered on the dedication of the Magnolia Cemetery, 19th November, 1850.* Charleston, SC: Walker & James.

Frederic, J. (1865). [Letter] To the reverend clergy and faithful of the diocese of Philadelphia. In J. G. Shea, ed., *The Lincoln memorial: A record of the life, assassination and obsequies of the martyred president* (pp. 144–45). NY: Bunce & Huntington.

French, S. (1974). The cemetery as cultural institution: The establishment of Mount Auburn and the 'rural cemetery' movement. In D. E. Stannard, ed., *Death in America* (pp. 69–91). Philadelphia: University of Pennsylvania Press.

Freud, S. (1953). Thoughts for the times on war and death. In J. Rickman, ed., *Civilization, war, and death* (pp. 1–25). London: Hogarth.

Fromm, E. (1973). *The anatomy of human destructiveness.* NY: Holt, Rinehart & Winston.

Fulton, J. D. (1865). Sermon. In J. E. Tilton, comp., *Sermons preached in Boston on the death of Abraham Lincoln* (pp. 359–79). Boston: Tilton & Co.

Gaonkar, D. (1988). The quarrel between philosophy and rhetoric. Paper presented at the meeting of the Eastern Communication Association. Baltimore, MD.

Garrett, W. D., (1969). *The arts in America: The nineteenth century.* NY: Scribner.

Garrison, J. F. (1865). *The teachings of the crisis: Address delivered in St. Paul's Church, Camden, N.J., on the occasion of the funeral of Abraham Lincoln, April 19, 1865.* Camden: West Jersey Press.

Gaustad, E., ed. (1982). *A documentary history of religion in America to the Civil War.* Grand Rapids, MI: Eerdmans.

Gayle, M. (1990). A portfolio of Harriette Forbes's cast iron gates. *Markers VII,* 19–33.

Geddes, G. E. (1976, 1981). *Welcome joy: Death in Puritan New England.* Ann Arbor, MI: University Microfilms International Press.

Geertz, C. (1973). *The interpretation of cultures.* NY: Basic Books.

George, D. H. and M. A. Nelson (1979/80). Resurrecting the epitaph. *Markers I,* 85–95.

George, D. H. and M. A. Nelson (1982). Grinning skulls, smiling cherubs, bitter words. *Journal of Popular Culture 15,* 163-74.

George, D. H. and M. A. Nelson (1983). *Epitaph and icon: A field guide to the old burying grounds of Cape Cod, Martha's Vineyard, and Nantucket.* Orleans, MA: Parnassus Imprints.

Gerzon, M. (1992). *A choice of heroes: The changing faces of American manhood.* NY: Houghton Mifflin.

Gleason, Mr. (1865). Remarks of Mr. Gleason. In J. B. Cushman, comp., *Legislative honors to the memory of president Lincoln* (pp. 41-46). Albany, NY: Weed, Parsons & Co.

Goebel, D. B. (1926). *William Henry Harrison: A political biography.* Indianapolis: Historical Bureau of the Indiana Library and Historical Department.

Goodrich, M. (1865). Resolutions [of the citizens of New York in Washington City]. In B. F. Morris, ed., *Memorial record of the nation's tribute to Abraham Lincoln* (p. 130). Washington, DC: Morrison.

Goody, J. (1974). Death and the interpretation of culture: A bibliographic overview. In D. E. Stannard, ed., *Death in America* (pp. 1-8). Philadelphia: University of Pennsylvania Press.

Gordon, D. C. (1970). *Overcoming the fear of death.* NY: Macmillan.

Gordon, M. B. (1949). *Aesculapius comes to the colonies: The story of the early days in the thirteen original colonies.* Ventnor, NJ: Ventnor.

Gorer, G. (1965). *Death, grief, and mourning.* NY: Doubleday.

Gorman, F. and M. DiBlasi (1977). Nonchronological sources of variation in the seriation of gravestone motifs in the northeast and southeast colonies. In P. Benes, ed., *Puritan gravestone art* (pp. 79-87). Boston: Boston University Press.

Gosnell, L. and S. Gott (1989). San Fernando Cemetery: Decorations of love and loss in a Mexican-American community. In R. E. Meyer, ed., *Cemeteries and gravemarkers: Voices of American culture* (pp. 217-36). Ann Arbor: University of Michigan Research Press.

Gramsci, A. (1971). *Selections from the prison notebooks of Antonio Gramsci.* Q. Hoare and G. N. Smith, eds. and trans. NY: International Publishers.

Grant, U. S. III. (1960). Lincoln: Commander-in-chief. In R. G. Newman, ed., *Lincoln for the ages* (pp. 242–47). NY: Doubleday.

Graves, T. E. (1988). Pennsylvania German gravestones: An introduction. *Markers V,* 60–95.

Gray, F. T. (1847). *New Years' sermons, preached in the Bulfinch Street Church, on Sunday, January 3, 1847.* Boston: Hall & Co.

Grice, S. E. (1982). Death in the writings of Henry David Thoreau. Diss. Southern Illinois University.

Griswold, R. W., comp. (1842). *The poets and poetry of America.* 8 vols. Philadelphia: Carey.

*Guide to Laurel Hill Cemetery, near Philadelphia, with a list of lotholders.* (c. 1860). Philadelphia: Laurel Hill Cemetery.

Gunther, J. (1949). *Death be not proud.* NY: Harper & Row.

Gurley, P. D. (1865a). Faith in God: A sermon delivered in the East Room of the Executive Mansion, Wednesday, April 19th, 1865, at the funeral of Abraham Lincoln, President of the U. States. In J. E. Tilton, comp., *Sermons preached in Boston on the death of Abraham Lincoln* (pp. 16–28). Boston: Tilton & Co.

Gurley, P. D. (1865b). Sermon. In J. G. Shea, ed., *The Lincoln memorial: A record of the life, assassination and obsequies of the martyred President* (pp. 88–89). NY: Bunce & Huntington.

Gurley, P. D. (1865c). Prayer. In J. G. Shea, ed., *The Lincoln memorial: A record of the life, assassination and obsequies of the martyred President* (pp. 136–37). NY: Bunce & Huntington.

Gurley, P. D. (1865d). Prayer. In J. G. Shea, ed., *The Lincoln memorial: A record of the life, assassination and obsequies of the martyred President* (p. 164). NY: Bunce & Huntington.

Gurley, P. D. (1865e). Prayer. In J. G. Shea, ed., *The Lincoln memorial: A record of the life, assassination and obsequies of the martyred President* (pp. 165–66). NY: Bunce & Huntington.

Habinstein, R. W. and W. M. Lamers, Sr. (1955). *The history of American funeral directing.* Milwaukee: Bulfin.

Habinstein, R. W. and W. M. Lamers, Sr. (1960). *Funeral customs the world over*. Milwaukee: Bulfin.

Hague, W. (1865). Sermon. In J. E. Tilton, comp., *Sermons preached in Boston on the death of Abraham Lincoln* (pp. 120–42). Boston: Tilton & Co.

Hale, A. (1865). Prayer. In B. F. Morris, ed., *Memorial record of the nation's tribute to Abraham Lincoln* (pp. 225–27). Washington, DC: Morrison.

Hale, E. E. (1865). Sermon. In J. E. Tilton, comp., *Sermons preached in Boston on the death of Abraham Lincoln* (pp. 267–79). Boston: Tilton & Co.

Hall, C. H. (1865). Episcopal Burial Service. In J. E. Tilton, comp., *Sermons Preached in Boston on the death of Abraham Lincoln* (pp. 7–9). Boston: Tilton & Co.

Hall, D. D. (1977). The gravestone image as a Puritan cultural code. In P. Benes, ed., *Puritan gravestone art* (pp. 23–30). Boston: Boston University Press.

Haller, J. S., Jr. (1981). *American medicine in transition, 1840–1910*. Chicago: University of Illinois Press.

Halley, Rev. (1865). Rev. Dr. Halley's Prayer. In J. B. Cushman, comp., *Legislative honors to the memory of President Lincoln* (pp. 8–15). Albany, NY: Weed, Parsons & Co.

Halsted, B. D. (1880). *History of the Massachusetts Horticultural Society, 1829–1878*. Boston: Rand, Avery & Co.

Hamill, S. M. (1865). *President Lincoln, a faithful son: An address delivered before the high school, at Lawrenceville, NJ*. Trenton, NJ: Murphy & Bechtel.

Hanchett, W. (1983). *The Lincoln murder conspiracies*. Chicago: University of Illinois Press.

Hannon, T. J. (1989). Western Pennsylvania cemeteries in transition: A model for subregional analysis. In R. E. Meyer, ed., *Cemeteries and gravemarkers: Voices of American culture* (pp. 237–57). Ann Arbor: University of Michigan Research Press.

Harding, W. E. (1977). Zerubbabel Collins' successor and his work in Bennington County, Vermont. In P. Benes, ed., *Puritan gravestone art* (pp. 14–21). Boston: Boston University Press.

Harris, K. (1971). The political meaning of death: An existential overview. *Omega 2, 227–39.*

Harris, N. (1966). *The artist in American society: The formative years, 1790–1860.* NY: Braziller.

Havens, Mr. (1865). Remarks of Mr. Havens. In J. B. Cushman, comp., *Legislative honors to the memory of President Lincoln* (pp. 113–15). Albany, NY: Weed, Parsons, & Co.

Haynie, I. N., (1865). Resolutions [of the citizens of Illinois in Washington City]. In B. F. Morris, ed., *Memorial record of the nation's tribute to Abraham Lincoln* (pp. 136–37). Washington, D.C.: Morrison.

Heidegger, M. (1962). *Being and time.* J. Macquarrie and E. Robinson, trans. NY: Harper & Row.

Helm, K. (1923). *The true story of Mary, wife of Lincoln.* NY: Harper & Brothers.

Hepworth, G. H. (1865). Sermon. In J. E. Tilton, comp., *Sermons sreached in Boston on the death of Abraham Lincoln* (pp. 100–121). Boston: Tilton & Co.

Hinkel, J. V. (1967/1970). *Arlington: Monument to heroes.* Englewood Cliffs, NJ: Prentice-Hall.

*Historical sketch and matters appertaining to the Copp's Hill Burial-Ground.* (1901). Boston: Municipal Printing Office.

Holland, J. G. (1866). *The life of Abraham Lincoln.* Springfield, MA: Gurdon Bill.

Holmes, F. L. (1930). *Abraham Lincoln traveled this way.* Boston: Page & Co.

Hosley, W. N., Jr. (1978). The Rockingham stonecarvers: Patterns of stylistic concentration and diffusion in the Upper Connecticut River Valley, 1790–1817. In P. Benes, ed., *Puritan gravestone art II* (pp. 66–78). Boston: Boston University Press.

Howe, D. W. (1970). *The Unitarian conscience: Harvard moral philosophy, 1805–1861.* Cambridge: Harvard University Press.

Howett, C. (1977). Living landscapes for the dead. *Landscape 21,* 9–17.

Humphrey, E. P. (1848). *Address on the dedication of the Cave Hill*

*Cemetery near Louisville, July 25, 1848*. Louisville, KY: Courier Job Room.

Hunt, A. S. (1865). Sermon. In *Our martyr president, Abraham Lincoln* (pp. 317–28). NY: Tibbals & Whiting.

Huntington, F. D. (1865). Sermon. In J. E. Tilton, comp., *Sermons preached in Boston on the death of Abraham Lincoln* (pp. 193–96). Boston: Tilton & Co.

Huth, H. (1972; 1957). *Nature and the Americans: Three centuries of changing attitudes*. Lincoln: University of Nebraska Press.

Illowy, B. (1927). Abraham Lincoln. In E. Hertz, ed., *Abraham Lincoln: The tribute of the synagogue* (pp. 160–63). NY: Bloch.

Irion, P. E. (1954). *The funeral and the mourners*. Nashville: Abingdon.

Irion, P. E. (1966/1977). *The funeral: Vestige or value?* NY: Arno.

Isaacs, S. M. (1865). Prayer. In B. F. Morris, ed., *Memorial record of the nation's tribute to Abraham Lincoln* (pp. 176–78). Washington, DC: Morrison.

Isaacs, S. M. (1927). The President's Death. In E. Hertz, ed., *Abraham Lincoln: The tribute of the synagogue* (pp. 71–79). NY: Bloch.

Jackson, E. N. (1957). *Understanding grief: Its roots, dynamics, and treatment*. NY: Abingdon.

Jackson, E. N. (1959). Grief and religion. In H. Feifel, ed., *The meaning of death* (pp. 218–33). NY: McGraw-Hill.

Jackson, J. B. (1972). *American space: The centennial years, 1865–1876*. NY: Norton.

Jeane, D. G.. (1987). Rural southern gravestones: Sacred artifacts of the Upland South Folk cemetery. *Markers IV*, 55–84.

Jeane, D. G. (1989). The Upland South Folk cemetery complex: Some suggestions of origins. In R. E. Meyer, ed., *Cemeteries and gravemarkers: Voices of American culture* (p. 107–36). Ann Arbor: University of Michigan Research Press.

Joachimsen, P. J. (1927). An address delivered on request of the congregation, . . . at the place of worship of the Hebrew Association, Temimi Derech, at New Orleans, on Saturday, April 29th, 1865. In E. Hertz, ed., *Abraham Lincoln: The tribute of the synagogue* (pp. 29–38). NY: Bloch.

Johnson, A. (1865). A proclamation. In B. F. Morris, ed., *Memorial record of the nation's tribute to Abraham Lincoln* (pp. 261–62). Washington, DC: Morrison.

Jones, A. T. (1927). Eulogy on Abraham Lincoln. In E. Hertz, ed., *Abraham Lincoln: The tribute of the synagogue* (pp. 151–59). NY Bloch.

Jones, C. R. (1979/80). Ithamar Spauldin, stonecarver of Concord, Massachusetts, 1795–1800. *Markers I*, 51–55.

Jordan, T. G. (1982). *Texas graveyards: A cultural legacy*. Austin: University of Texas Press.

Jung, C. (1959). The soul and death. In H. Feifel, ed., *The meaning of death* (pp. 3–15). NY: McGraw-Hill.

Kallas, P. (1983). The carvers of Portage County, Wisconsin, 1850–1900. *Markers II*, 187–202.

Kammen, M. (1991). *Mystic chords of memory: The transformation of tradition in American culture*. NY: Knopf.

Kastenbaum, R. (1977). Death and development through the life-span. In H. Feifel, ed., *New meanings of death* (pp. 18–45). NY: McGraw-Hill.

Kastenbaum, R. and R. Miller (1972). *The psychology of death*. NY: Springer.

Keck, L. E. (1969). New Testament views of death. In L. O. Mills, ed., *Perspectives on death* (pp. 33–98). NY: Abingdon.

Kelly, S. and A. Williams (1983). 'And the men who made them': The signed gravestones of New England. *Markers II*, 1–103.

Kenny, D. J. (1875). *Illustrated Cincinnati: A pictorial hand-book of the Queen City*. Cincinnati: Clarke & Co.

Kett, J. F. (1968/1980). *The formation of the American medical profession: The role of institutions, 1790–1860*. Westport, CT: Greenwood.

King, M. (1883). *Mount Auburn cemetery, including also a brief history and description of Cambridge, Harvard University, and the Union Railway Company*. 19th ed. Cambridge: Moses King.

Kirk, E. N. (1865). Be still and know that I am God. In J.E. Tilton, comp., *Sermons preached in Boston on the death of Abraham Lincoln* (pp. 33–47). Boston: Tilton & Co.

Koestenbaum, P. (1964). The vitality of death. *The Journal of Existentialism 5*, 139–66.

Koestenbaum, P. (1971). *The vitality of death: Essays in existential psychology and philosophy*. Westport, CT: Greenwood.

Kolodny, A. (1975). *The lay of the land: Metaphor as experience and history in American life and letters*. Chapel Hill: University of North Carolina Press.

Kroeber, A. L. (1927). Disposal of the dead. *American Anthropologist 29*, 30–315.

Kruger-Kaholoula, A. (1989). Tributes in stone and lapidary lapses: Commemorating Black People in eighteenth- and nineteenth-century America. *Markers VI*, 33–100.

Krupat, A. (1992). *Ethnocriticism: Ethnography, history, literature*. Berkeley: University of California.

Kubler-Ross, E. (1969). *On death and dying*. NY: Macmillan.

Kubler-Ross, E. (1974). *Questions and answers on death and dying*. NY: Collier.

Kubler-Ross, E., ed. (1975). *Death: The final stage of growth*. Englewood Cliffs, NJ: Prentice-Hall.

Kunhardt, D. M. and P. B. Kunhardt, Jr. (1965/1985). *Twenty days: A narrative in text and pictures of the assassination of Abraham Lincoln and the twenty days and nights that followed—The nation in mourning, the long trip home to Springfield*. N. Hollywood, CA: Newcastle.

Lamm, M. (1969). *The Jewish way in death and mourning*. NY: Jonathan David.

Lamm, M. and N. Eskreis (1966). Viewing the remains: A new American custom. *Journal of Religion and Health 5*, 137–43.

Leeser, I. (1927). Lincoln's death. In E. Hertz, ed., *Abraham Lincoln: The tribute of the synagogue* (pp. 133–37). NY: Bloch.

Levine, G. S. (1978). Colonial Long Island grave stones: Trade network indicators, 1670–1799. In P. Benes, ed., *Puritan grave-stone art II* (pp. 46–57). Boston: Boston University Press.

Lilienthal, M. (1927a). The assassination of Lincoln. In E. Hertz, ed., *Abraham Lincoln: The tribute of the synagogue* (pp. 110–21). NY: Bloch.

Lilienthal, M. (1927b). Lincoln—An appreciation. In E. Hertz, ed., *Abraham Lincoln: The tribute of the synagogue* (pp. 122–32). NY: Bloch.

Lincoln, L. (1838). *An address delivered on the consecration of the Worcester rural cemetery, September 8, 1838.* Boston: Dutton & Wentworth.

Lindemann, E. (1944/1977). Symptomatology and the management of acute grief. In A. Wilcox and M. Sutton, eds., *Understanding death and dying: An interdisciplinary approach* (pp. 166–81). Dominguez Hills, CA: Alfred.

Linden, B. M. G. (1979/80). The willow tree and urn motif: Changing ideas about death and nature. *Markers I,* 149–55.

Linden-Ward, B. (1986). Putting the past under grass: History as death and commemoration. *Prospects 10,* 279–313.

Linden-Ward, B. (1989a). *Silent city on a hill: Landscapes of memory and Boston's Mount Auburn Cemetery.* Columbus: Ohio State University Press.

Linden-Ward, B. (1989b). Strange but genteel pleasure grounds: Tourist and leisure uses of nineteenth-century cemeteries. In R. E. Meyer, ed., *Cemeteries and gravemarkers: Voices of American culture* (pp. 293–328). Ann Arbor: University of Michigan Research Press.

Linden-Ward, B. (1990). 'The fencing mania': The rise and fall of nineteenth-century funerary enclosures. *Markers VII,* 35–58.

Little, M. R. (1989). Afro-American Gravemarkers in North Carolina. *Markers IV,* 103–34.

Littlejohn, A. N. (1865). Sermon. In *Our martyr president, Abraham Lincoln* (pp. 145–58). NY: Tibbals & Whiting.

Lothrop, S. K. (1865). Sermon. In J. E. Tilton, comp., *Sermons preached in Boston on the death of Abraham Lincoln* (pp. 245–63). Boston: Tilton & Co.

Low, Mr. (1865). Remarks of Mr. Low. In J. B. Cushman, comp., *Legislative honors to the memory of President Lincoln* (pp. 104–7). Albany, NY: Weed, Parsons & Co.

Lowenfels, W., ed. (1960). *Walt Whitman's Civil War.* NY: Knopf.

Lowry, R. (1865). Sermon. In *Our martyr President, Abraham Lincoln* (pp. 303-15). NY: Tibbals & Whiting.

Lucas, J. (1990). Stonecarvers of Monroe County, Indiana, 1827-1890. *Markers VII,* 195-212.

Ludwig, A. I. (1966). *Graven images: New England stonecarving and its images, 1650-1815.* Middletown, CT: Wesleyan University Press.

Ludwig, A. I. (1977). Eros and agape: Classical and early Christian survivals in New England stonecarving (pp. 41-56). In P. Benes, ed., *Puritan gravestone art.* Boston: Boston University Press.

Ludwig, A. I. and D. D. Hall (1978). Aspects of music, poetry, stonecarving, and death in early New England (pp. 18-24). In P. Benes, ed., *Puritan gravestone art II.* Boston: Boston University Press.

Luti, V. F. (1983). Stonecarvers of the Narragansett Basin: Stephen and Charles Hartshorne of Providence. *Markers, II,* 149-69.

McCarthy, J. B. (1979). *Fearful living: The fear of death.* NY: Irvington.

McCarthy, J. B. (1980). *Death anxiety: The loss of self.* NY: Halsted.

M'Clintock, J. (1865). Sermon. In *Our martyr President, Abraham Lincoln* (pp. 129-44). NY: Tibbals & Whiting.

McCloskey, J. (1865a). Sermon. In J. G. Shea, ed., *The Lincoln memorial: A record of the life, assassination and obsequies of the martyred President* (pp. 99-101). NY: Bunce & Huntington.

McCloskey, J. (1865b). Letter. In J. G. Shea, ed., *The Lincoln memorial: A record of the life, assassination and obsequies of the martyred President* (pp. 143-44). NY: Bunce & Huntington.

McDannell, C. (1987). The religious symbolism of Laurel Hill Cemetery. *The Pennsylvania Magazine of History and Biography, 111,* 275-303.

MacDonald, E. (1885). *Old Copp's Hill and burial ground; with historical sketches.* Boston: Park.

McDowell, P. (1989). J. N. B. de Pouilly and French sources of revival style design in New Orleans cemetery architecture (pp. 137–58). In R. E. Meyer, ed., *Cemeteries and gravemarkers: Voices of American culture.* Ann Arbor: University of Michigan Research Press.

McGrath, R. L. (1987). Death Italo-American style: Reflections on modern martyrdom. *Markers IV,* 107–13.

McIlvaine, C. P. (1865). Burial service of the Episcopal church. In B. F. Morris, ed., *Memorial record of the nation's tribute to Abraham Lincoln.* Washington, DC: Morrison.

McNickle, D. (1973). *Native American tribalism: Indian survivals and renewals.* NY: Oxford University Press.

MacIntyre, A. (1981). *After Virtue.* Notre Dame: University of Notre Dame Press.

Mack, A., ed. (1973). *Death in American experience.* NY: Schocken.

Mandelbaum, D. (1959). Social uses of funeral rites. In H. Feifel, ed., *The meaning of death* (pp. 187–217). NY: McGraw-Hill.

Manning J. M. (1865). Sermon. In J. E. Tilton, comp., *Sermons preached in Boston on the death of Abraham Lincoln* (pp. 59–72). Boston: Tilton & Co.

Manning, R. (1880). *History of the Massachusetts horticultural society.* Boston: Rand, Avery & Co.

Marcuse, H. (1959). The ideology of death. In H. Feifel, ed., *The meaning of death* (pp. 64–76). NY: McGraw-Hill.

Marsden, G. M. (1970). *The evangelical mind and the new school Presbyterian experience: A case study of thought and theology in nineteenth-century America.* New Haven: Yale University Press.

Marshall, H. (1855). Address of Col. Marshall upon the life and character of Capt. Ballard. *Obituary addresses delivered upon the occasion of the re-interment of the remains of Gen. Chas. Scott, Maj. Wm. T. Barry, and Capt. Bland Ballard and wife, in the cemetery of Frankfort, November 8, 1854* (pp. 43–54). Frankfort, KY: Hodges.

Massachusetts Medical Society. (1831). Address to the community on the necessity of legalizing the study of anatomy. *North American review 32,* 64–73.

Mather, C. (ND). *Essays to do good; addressed to all Christians, whether in public or private capacities.* NY: American Tract Society.

Mather, C. (1693). *Wonders of the invisible world: Being an account of the tryals of several witches, lately executed in New-England.* London: Dunton.

Mather, C. (1970). *Days of humiliation, times of affliction and disaster: Nine sermons for restoring favor with an angry God, 1696–1727.* Gainsville, FL: Scholar's Facsimiles & Reprints.

May, W. F. (1969). The sacral power of death in contemporary experience. In L. O. Mills, ed., *Perspectives on death* (pp. 168–96). NY: Abingdon.

May, W. F. (1973). The sacral power of death in contemporary experience. In A. Mack, ed., *Death in American experience* (pp. 97–122). NY: Schocken.

Mayer, L. R. (1978). An alternative to Panofskyism: New England grave stones and the European folk art tradition. In P. Benes, ed., *Puritan gravestone art II* (pp. 5–17). Boston: Boston University Press.

Mead, S. E. (1963). *The lively experiment: The shaping of Christianity in America.* NY: Harper & Row.

Meyer, R. E., ed. (1989a). *Cemeteries and gravemarkers: Voices of American culture.* Ann Arbor: University of Michigan Research Press.

Meyer, R. E., ed. (1989b). Introduction. In R. E. Meyer, ed., *Cemeteries and gravemarkers: Voices of American culture* (pp. 1–6). Ann Arbor: University of Michigan Research Press.

Meyer, R. E., ed. (1989c). Images of logging on contemporary Pacific Northwest gravemarkers. In R. E. Meyer, ed., *Cemeteries and gravemarkers: Voices of American culture* (pp. 61–85). Ann Arbor: University of Michigan Research Press.

Meyer, R. E., ed. (1989d). Origins and influences. In R. E. Meyer, ed., *Cemeteries and gravemarkers: Voices of American culture* (p. 105). Ann Arbor: University of Michigan Research Press.

Midgley. R. L.(1856). *Sights in Boston and suburbs, or guide to the stranger.* Boston: Jewett & Co.

Miller, P. P., ed. (1992). *Reclaiming the past: Landmarks of Women's history.* Bloomington: Indiana University Press.

Mills, L. O., ed. (1969). *Perspectives on death.* NY: Abingdon.

Milmoe, J. (1979/80). Colorado wooden markers. *Markers I,* 57-61.

Miner, A. A. (1865). Sermon. In J. E. Tilton, comp., *Sermons preached in Boston on the death of Abraham Lincoln* (pp. 279-91). Boston: Tilton & Co.

Mitford, J. (1963). *The American way of death.* NY: Simon & Schuster.

Morais, S. (1927a). An address on the death of Abraham Lincoln, President of the United States, delivered before the congregation Mikve Israel of Philadelphia, . . . on Wednesday, April 19th, 1865. In E. Hertz, ed., *Abraham Lincoln: The tribute of the synagogue* (pp. 1-6). NY: Bloch.

Morais, S. (1927b). A discourse delivered before the Congregation Mikve Israel of Philadelphia, at their synagogue in Seventh Street on Thursday, June 1, 1865. . . . In E. Hertz, ed., *Abraham Lincoln: The tribute of the synagogue* (pp. 7-12). NY: Bloch.

Morford, H. (1865). Poem. In J. G. Shea, ed., *The Lincoln memorial: A record of the life, assassination and obsequies of the martyred president* (p. 110). NY: Bunce & Huntington.

Morgan, E. (1980). *A manual of death education and simple burial.* Burnsville, NC: Celo.

Morgan, F. H., J. C. Tasker, and W. H. H. Allen (1865). Resolutions [of the citizens of New Hampshire in Washington City]. In B. F. Morris, ed., *Memorial record of the nation's tribute to Abraham Lincoln* (pp. 123-25). Washington, DC: Morrison.

Morgan, W. F. (1865a). Joy darkened: Sermon preached in St. Thomas' Church, New York, Easter Sunday morning, April 16th, 1865. *In memoriam* (pp 7-22). [NY: Baker & Godwin].

Morgan, W. F. (1865b). Address. *In memoriam* (pp. 27–31). [NY: Baker & Godwin].

Morgan, W. F. (1865c). The prolonged lament: Sermon preached in St. Thomas' Church, New York, on the 1st Sunday after Easter, April 23d, 1865. *In Memoriam* (pp. 35–47). [NY: Baker & Godwin].

Morgenthau, H. J. (1961). Death in the nuclear age. *Commentary 32,* 231–34.

Morris, B. F., ed. (1865). *Memorial record of the nation's tribute to Abraham Lincoln.* Washington, DC: Morrison.

Morris, R. (1985). The Vietnam Veterans Memorial as cultural institution. Paper presented to the Eastern Communication Association Convention. Providence, RI.

Morris, R. (1986a). Memorializing among Americans: The case of Lincoln's assassination. Diss. University of Wisconsin.

Morris, R. (1986b). The Vietnam Veterans Memorial: A study in cultural conflict and resolution. Paper presented to the Conference on the cultural legacy of Vietnam. New Brunswick, NJ.

Morris, R. (1987). Memorializing among Americans. Paper presented to the International Society for the History of Rhetoric, American Branch. Boston, MA.

Morris, R. (1990). The Vietnam Veterans Memorial and the myth of superiority. In R. Morris and P. Ehrenhaus, eds., *Cultural legacies of Vietnam: Uses of the past in the present* (pp. 199–222). Norwood, NJ: Ablex.

Morris, R. (1995). Sinners, lovers, and heroes: A rhetorical ethnology of memorializing in three American cultures. Paper presented to the Western States Communication Association. Portland, OR.

Morton, O. H. P. (1865). Letter to the citizens of Indiana. In B. F. Morris, ed., *Memorial record of the nation's tribute to Abraham Lincoln* (p. 135). Washington, DC: Morrison.

Murphy, H. C. (1865). Remarks of Mr. Murphy. In J. B. Cushman, comp., *Legislative honors to the memory of President Lincoln* (pp. 80–84). Albany, NY: Weed, Parsons & Co.

Myer, I. S. (1927). The President's death. In E. Hertz, ed., *Abraham Lincoln: The tribute of the synagogue* (pp. 71–77). NY: Bloch.

Natanson, M. (1966). Death and mundanity. *Omega, 1,* 20–22.

Neale, R. H. (1865). Sermon. In J. E. Tilton, comp., *Sermons preached in Boston on the death of Abraham Lincoln* (pp. 163–75). Boston: Tilton & Co.

Nerone, J. (1989). Professional history and social memory. *Communication 11,* 89–104.

Nicholson, W. R. (1865). Address. In J. E. Tilton, comp., *Sermons preached in Boston on the death of Abraham Lincoln* (pp. 125–26). Boston: Tilton & Co.

Nicolay, J. G. and J. Hay. (1890). *Abraham Lincoln: A history.* NY: Century.

Norris, D. A. (1988). Ontario gravestones. *Markers V,* 122–49.

Nye, R. B. (1974). *Society and culture in America, 1830–1860.* NY: Harper & Row.

O'Hara, T. (1855). Address of Col. O'Hara upon the life and character of Hon. W. T. Barry. In *Obituary addresses delivered upon the occasion of the re-interment of the remains of Gen. Chas. Scott, Maj. Wm. T. Barry, and Capt. Bland Ballard and wife, in the cemetery at Frankfort, November 8, 1854* (pp. 23–42). Frankfort, KY: Hodges.

*Old Copp's Hill and Burial Ground; with historical sketches.* (1885). Boston: Benjamin Parks.

Oring, E. (1982). Forest Lawn and the iconography of American death. *Southwest Folklore 6,* 62–72.

Osler, W. (1904). *Science and immortality.* NY: Houghton-Mifflin.

Parker, G. T., ed. (1972). *The oven birds: American women on womanhood, 1820–1920.* NY: Anchor.

Parker, G. T. (1973). *Mind cure in New England: From the Civil War to World War I.* Hanover: University of New England Press.

Patterson, N. (1989). United above though parted below: The hand as symbol on nineteenth-century Southwest Ontario gravestones. *Markers VI,* 181–206.

Peabody, W. B. O. (1831). Mount Auburn cemetery. *North American Review 33,* 397–406.

Perelman, C. and L. Olbrechts-Tyteca. (1971). *The New Rhetoric.* Trans. Wilkinson and Weaver. Notre Dame University Press.

Perkins, F. B. (1871). Sepulture, its ideas and practices. *The Galaxy XI* (June): 840–51.

Peterson, M. (1994). *Lincoln in American memory.* NY: Oxford.

Philipson, D. (1915). *Max Lilienthal, American Rabbi: Life and writings.* NY: Bloch.

*Picturesque pocket companion and visitor's guide through Mt. Auburn.* (1829). Boston: n.p.

Pierce, F. (1865). Speech of ex-President Pierce. In. J. G. Shea, ed., *The Lincoln memorial: A record of the life, assassination and obsequies of the martyred President* (pp. 86–87). NY: Bunce & Huntington.

Pierpont, J. (1841). *The garden of graves.* Dedham, MA: Mann.

Pine, V. (1975). *Caretaker of the dead.* NY: Irvington.

Pine, V. et al., eds. (1976). *Acute grief and the funeral.* Springfield, IL: Thomas.

Pine, V. and D. L. Phillips (1970). The cost of dying: A sociological analysis of funeral expenditures. *Social Problems 17,* 405–17.

Pitman, B. (1865). *The assassination of President Lincoln and the trial of the conspirators.* NY: Moore, Wilstach & Baldwin.

Pitts, Mr. (1865). Remarks of Mr. Pitts. In J. B. Cushman, comp., *Legislative honors to the memory of President Lincoln* (pp. 46–51). Albany, NY: Weed, Parsons.

Poor, B. P., I. E. Farbank and G. White (1865). Resolutions [of the citizens of Massachusetts in Washington City]. In B. F. Morris, ed., *Memorial record of the nation's tribute to Abraham Lincoln* (pp. 125–26). Washington, DC: Morrison.

Porter, E. S. (1865). Sermon. In *Our martyr President, Abraham Lincoln* (pp. 233–40). NY: Tibbals & Whiting.

Post, T. M. (1856). *The skeptical era in modern history; or, the infidelity of the eighteenth century, the product of spiritual despotism.* NY: Scribner.

Potter, H. (1865). [Letter] To the clergy and laity of the diocese of New York. In J. G. Shea, ed., *The Lincoln memorial: A record of the life, assassination and obsequies of the martyred President* (pp. 141–42). NY: Bunce & Huntington.

Potter, D. M. (1976). *The impending crisis, 1848–1861.* NY: Harper & Row.

Powell, L. W. (1855). Gov. Powell's introductory address. *Obituary addresses delivered upon the occasion of the re-interment of the remains of Gen. Chas. Scott, Maj. Wm. T. Barry, and Capt. Bland Ballard and wife, in the cemetery at Frankfort, November 8, 1854* (pp. 7–10). Frankfort, KY: Hodges.

Prefatory. (1865). Sermon. In *Our martyr president, Abraham Lincoln* (pp.vii–viii). NY: Tibbals & Whiting, 1865.

Prestiano, R. (1983). The example of D. Aldo Pitassi: Evolutionary thought and practice in contemporary memorial design. *Markers II,* 203–20.

Puckle, B. S. (1926). *Funeral customs: Their origin and development.* NY: Stokes.

Putnam, G. (1865). Address. In J. E. Tilton, comp., *Sermons preached in Boston on the death of Abraham Lincoln* (pp. 309–21). Boston: Tilton & Co.

Raether, H. C. (1971). The place of the funeral director in contemporary America. *Omega 2,* 136144.

Raether, H. C. and R. C. Slater (1974). *The funeral: Facing death as an experience of life.* Milwaukee: National Funeral Directors Association.

Raether, H. C. and R. C. Slater (1977). Immediate post-death activities in the United States. In H. Feifel, ed., *New meanings of death* (pp. 234–48). NY: McGraw-Hill.

Rakoff, V. M. (1973). Psychiatric aspects of death in America. In A. Mack, ed., *Death in American experience* (pp. 149–61). NY: Schocken.

Randall, R. P. (1953). *Mary Lincoln: Biography of a marriage.* Boston: Little, Brown & Co.

Raphall, M. J. (1927). Abraham Lincoln. In E. Hertz, ed., *Abraham Lincoln: The tribute of the synagogue* (pp. 169–72). NY: Bloch.

Rathbone, H. (1865). Testimony of Major Rathbone. In J. G. Shea, comp., *The Lincoln memorial: A record of the life, assassination and obsequies of the martyred president* (pp. 62-63). NY: Bunce & Huntington.

Raymond, H. J. (1865). *The life and public services of Abraham Lincoln.* NY: Derby & Miller.

Redington, Mr. (1865). Remarks of Mr. Redington. In J. B Cushman, comp., *Legislative honors to the memory of President Lincoln* (pp. 25-30). Albany, NY: Weed, Parsons & Co.

Reed, J. (1865). Address. In J. E. Tilton, comp., *Sermons preached in Boston on the death of Abraham Lincoln* (pp. 295-305). Boston: Tilton & Co.

Richardson, J. B. III and R. C. Carlisle (1979/80). The archaeological significance of mausoleums in the Allegheny and Homewood cemeteries of Pittsburgh: A preliminary statement. *Markers I,* 157-65.

Robbins, C. (1865). Sermon. In J. E. Tilton, comp., *Sermons preached in Boston on the death of Abraham Lincoln* (pp. 215-23). Boston: Tilton & Co.

Robbins, T. (1886). *Diary of Thomas Robbins, D.D., 1796-1854.* 2 vols. Ed. I. N. Tarbox. Boston: Beacon.

Roberts, W. E. (1990). Notes on the production of rustic monuments in the limestone belt of Indiana. *Markers VII,* 173-93.

Robinson, C. S. (1865). Sermon. In *Our martyr President, Abraham Lincoln* (pp. 85-109). NY: Tibbals & Whiting.

Rockwell, J. E. (1865). Sermon. In *Our martyr President, Abraham Lincoln* (pp. 273-87). NY: Tibbals & Whiting.

Rogers, A. P. (1865). Sermon. In *Our martyr President, Abraham Lincoln* (pp. 241-54). NY: Tibbals & Whiting.

Rogers, E. P. (1865). Prayer. In *Our martyr President, Abraham Lincoln* (pp. 473-76). NY: Tibbals & Whiting.

Rosenberg, C. E. (1962/1974). *The cholera years: The United States in 1832, 1849, and 1866.* Chicago: University of Chicago Press.

Rosenberg, C. E. (1976). *No other gods: On science and American social thought.* Baltimore: Johns Hopkins University Press.

Ross, I. (1973). *The President's wife, Mary Todd Lincoln: A biography.* NY: Putnam.

Rothstein, W. G. (1972). *American physicians in the nineteenth century: From sects to science.* Baltimore: Johns Hopkins University Press.

Rotunda, B. (1973). The rural cemetery movement. *Essex institute historical collections 109,* 231–40.

Rotunda, B. (1989). Monumental bronze: A representative American company. In R. E. Meyer, ed., *Cemeteries and gravemarkers: Voices of American culture* (pp. 263–91). Ann Arbor: University of Michigan Research Press.

Sample, R. F. (1865). *The curtained throne: A sermon, suggested by the death of President Lincoln, preached in the Presbyterian church of Bedford, Pa., April 23, 1865, and repeated April 30, 1865.* Philadelphia: Claxton.

Sanborn, L. S. (1989). Compasantos: Sacred places of the Southwest. *Markers VI,* 159–79.

Sandburg, C. (1960). The most enduring memorial to Lincoln. In R. G. Newman, ed., *Lincoln for the ages* (pp. 33–35). NY: Doubleday. [Reprint of the Sesquicentennial Tribute before the Joint Session of the Congress of the United States. February 12, 1959.]

Sandburg, C. and P. M. Angle (1932/1960). *Mary Lincoln: Wife and widow.* NY: Harcourt, Brace & World.

Sargent, N. (1865). Resolutions [of the Levy Court of the county of Washington]. In B. F. Morris, ed., *Memorial record of the nation's tribute to Abraham Lincoln* (pp. 147–48). Washington, DC: Morrison.

Saum, L. O. (1975). Death in the popular mind of pre-Civil War America. In D. E. Stannard, ed., *Death in America* (pp. 30–48). Philadelphia: University of Pennsylvania Press.

Scharf, F. A. (1961). The garden cemetery and American sculpture. *Art Quarterly 24,* 88–92.

Schwartz, B. (1990). The reconstruction of Abraham Lincoln. In D. Middleton and D. Edwards, eds., *Collective remembering* (pp. 81–107). London: Sage.

Schlesinger, M. (1927). Abraham Lincoln. In E. Hertz, ed., *Abraham Lincoln: The tribute of the synagogue* (pp. 106–9). NY: Bloch.

Scott, D. M. (1978). *From office to profession: The New England ministry, 1750–1850.* Philadelphia: University of Pennsylvania Press.

Scudder, J. M. (1879). A brief history of eclectic medicine. *Eclectic Medical Journal 39*, 295–318.

Segal, R. A. (1990). Introduction: In quest of the hero. In R. A. Segal, *In quest of the hero.* Princeton University Press.

Sewall, S. (1967). *The diary of Samuel Sewall.* Ed. Harvey Wish. NY: Putnam's Sons.

Shea, J. G., ed. (1865). *The Lincoln memorial: A record of the life, assassination and obsequies of the martyred President.* NY: Bunce & Huntington.

Shepard, Mr. (1865). Remarks of Mr. Shepard. In J. B. Cushman, comp., *Legislative honors to the memory of President Lincoln* (pp. 56–58). Albany, NY: Weed, Parsons & Co.

Sheskin, A. and S. Wallace (1976). Differing bereavements: Suicide, natural, and accidental death. *Omega 7*, 229–42.

Shudson, M. (1989). The present in the past versus the past in the present. *Communication 11*, 105–13.

Simons, B. G. (1979). *A time to grieve.* NY: Irvington.

Simpson, M. (1865a). Funeral oration. In J. G. Shea, ed., *The Lincoln memorial: A record of the life, assassination and obsequies of the martyred President* (pp. 229–39). NY: Bunce & Huntington.

Simpson, M. (1865b). Prayer. In J. E. Tilton, comp., *Sermons preached in Boston on the death of Abraham Lincoln* (pp. 9–16). Boston: Tilton and Co.

Slater, J. (1977). Principles and methods for the work of individual carvers. In P. Benes, ed., *Puritan gravestone art* (pp. 9–13). Boston: Boston University Press.

Slater, J., R. L. Tucker, and D. Farmber (1978). The colonial gravestone carvings of John Hartshorne. In P. Benes, ed., *Puritan gravestone art II* (pp. 79–146). Boston: Boston University Press.

Smart, N. (1968a). Death in the Judaeo-Christian tradition. In A. Toynbee et al., *Man's concern with death* (pp. 116–21). London: Hodder & Stoughton.

Smart, N. (1968b). Death and the decline of religion in Western society. In A. Toynbee et al., *Man's concern with death* (pp. 138–44). London: Hodder & Stoughton.

Smith, A. E. (1901). *Historical sketch and matters appertaining to the Copp's Hill burial-ground.* Boston: Municipal Printing Office.

Smith, D. (1987). 'Safe in the arms of Jesus': Consolation on Delaware children's gravestones, 1840-99. *Markers IV,* 85–106.

Smith, H. S., R. T. Handy and L. A. Loetscher (1960). *American Christianity: An historical interpretation with representative documents, Vol. I, 1607-1820.* NY: Scribner.

Smith, H. B. (1865). Sermon. In *Our martyr President, Abraham Lincoln* (pp. 359–81). NY: Tibbals & Whiting.

Smith, H. N., ed. (1967). *Popular culture and industrialism, 1865-1890.* NY: New York University Press.

Smith, H. N. (1971; 1950). *Virgin land: The American west as symbol and myth.* Cambridge: Harvard University Press.

Snyder, E. M. (1989). Innocents in a worldly world: Victorian children's gravemarkers. In R. E. Meyer, ed., *Cemeteries and gravemarkers: Voices of American culture* (pp. 11–29). Ann Arbor: University of Michigan Research Press.

Somkin, F. (1967). *Unquiet eagle: Memory and desire in the idea of American freedom, 1815-1860.* Ithaca: Cornell University Press.

Spalding, M. J. (1865). Letter. In J. G. Shea, ed., *The Lincoln memorial: A record of the life, assassination and obsequies of the martyred President* (p. 143). NY: Bunce & Huntington.

Spear, S. T. (1865). Sermon. In *Our Martyr President, Abraham Lincoln* (pp. 289–301). NY: Tibbals & Whiting.

Sprague, W. B. (1832). *Lectures on revivals of religion.* Albany, NY: Webster & Skinners.

Sprague, W. B., comp. (1857/1869). *Annals of the American pulpit.* 8 vols. NY: Carter.

Sprague, W. B. (1865). Rev. Dr. Sprague's Prayer. In J. B. Cushman, comp., *Legislative honors to the memory of President Lincoln* (pp. 67–71). Albany, NY: Weed, Parsons & Co.

Stamp, K. M. (1956). *The peculiar institution: Slavery in the ante-Bellum South.* NY: Vintage.

Stannard, D. E. (1975a). Death and the Puritan child. In D. E. Stannard, ed., *Death in America* (pp. 9–29). Philadelphia: University of Pennsylvania Press.

Stannard, D. E., ed. (1975b). *Death in America.* Philadelphia: University of Pennsylvania Press.

Stannard, D. E. (1977). *The Puritan way of death.* NY: Oxford University Press.

Steele, R. H. (1865). *Victory and mourning: A sermon occasioned by the death of Abraham Lincoln, late President of the United States; preached in the First Reformed Dutch Church, New-Brunswick, N.J., June 1st, 1865.* New Brunswick, NJ: Terhune & Van Anglen.

Stevenson, J. E. (1865). Address. In B. F. Morris, ed., *Memorial record of the nation's tribute to Abraham Lincoln* (pp. 191–93). Washington, DC: Morrison.

Stewart, C. A. and W. H. Wormley (1865). Resolutions [of the Colored Citizens in Washington City]. In B. F. Morris, ed., *Memorial record of the nation's tribute to Abraham Lincoln* (pp. 153–54). Washington, DC: Morrison.

Stewart, C. J. (1963). A rhetorical study of the reaction of the Protestant pulpit in the North to Lincoln's assassination. Diss. University of Illinois.

Stewart, C. J. (1964). The pulpit and the assassination of Lincoln. *Quarterly Journal of Speech 50,* 299–307.

Stewart, C. J. (1965). The pulpit in time of crisis: 1865 and 1963. *Communication Monographs 32,* 427–34.

Stoddard, R. H. (1865). Abraham Lincoln—An Horatian ode. In J. G. Shea, ed., *The Lincoln memorial: A record of the life, assassination and obsequies of the martyred President* (pp. 273–78). NY: Bunce & Huntington.

Stone, A. L. (1865). Sermon. In J. E. Tilton, comp., *Sermons preached in Boston on the death of Abraham Lincoln* (pp. 337–55). Boston: Tilton & Co.

Stone, W. M. (1865). Letter to the people of Iowa. In B. F. Morris, ed., *Memorial record of the nation's tribute to Abraham Lincoln* (p. 138). Washington, DC: Morrison.

Storrs, R. S. (1865). Oration. In *Our martyr President, Abraham Lincoln* (pp. 411–65). NY: Tibbals & Whiting.

Story, J. (1859a). An address delivered on the dedication of the cemetery at Mount Auburn, September 24th, 1831. In Jacob Bigelow, *A history of the cemetery of Mount Auburn* (pp. 143–67). Boston: Munroe & Co.

Story, J. (1859b). Report of the garden and cemetery committee of the Massachusetts horticultural society, at a meeting held on Saturday, September 17, 1834. In Jacob Bigelow, *A history of the cemetery of Mount Auburn* (pp. 196–203). Boston: Munroe & Co.

Strauch, A. (1869). *Spring Grove cemetery: Its history and improvements, with observations on ancient and modern places of sepulture.* Cincinnati: Clarke & Co.

Strong, Mr. (1865). Remarks of Mr. Strong. In J. B. Cushman, comp., *Legislative honors to the memory of President Lincoln* (p. 116). Albany, NY: Weed, Parsons & Co.

Studley, W. S. (1865). Sermon. In J. E. Tilton, comp., *Sermons preached in Boston on the death of Abraham Lincoln* (pp. 227–32). Boston: Tilton & Co.

Sudnow, D. (1967). *Passing on: The social organization of dying.* Engewood Cliffs, NJ: Prentice-Hall.

Sweeney, K. M. (1985). Where the bay meets the river: Gravestones and stonecutters in the river towns of Western Massachusetts, 1690–1810. *Markers III,* 1–46.

Sweet, G. (1945). Iron island: Burial plot enclosures of Edgartown, Martha's Vineyard. *Magazine of Art 38,* 89–91.

Takaki, R. (1993). *A different mirror: A history of multicultural America.* NY: Little, Brown & Co.

Tashjian, A. and D. Tashjian. (1989). The Afro-American section of Newport, Rhode Island's common burying ground." In R.E. Meyer, ed., *Cemeteries and gravemarkers: Voices of American culture* (pp. 164-96). Ann Arbor: University of Michigan Research Press.

Tashjian, D. (1978). Puritan attitudes toward iconoclasm. In P. Benes, ed., *Puritan gravestone art II* (pp. 37-45). Boston: Boston University Press.

Tashjian, D. and A. Tashjian (1974). *Memorials for children of change: The art of early New England stone carving.* Middleton, CT: Wesleyan University Press.

Tatum, G. B. (1951). The beautiful and the picturesque. *American Quarterly 3,* 36-51.

Tatum, G B. (1974). "New introduction." In G.W. Curtis, ed., *Rural essays by Andrew Jackson Downing.* New York: Da Capo.

Temes, R. (1980). *Living with an empty chair.* NY: Irvington.

Thomas, J. W. and R. A. Dixon (1973). Cemetery ecology. *Natural history 82,* 60-67.

Thompson, J. P. (1865). Sermon. In *Our martyr President, Abraham Lincoln* (pp. 173-217). NY: Tibbals & Whiting.

Thoreau, H. D. (1906). *A week on the Concord and Merrimack rivers.* Boston: Houghton-Mifflin.

Tillich, P. (1959). The eternal now. In H. Feifel, ed., *The meaning of death* (pp. 30-38). NY: McGraw-Hill.

Todd, John E. (1865). President Lincoln. In J.E. Tilton, comp., *Sermons preached in Boston on the death of Abraham Lincoln* (pp. 75-87). Boston: Tilton & Co.

Toynbee, A. J. (1968a). Changing attitudes towards death in the modern world. In A. Toynbee et al., eds., *Man's concern with death* (pp. 122-33). London: Hodder & Stoughton, 1968.

Toynbee, A. J. (1968b). Death in war. In A. Toynbee et al., eds., *Man's concern with death* (pp. 145-52). London: Hodder & Stoughton.

Trask, D. (1978). 'J.W.' Folk carver of Hants County, Nova Scotia. In P. Benes, ed., *Puritan gravestone art II* (pp. 58-65). Boston: Boston University Press.

Tucker, B. (1948). *Address of Beverley Tucker, Esq., to the people of the United States, with appendix relating to President Johnson's proclamation of 2nd May, 1865.* Atlanta, GA: Emory University Press.

Tuckerman, H. T.(1865). Poem. In J. G. Shea, ed., *The Lincoln memorial: A record of the life, assassination and obsequies of the martyred President* (p. 162). NY: Bunce & Huntington.

Turner, J. and L. L. Turner (1972). *Mary Todd Lincoln: Her life and letters.* NY: Knopf.

Turner, T. R. (1982). *Beware the People Weeping: Public Opinion and the Assassination of Abraham Lincoln.* Baton Rouge: Louisiana State University Press.

Tyng, S. H. (1865a). Prayer. In *Our martyr President, Abraham Lincoln* (467–71). NY: Tibbals & Whiting.

Tyng, S. H. (1865b). Sermon. In *Our martyr President, Abraham Lincoln* (pp. 65–84). NY: Tibbals & Whiting.

Tyng, S. H. (1881). Life-assurance does assure. *Harper's Monthly 62* (April): 754–59.

Tyng, S. H. (1893). Modern insurance and its possibilities. *North American Review 156* (March): 303–4.

U.S. Department of Health, Education, and Welfare. (1970). *Facts of life and death.* Washington, DC: GPO, PHS Publication No. 600.

Van Buren, T. B. (1865). Remarks of Mr. Van Buren. In J. B. Cushman, comp., *Legislative honors to the memory of President Lincoln* (pp. 17–21). Albany, NY: Weed, Parsons & Co.

Vermeul, E. (1981). *Aspects of death in early Greek art and poetry.* Berkeley: University of California Press.

Vernon, G. M. (1970). *Sociology of death: An analysis of death-related behavior.* NY: Ronald.

Vidaver, H. (1927). Discourse. In E. Hertz, ed., *Abraham Lincoln: The tribute of the synagogue* (pp. 48–55). NY: Bloch.

Vidutis, R. and V. A. P. Lowe. The cemetery as a cultural text. *Kentucky Folklore Record 26:* 103–113.

Vinovskis, M. A. (1973). Angel's heads and weeping willows: Death in early America. In M. Gordon, ed., *The American family in social historical perspective*. NY: St. Martin's.

Wakeley, J. B. (1856). *The heroes of Methodism, containing sketches of eminent Methodist ministers and characteristic anecdotes of their personal history*. NY: Carlton & Phillips.

Waldo, O.H., et al. (1865). Resolutions [of the citizens of Wisconsin in Washington City]. In B. F. Morris (Ed.), *Memorial record of the nation's tribute to Abraham Lincoln* (pp. 139140). Washington, DC: Morrison.

Walsh, E. R. (1975). Cemeteries: Recreation's new space frontier. *Parks and recreation 10*, 28-29, 53-54.

Walter, C. W. (1850). *Mount Auburn illustrated*. NY: Martin.

Warner, W. L. (1959). *The living and the dead: A study of the symbolic life of Americans*. New Haven: Yale University Press.

Warren, N. H. (1987). New Mexico village camposantos. *Markers IV*, 115-29.

Watters, D. H. (1979/80). Gravestones and historical archaeology: A review essay. *Markers I*, 174-79.

Watters, D. H. (1983). The JN Carver. *Markers II*, 115-31.

Weaver, Mr. (1865). Remarks of Mr. Weaver. In J. B. Cushman, comp., *Legislative honors to the memory of President Lincoln* (pp. 21-25). Albany, NY: Weed, Parsons & Co.

Webb, E. B. (1865). Sermon. In J. E. Tilton, comp., *Sermons preached in Boston on the death of Abraham Lincoln* (pp. 145-60). Boston: Tilton & Co.

Weed, E. E. (1912). *Modern Park Cemeteries*. Chicago: R. J. Haight.

Weed, Mr. (1865). Announcement [to the United States Court of Claims]. In B. F Morris, ed., *Memorial record of the nation's tribute to Abraham Lincoln* (pp. 145-46). Washington, DC: Morrison.

Welsh, R. P. (1987). The New York and New Jersey gravestone carving tradition. *Markers IV*, 1-54.

Welter, Barbara. (1974). The feminization of American religion. In M. Hartman and L. W. Banner, eds., *Clio's consciousness raised: New perspectives on the history of women*. NY: Harper.

West, E. S. (1989). The John Dwight workshop in Shirley, Massachusetts, 1770–1816. *Markers VI*, 1–31.

White, E. A. (1968; 1952). *Science and religion in American thought: The impact of naturalism.* NY: AMS Press.

White, E. E. (1972). *Puritan rhetoric: The issue of emotion in religion.* Carbondale, IL: Southern Illinois University Press.

White, Mr. (1865). Remarks of Mr. White. In J. B. Cushman, comp., *Legislative honors to the memory of President Lincoln* (pp. 92–98). Albany, NY: Weed, Parsons & Co.

Whitman, W. (1960a). O captain! My captain! In Walter Lowenfels, ed., *Walt Whitman's Civil War* (pp. 279–80). NY: Knopf.

Whitman, W. (1960b). When lilacs last in the dooryard bloom'd. In Walter Lowenfels, ed., *Walt Whitman's Civil War* (pp. 326–33). NY: Knopf.

Whitman, W. (1962). Death of Abraham Lincoln. In R. P. Basler, ed., *Walt Whitman's 'Memoranda during the Civil War [and] death of Abraham Lincoln'* (pp. 1–14). Bloomington, IN: Indiana University Press.

Whitney, F. C. (1850). *Address delivered at the consecration of Evergreen cemetery, August 7, 1850.* Boston: Wilson.

Wilbur, Mr. (1865). Remarks of Mr. Wilbur. In J. B. Cushman, comp., *Legislative honors to the memory of President Lincoln* (pp. 52–56). Albany, NY: Weed, Parsons & Co.

Wilcox, A. G. and M. Sutton, eds (1977). *Understanding death and dying: An interdisciplinary approach.* Domenguez Hills, CA: Alfred.

Williams, D. D. (1970; 1941). *The Andover liberals: A study in American theology.* NY: Octagon.

Williams, M. M. and G. Williams, Jr.. (1988). 'MD by Thos. Gold': The gravestones of a New Haven Carver." *Markers V*, 1–59.

Williams, Mr. (1865). Remarks of Mr. Williams. In J. B. Cushman, comp., *Legislative honors to the memory of President Lincoln* (pp. 107–13). Albany, NY: Weed, Parsons & Co.

Williams, R. H. (1973). *To live and to die—when, why and how.* NY: Springer-Verlag.

Williams, W. R. (1865). Sermon. In *Our martyr President, Abraham Lincoln* (pp. 9–32). NY: Tibbals & Whiting.

Williamson, D. B. (1865). *Illustrated life, services, martyrdom, and funeral services of Abraham Lincoln, sixteenth President of the United States, with a portrait of President Lincoln, and other illustrative engravings of the assassination, etc.* Philadelphia: Peterson & Brothers.

Willshire, B. (1983). Scottish gravestones and the New England winged skulls. *Markers II*, 105–14.

Wise, I. M. (1927). Funeral address. In E. Hertz, ed., *Abraham Lincoln: The tribute of the synagogue* (pp. 92–99). NY: Bloch.

Wood, A. D. (1973). 'The fashionable diseases,' women's complaints and their treatment in nineteenth-century America. *Journal of Interdisciplinary History 4*, 25–52.

Wright, R. A. (1988). Poems in stone: The tombs of Henri Sullivan. *Markers V*, 169–208.

Young, F. W. (1960). Graveyards and social structure. *Rural Sociology 25*, 446–50.

Zaniello, T. A. (1977). Chips from Hawthorne's workshop: The icon and cultural studies. In P. Benes, ed., *Puritan gravestone art* (pp. 68–78). Boston: Boston University Press.

Zilboorg, G. (1943). Fear of death. *Psychoanalytic Quarterly 12*, 465–75.

Zuckerman, M. (1970). *Peaceable kingdoms: New England towns in the eighteenth century*. NY: Knopf.

# INDEX

Abbott, Dr. E. W., 176 n. 4
actions, and immortality, 123, 124, 134, 144, 151, 154, 166; as divine significations, 46, 74, 155; as emotion, 125; as inconsistent with reflection, 137; as life, 137; as speaking louder than words, 123, 140; heroic, 67, 116, 121, 122, 123, 125, 130, 131, 132, 133, 137, 139, 140, 143, 144, 151, 154, 158, 166 natural/un- natural, 87, 163, 167. *See also* contemplation, death, and thinking
Adams, John Quincy, 177 n. 11
Adams, Samuel, memorial of, 71–73, 161
Agosta, Lucien L., 66
Allegheny Cemetery, 104
Alexander, Dr., 7

Allen, W. H. H., 123
alterity, transformed into sameness through singularity, 171
America, as a singularity, 2, 32, 34, 35, 44, 171; as not monocultural, 25, 171
America's hegemonic voice, xii, 36, 45, 46, 63, 64, 68, 73–74, 76, 90, 91, 113, 137–38, 141, 150, 154, 160, 172
Andrew, John Albion, 119
Appleton, Samuel, 100
Archer, Judith, memorial of, 93
Aristotle, 115
Austin, James T., 100

Baker, John, 94
Bakhtin, Mikhail, 153

Bancroft, George, 117–18, 125
Barnes, Dr., 7
Barrett, Humphrey, memorial of, 73
Barrett, James, memorial of, 73
Barrett, Joseph, memorial of, 71
Becker, Ernest, 21, 23, 40
Beecher, Henry Ward, 96–97
Belknap, William Worth, memorial
   of, 138–39
Bell, Edward, 95
Bellah, Robert, 26
Bigelow, Jacob, 63–64, 99, 100, 106
Black Easter, 9
Black, Edwin, xiv
Bodnar, John, 25
Bond, George, 99, 100
Booth, John Wilkes, 3
Bradlee, Joseph P., 19
Branch, E. Douglas, 90
Brazee, M. P., 106
Brazil, Matthew, 147
Brimmer, George W., 99, 100
Broad, Milton C., memorial of, 149
Brown, Dr., 7
Buchanan, William H., memorial of,
   149
Budington, William Ives, 51
Burke, Kenneth, xiv
Burnham, Alfred Avery, 123

Campbell, Ernest, 23
Carse, James, 125
Cattell, Harry P., and preparation of
   Lincoln's corpse, 7
Cave Hill Cemetery, 104
Chaney, George, 117
Chattanooga (TN) *Daily Rebel*, 19
Civil Rights Memorial (National), 111
Civil Rights Movement, 111
Civil War Memorial (Washington,
   D.C.), 144
Clark, William T., 5

Clarke, James Freeman, 82–89
Clusca, Lowel M., memorial of, 67
Colfax, Schuyler, 18, 49, 50
collective memory. *See* memory, col-
   lective
Conant, Andrew, memorial of, 92
Conant, Catherrine, memorial of, 91
Cone, Warren, 109
Congress (39th), 8; determines route
   for Lincoln's funeral cortege, 9
contemplation, appropriate in the
   Romanticist gravescape, 103,
   138, 139, 159; inconsistent with
   action, 133, 137, 141; necessary
   in preparing for death, 54. *See
   also* thinking
Cook, Zebedee, 100
Crane, Dr., 7
Crawford, Thomas, 106
Cromwell, Doraty, memorial of,
   70–71
Cudworth, Warren, 17, 47
cultural ascendency, 1, 42, 90, 92, 93,
   94, 136, 137, 140, 141, 144, 152
cultural conflict, 24, 29, 31, 42, 154,
   160, 170, 171–74
cultural dominance, 1, 26, 41, 141,
   142, 152
cultural exchange, 25, 33
cultural influence, 25, 41, 91, 136, 149
cultural interchange, 25
cultural memory. *See* memory, cultural
cultural transformation, 1–3, 23, 25,
   26, 27, 29, 41, 45, 76, 113, 135,
   153, 156, 160, 173, 174
culture, and collective memory, 27;
   and demographic categories,
   34–36; and public memory, 26,
   27; and sacred symbols, 28, 31;
   as dynamic, 36, 43; as generalization, 35; df. of, 28; not an
   entity, 43; predefined, 34

Curtis, Charles P., 100
Curtis, Dr., 7
Cutting, Frank Brockholst, 122
Cuyler, Theodore L., 78

Daggett, O. E., 22, 51–52
Daily, Maria, 17
Davidson, James, 16
Dawes, Bernadine, xv
Dawes, L.W., 13
Dearborn, H.A.S., 100
death, 169–170; action as an appro-
    priate response, 137; and grief
    (see grief); and harmony, 80,
    81, 85, 88, 106, 157, 159; and
    memory, 63–74; as a cultural
    event, 27; as a moment immer-
    sed in natural processes, 77; as
    beautiful, 77, 80, 81, 82, 83, 89,
    116, 138, 156, 157; as culturally
    illuminating, 27; as having a
    divine purpose, 155–56, 46–74,
    77; as homeopathic, 81, 89, 111,
    138, 162, 170; as inspiring as
    life, 77, 89; as liminality, 24; as
    natural, 77, 80, 81, 85, 116, 129,
    136, 157, 169; as opportunity,
    170; as regenerative, 82, 83, 93,
    169; ignominious, 52, 55, 56,
    58, 60, 155; sacral power of, 40;
    should not disrupt the flow of
    life, 137; silence as an appropri-
    ate response to, 122, 139, 140,
    149. See also Lincoln's death
Deetz, James, 32, 33
defamation, df. of, 31
desecration, df. of, 31
Dethlefsen, Edwin, 32
Dexter, Franklin, 100
Donne, John, 45
Downing, Andrew Jackson, 104,
    105–6, 144–45

Dudley, Abigail, memorial of, 92–93
Dunlap, Andrew, memorial of, 140

efficiency, as rationale for eliminating
    diversity, 137, 146, 147, 151, 162;
    as fundamental measure of suc-
    cess, 152, 162
election of 1860, 14
election of 1864, 14
Emancipation Proclamation, 153
Emerson, Ralph Waldo, 15, 78, 79
emotions, as an uneasy composite of
    mortality and immortality, 168;
    as homeopathic, 77, 81, 82, 85,
    89, 92, 122, 162, 156, 168; as
    incapacitating, 56, 63, 115, 123,
    131, 133, 134, 151, 159, 168, 169,
    170; as leading to greater
    beauty, 81, 82, 85, 92, 101, 103,
    105, 168, 170; as leading to
    greater unity, 81, 82, 85, 88, 92,
    122, 168, 170; as morally salu-
    brious or insalubrious, 56, 57,
    59, 60, 61, 159, 168; as motive,
    169; as offensive, 6; as primor-
    dial, 81, 87, 168, 170; as untrust-
    worthy, 56, 63, 123, 124, 125,
    126, 133, 134, 151, 159, 168, 169
ethos, and cultural memory, 26, 42,
    46, 54, 75, 77, 82, 90, 94, 116,
    125, 134, 137, 155, 157, 160; and
    culture, 27, 35, 36, 41, 43, 44,
    171; and demographic cate-
    gories, 35, 36; and dominance,
    41, 90; and public memory, 172;
    and the rise and fall of cultures,
    27, 41, 82, 90, 93, 140, 144, 150;
    and sacred symbols, 28;  and the
    problem of compromise, 161; as
    boundary and discipline,
    151–52, 160; disciplined by
    worldview, 113; freedoms of,

ethos *(continued)*
      113; Heroist *(see* Heroism); pos-
      sesses possibility, 75; Religionist
      *(see* Religionism); Romanticist
      *(see* Romanticism);
      symbolically articulated, 24, 27,
      41, 43, 54, 82, 90, 93, 94, 100,
      107, 112, 137, 144, 149, 150
evangelical behavior, as a sign of sta-
      tus and authority, 59, 76, 165; as
      an index of the right and obliga-
      tion to speak, 59, 76, 165
Everett, A.H., 100
Everett, Edward, 17, 99, 100

Farnsworth, Gen., 6
Farrell, James J., 27, 136
Farrer, Claire, 43
Field, Maunsell, 6, 176 n. 4
Finney, Charles Grandison, 65
Floyd, Nolia E., memorial of, 149
Folger, Charles, 123
Foote, Henry, 20, 121
Ford's theater, 3, 4, 52
Fox, Henry J., 22, 52
fragmentation, 36, 44, 152, 173; as
      indicative of the postmodern
      condition, 1
Franklin, Benjamin, 126
French, Stanley, 64, 104
Freud, Sigmund, 19
*fugit hora*, trans. of, 69
Fulton, J. D., 16, 50

Gaonkar, Dilip, 39
Gardiner, Samuel P., 99
Geertz, Clifford, xv, 27-28, 36, 44
George, Diane, 73
Graceland, 111, 181 n. 11
Grant, Ulysses S., 21, 54; memorial
      (Washington, D.C.), 144
gravescape(s) as sociological and cli-

matological drain, x; df. of, 63;
      segregated, x
Heroist, 137-50; development
      of, 137-50; eliminates "death,
      sorrow, and pain," 147; hege-
      mony in, 64, 137, 141, 150, 160,
      164;
Religionist, 63-74; and the formal
      capacity to evoke memory of
      death, 64-65; as institutions/
      places of learning, 68-69; hege-
      mony in, 45, 46, 63-76, 90, 113,
      137-38, 141, 154, 160; ostensibly
      neglected condition of, 65
Romanticist, 90-112; development
      of, 90-112; hegemony in, 64, 90,
      113, 137-38, 141, 154, 160; rapid
      emergence of, 103-5. *See also*
      memorials; Heroism; Religion-
      ism; and Romanticism
Gray, E. H., 10
Greenmount Cemetery, 104
Greenough, Richard, 106
grief, 9, 10, 23, 54, 61, 77, 80, 81, 82,
      89, 99, 102, 110, 115, 123, 125,
      137
Gurley, Phineas Densmore, 6, 10, 11,
      13, 48, 53; delivers benediction,
      13; delivers closing prayer, 11, 13;
      delivers death-bed prayer, 6

*Habits of the Heart,* 26
Hale, Albert, 10, 13
Hale, Nathan, 99
Hall, David D., 34
Hall, G. R., 11
Halsted, B. D., 96
Hamilton, Emmert, memorial of, 109
Hanchett, William, 14, 18
Harden, William Frederick, memorial
      of, 109
Hare, Sidney, 147
Harris, A. D., memorial of, 108

Harris, Clara, 3
Haynes, John, memorial of, 67
Hayward, Josiah, memorial of, 67
hegemonic bloc, 2
Heidegger, Martin, 39
Hepworth, George, 16
Heroism 115–52, 153–74; and becoming, 152; and cultivation of homogeneity and fragmentation, 152; and death, 137, 170; and efficiency as a central characteristic, 147; and efficiency as rationale for eliminating diversity, 147; and emotion, 6, 56, 63, 115, 123, 131, 133, 134, 151, 159, 168, 169, 170; and immortality, 119, 123, 124, 134, 135, 136, 137, 142, 151, 158, 159, 162, 164, 166, 167; and mode, 165–66; and nature, 167; and the reordering of the Religionist gravescape, 64; and space/place, 164; and time, 162; and silence, 149; and standing larger than life, 134; dichotomy as synecdoche for, 151; efficiency as fundamental measure of success, 152; elimination of diversity as characteristic of, 146–47; ethos of, 116, 118, 121, 125, 134, 137, 140, 144, 149, 150, 151, 152; hegemonic authority of, 64, 137, 141, 150, 160, 164; homogeneity as mechanism for announcing power and dominance of, 152; measurement of success necessary to, 151; memorializing beyond the gravescape as a development of, 141; quantity as primary principle for determining individual worth, 152; worldview of, 121, 124, 125, 132, 134, 135, 136, 137, 140, 144, 147, 149, 150, 151, 152, 158, 164, 166, 167. See also

gravescape(s); Lincoln; Lincoln, Mary Todd; Lincoln's death; Romanticism; thinking; and transculturation
history, as unavoidably a site of ideological struggle, 39
Hooker, Roger, memorial of, 67
Hubbard, A. C., 13
Hutchinson, Thomas, 94

Illowy, Bernard, 50
immortality, and cultural memory, 134, 135, 137, 142, 159, 164, 166, 167; and deity, 53, 58, 62, 155, 156, 159–60, 166, 168; blissful, 73, 83; natural, 10, 83, 84, 87, 159; necessary, 57; physical, 136; species, 119, 123, 124, 134, 135, 137, 151, 158, 159, 162, 164, 166, 167
ironmongery, 144–45

Jamieson, Kathleeen, xv
Jefferson, Thomas, 126; memorial for (Washington, D.C.), 143
Joachimsen, Philip, 119
Johnson, Andrew, 7, 18; determines date and place of Lincoln's funeral, 7
Jones, Alfred T., 20
Jones, Alice, memorial of, 74
Jones, Ephraim, memorial of, 91

King, Martin Luther, Jr., memorial to, 111
Kinney, Miss, 6
Kirk, Edward Norris, 54–63
Krupat, Arnold, 2

LaCross (WI) Democrat, 17

Laurel Hill Cemetery (Philadelphia)
104, 105, 145. *See also* Notman,
John
lawn cemetery. *See* gravescape(s),
Heroist
Lawrence, Abbott, 100
Lawrence, James, memorial of, 108
Lee, Robert E., 21
Lilienthal, Max, 125–37
Lincoln, as a moderately popular
president, 14; as "a sincere
Christian," 49; as an American
Christ/Moses, 50–52, 55, 156; as
being of Hebrew parentage, 50;
as Heroist, 116–25, 129, 158; as
Religionist, 46–54, 157; as
Romanticist, 78–82, 157; as an
integral part of the nation's
image, 13; as deity's "gift for the
crisis"; 48–49; as father to the
nation, 86; as "first laborer-
President," 127; as natural, 78; as
rail-splitter, 25, 26, 42, 78, 82,
87, 157
    attacked, as a "barbarian,
    Scythian, or gorilla," 16; as
    "a Black Republican," 15; as
    "a clod," 17; as a coward, 15; as a
    mediocre orator, 17; as a "vulgar
    monkey," 16; as an object of
    hatred, 14; as an "uneducated
    boor," 17; as not being a "great
    man," 16; as "the rottenest,
    most stinking, ruinworking pox
    ever conceived by friends or
    mortals," 17; as too forgiving,
    86, 88; as too gentle, 20; as
    unimaginative, 17, 86; as un-
    trained and without culture, 16;
    for "official awkwardness," 16;
    for peculiar mannerisms, 16; for
    "philosophy of jacoseness," 16
    not comparable with Adams,

John Quincy, 17;  Caesar,
131; Hamilton, Alexander, 17;
Clay, Henry, 17; Everett, Edward,
17; Franklin, Benjamin, 126;
Henry IV, 131; Jackson, Andrew,
126; Jefferson, Thomas, 126;
Webster, Daniel, 17; William of
Orange, 131; Washington,
George, 17, 126
    rose to greatness through his own
    energies, 127
Lincoln myth, 22–28; three dominant
elements of, 24–25
Lincoln, Mary Todd, 3, 4, 6, 7, 8, 9,
11; disturbed by funeral prepa-
rations, 8; kept from President's
side, 6–7, marginalized by
Heroists, 6–7, 8–9, 176 n. 7
Lincoln, Robert, 5, 6, 11
Lincoln, Tad, 11
Lincoln, Willie, 7, 11
Lincoln's assassination, described,
3–4; coffin, 7, 13
    corpse, prepared, 7; removed
    to the White House, 7
    death, 2, 3–15, 19–23, 27, 42, 46,
    47, 51, 52, 53, 54, 55, 56, 67, 59,
    60, 62, 75, 76, 78, 79, 80; and
    the emergence of disparate
    voices, 3; and the physician's
    notes, 5–6; and the rupture of
    social structure, 2; as a cultural
    event, 2; as a divine message to
    the community, 51–54, 58–63;
    as a Heroist lesson, 129; as a
    Religionist lesson, 46–63; as a
    Romanticist lesson, 82–90; as a
    shock to Northerners, 21; as
    beautiful, 80; as unity, 87; as
    unprecedented, 21, 126; caused
    by deity, 51–52, 55; compared
    with Christ, 22, 87–88; com-
    pared with Harrison, William

Henry, 22; compared with Moses, 22; compared with William of Orange, 21; compared with Taylor, Zachary, 22; compared with Washington, George, 22; not ignominious, 52-54, 155; time of, 6

death-bed scene described, 6

funeral services in Baltimore, 11; in Chicago, 12; in Cleaveland, 11; in Columbus, 11; in Harrisburg, 11; in Indianapolis, 12; in Philadelphia, 11; in Washington, D.C., 8, 9, 10, 11

funeral train, arrives in Springfield, 12; begins its journey to Springfield, 11

Heroist ethos of, 116-25; humble beginnings as symbolic of a deity's influence, 47-48; Religionist ethos of, 46-54; Romanticist ethos of, 78-82; political beginnings as symbolic of deity's influence, 48

Linden-Ward, Blanche, 64, 105

Littlejohn, A. N., 16, 17, 119-21

Lorraine Motel, 111

Lowell, Charles, 100

Lowell, John, 99

Lowry, Robert, 48

Ludwig, Allan, 29-30; and Hall, 34


M'Clintock, John, 51

MacDonald, E., 180 n. 5

MacIntyre, Alasdar, 161

Madsen, Richard, 26

Mallory, Annie E., memorial of, 110

MAN stone, x-xi

Mandalbaum, David, 27

marginalization, of people of color, x; and the forgotten, xi; and subordination, 1

Marcuse, Herbert, 65

Marine Corps Memorial (Washington, D.C.), 144

Martyn, Edward, 94

Massachusetts Horticultural Society, 99-100

materialism, 45

Mather, Nathanael, memorial of, 69-70, 72, 73

May, William F., 40

McKee, Nancy, memorial of, 110

McKee, Thomas, memorial of, 110

McNickle, D'arcy, 35

Mechling, Elizabeth, xv

Mechling, Jay, xv

Melven, Jonathan, memorial of, 73

*memento mori*, trans. of, 69

*memor*, trans. of, 37

memorable, the, as that which deserves to be in memory, 38; df. of, 37

*memoria*, trans. of, 37

memorializing; American, xii-xiii; and aesthetic standards, x; and cultural membership, 40-41; as a consequence of the evangelical impulse, 76; as a third-order process, 37; as incomplete and partialized, 37; as more than remembering, 37; as necessarily an abstraction, 37; as necessarily evaluative, 37, 40; as representational, 37; as symbolic, 37, 40; cultural and rhetorical bases of, xi, xiii, 3; df. of, 37. *See also* memorials; gravescape(s); Heroism; Lincoln; Religionism; Romanticism

memorials; and defamation, 31; and desacration, 31; and efforts of the marginalized and the forgotten, xi; and evocative power, x; and layers of significance and

memorials *(continued)*
    meaning, x; and living in the
    moment, 112–13; and mummifi-
    cation, 111; as announcing cul-
    ture, xii; as answering needs, 40;
    as establishing patterns of com-
    munication, 39; as fundamen-
    tally aesthetic objects, 40; as
    fundamentally rhetorical and
    cultural forms of expression, xii,
    34; as instances of memorializ-
    ing, xi; as modes of rhetorical
    and cultural expression, xii; as
    not representative of all individ-
    uals or cultures, xiii; as poor
    aesthetic imitations, x; as sites
    of ideological struggle, xiii, 39,
    41; as speaking through cultural
    and rhetorical forms, xii, 40, 41;
    as Romanticist works of art,
    107–8; cultural and rhetorical
    significance of, xi, 28, 30–31;
    depend on the living for their
    voice, xii; discursive, xi; inscrip-
    tion-only, 67–68, 92, 149; mis-
    understood as aesthetic objects,
    29–31; misunderstood as histor-
    ical data, 29, 32–36; private,
    38–39; public, 38–39; single
    arch, 66; triple arch, 66. *See also*
    memorializing, (s), and grave-
    scape(s); Heroism; Lincoln;
    Religionism; Romanticism
memory, collective, xii, 24, 25, 26, 27,
    125, 142, 156
    cultural, xiii, 26, 27, 28, 76,
    125, 172; df. of, 26
    public, 3, 27, 41, 42, 45, 76, 113,
    153, 157, 160, 172; df of , 26
    *See also* memorial(s), memorial-
    izing
Meyer, Richard, 39
Miner, A. A., 115–16

Miner, N. W., 13
Mockridge, Elizabeth, memorial of,
    67
mode, 164–6
Moore, Albin, memorial of, 138
Moore, Mary, memorial of, 138
Moore, Thomas, memorial of, 138
More, Richard, memorial of, 67
Moremen, Robin, xv
Morgan, T. H., 123
Morias, Sabato, 49
Morris, Ian, xiv
Mount Auburn Cemetery, 12, 104,
    105, 106, 107; consecration of,
    100–103
Mount Hope Cemetery, 104
Mount Vernon Association, 142
Mount Vernon Memorial, as compe-
    tition for the Washington
    Monument, 142; as a living
    monument, 143

narrative, 2–3
National Civil Rights Museum, 111
naturalism, 45
nature/Nature, 166–67; and art, 77,
    88, 92, 93, 99, 103–8; and deity,
    46, 56, 57, 85, 88; and immor-
    tality, 83–84; and the unnatural,
    112–14; as a unified whole, 78,
    82, 84, 88–89; as commodity,
    167; as goodness, 167; as
    mechanical, 167; as metric
    against which all things are
    measured, 78, 157, 167; as
    morally neutral, 56, 166; as part
    of deity's language, 56; as regen-
    erative, 84. *See also* Romanti-
    cism
Nelson, Malcolm, 73
*New York Copperhead,* 18
*New York World,* 17

Nicholson, W. R., 52
*North American Review*, 97, 142
Notman, John, as landscape architect, of Spring Grove Cemetery (Cincinnati), 145; of Laurel Hill Cemetery (Philadelphia), 145
Oak Ridge Cemetery, compared with Mount Auburn Cemetery (Massachusetts), 12; compared with Greenwood Cemetery (New York), 12; described, 12-13
Oglesby, Richard, 8
Old City Cemetery, 108
Old Copp's Hill and Burying Ground, 94-96, 180 n. 5; redesigned by Romanticists, 95-96
Otis, James, 107
*Our American Cousin*, 3, 5
Owen, Richard, 142-43


Patton, Lois, xv
Peabody, William B. O., 97-98
Peterson, Merrill, 22, 24, 25
Peterson, William, 4
Pierpont, John, 100
place. *See* space/place
Pomeroy, Marcus "Brick," 17, 18
positivism, 45
postmodern condition, 1. *See also* fragmentation
Pratt, George W., 100
Presley, Elvis, 111
Presnell, Mick, xv
Prestiano, Robert, 140
public memory. *See* memory, public


Rad, Robert, memorial of, 71
Randall, Ruth Painter, 176 n. 6
Rathbone, Maj. Henry Reed, 3, 4
reason. *See* emotion
Reed, Paul, memorial of, 93

Religionism, 42-43, 45-76; and authority to speak as deriving from deity, 59, 76, 155; and death, 169-70; and emotion, 56, 57, 59, 60, 61, 63, 115, 168; and immortality, 53, 58, 62, 73, 155, 156, 159-60, 166, 168; and mode, 164-65; and nature, 166-67; and space/place, 163; and temporal icons as subordinate to death-related icons, 72; and time, 161-62; and universe as vertically structured, 46-76; ethos of, 46, 54, 56, 62, 63, 64, 65, 67, 68, 70, 74, 75, 77, 78, 135, 147, 155, 160, 165, 167, 169; hegemonic authority of, 45, 46, 63, 68, 73-74, 76, 90, 113, 137-38, 141, 154, 160; moral structure of the universe as key principle in, 46; rhetorical and cultural imperative of, 63; worldview of, 46, 54, 56, 62, 63, 64, 65, 67, 68, 70, 74, 75, 77, 78, 135, 147, 155, 160, 165, 167, 169. *See also* gravescape(s), Heroism, Lincoln, Lincoln's death, Romanticism, and transculturation
responses to Lincoln's assassination, akin to still photographs, 42; as instructive media, 3
rhetoric, df. of, 24
*Richmond* (VA) *Enquirer*, 15
Roberts, Luke, memorial of, 93
Robinson, Charles, 19
Rockwell, J. E., 22
Rogers, A. P., 22
Rogers, E. P., 50
Rogers, Randolph, 107
Romanticism, 42-43, 77-114, 153-71; and beautification of the Religionist gravescape, 64;

Romanticism *(continued)*
  and criticism of the Heroist
    memorial tradition, 142–43; and
    death, 77, 83, 88, 89, 92, 103,
    156, 157, 169–70
  and emotion, as homeopathic,
    77, 81, 82, 85, 89, 92, 122, 162,
    156, 168; as leading to greater
    beauty, 81, 82, 85, 92, 101, 103,
    105, 168, 170; as leading to
    greater unity, 81, 82, 85, 88, 92,
    122, 168, 170; as primordial, 81,
    87, 168, 170
  and immortality, 10, 83, 84, 87,
    159; and mode, 165; and
    Nature, 167; and opposition as a
    contradiction to unity, 89; and
    space/place, 163–64; and time,
    162; and the universe as hori-
    zontally unified through Nature,
    78; ethos of, 42, 77, 82, 90, 93,
    94, 100, 107, 112, 157, 160, 165,
    169; hegemonic authority of, 64,
    90, 113, 137–38, 141, 154–70;
    worldview of, 77, 78, 81, 82, 88,
    89, 90, 93, 94, 100, 107, 112, 113,
    116, 147, 156, 157, 162, 163, 165,
    167
  *See also* contemplation, grave-
    scape(s), Heroism, Lincoln,
    Lincoln's death, memorials, Old
    Copps Hill and Burying Ground,
    transculturation, and Washing-
    ton monument
Root, George F., 13
Ropes, George, 73
Rutgers University, ix


Sample, Robert F., 22, 48
Sargent, Isabel, memorial of, 109–10
Sargent, L. M., 100
Sargent, Nathan, memorial of,
    109–10
Scott, Gen. Winfield, 15

Second, Jane, memorial of, 67
Seifert, Marsha, xv
Selma (AL) *Dispatch*, 18
Seward, William, 14, 15, 18
Sewell, Hannah, 94
Sewell, Samuel, 94
Simons, Herb, xv
Simpson, Matthew, 10, 13, 47, 48
Sinkler, Ella Brock, memorial of, 67
Slater, James, 34
Smith, Henry B., 47
Smull, Eliza, memorial of, 110
social structure, rupture of, 1–2
Southern Christian Leadership
    Conference, 111
space/place, as always already sancti-
    fied, 163–64; and rhetoric of
    exhibitionism, 164; and witness-
    ing, 164; dual character of, 163;
    sanctified, 163
speaking. *See* speech; authority; and
    evangelical behavior
speech, as inadequate/inutile for
    responding to death, 122–23,
    126–27, 130, 140
Spring Grove Cemetery (Cincinnati,
    OH), 104, 145, 147–48. *See also*
    Notman, John
Springfield (IL) City Council, 9
stability, burden of, 172; first
    order of, 172; second order
    of, 172
Stannard, David, 27
Stanton, Edwin M., bars Mary
    Lincoln from death scene, 6
Steele, Richard, 21, 49
Stewart, Charles, 26
Stone, A. L., 79
Stone, Dr., 7
Storrs, Richard S., Jr., 78–79
Story, Joseph, 100, 104; consecration
    address of, 101–3
Strong, George Templeton, 16
Stuckey, Mary, xv
Sturgis, William, 99

Sullivan, William, 26
Swindler, Ann, 26
symbols, sacred, 28, 30–31, 36, 40–41.
    See also ethos, memorials,
    memorializing, and worldview

Taft, Dr., 7
Tappan, Charles, 100
Tappan, John, 99
Tashjian, Ann, xi, 30, 66, 68–69, 90
Tashjian, Dickran, xi, 30, 66, 68–69,
    90
Tasker, J. C., 123
Temple University, ix
Texas Republican, 19
thinking, as a means to Heroist
    action, 133. See also contempla-
    tion
Thoreau, Henry David, 77–78, 88, 89
Thornton, Timothy, 94
time, 161–62. See also Heroism,
    Religionism, and Romanticism
Tipton, Steven, 26
Todd, Gen., 6
transculturation, 33, 73, 74; between
    Heroism and Romanticism, 111,
    137–38; between Religion-ism
    and Romanticism, 73–74, 93–94
Turell, Daniel, 94
Turner, Thomas Reed, 18
tympanium, df. of, 69
Tyng, Stephen Higgison, 48–49

universe, as horizontally unified
    through Nature, 78, 113, 165; as
    resource, 165, 167, 169, 170; as
    vertically structured, 56, 59, 75,
    78, 164, 165, 167

Vidaver, Henry, 122
Vietnam Veterans Memorial
    (Washington, D.C.), 31

Walker, William Perkins, memorial
    of, 108
Wander, Philip, xiv
Ward, Thomas W., 99
Washington Monument
    (Washington, D.C.), 141–42;
    as a mere "pile," 142; as an
    accomplishment of labor than
    of artistic skill, 141; lack of
    funding for, 142; Romanticists
    opposed to construction of,
    142; speaks of power over, 142
Washington, George, 8, 17, 22, 119,
    129, 126, 128, 142, 143
Watson, Joseph, memorial of, 91–92
Watters, David H., 32
Webb, E. B., 122
Webster, Daniel, 17, 100
Weld, Benjamin, 95
Wells, Charles, 95
White House, 6, 7, 8, 9, 10, 11, 16, 18,
    25, 42, 135, 158; opened to the
    public, 9
winged death's head, 32, 33, 69, 71,
    72, 73; as symbol of hopeful-
    ness, 69, 70
Winthrop, John, 106
Wise, Isaac M., 50
Woodward, Dr., 7
Worcester Rural Cemetery, 104
worldview, 3, 24, 32, 35, 36, 37,
    41, 42, 43, 44, 46, 173; and
    cultural memory, 26; and
    culture, 3, 35, 36, 41, 44, 153,
    161; and dominance, 41, 152,
    160; and multicultural tensions,
    154, 174; and the problem of
    compromise, 161; as boundary,
    113; as culture premises, 40;
    conflict of, 160, 161, 171, 172;
    df. of, 28; Heroist (see Heroism);
    Religionist (see Religionism);
    Romanticist (see Romanticism);
    symbolically articulated, 24, 28,
    41, 90, 93, 94, 100, 107